Our Aging Parents

Our Aging Parents

A PRACTICAL GUIDE TO ELDERCARE

Edited by

COLETTE BROWNE

and

ROBERTA ONZUKA-ANDERSON

A Kolowalu Book

UNIVERSITY OF HAWAII PRESS

HONOLULU

Library of Congress Cataloging in Publication Data
Main entry under title:

Our aging parents.

  (A Kolowalu book)
  Bibliography: p.
  Includes index.
    1. Aged—Home care—United States. 2. Aged—Care
and hygiene—United States. 3. Aged—United States—
Family relationships. I. Browne, Colette, 1950–
II. Onzuka-Anderson, Roberta, 1951–   . [DNLM:
1. Family—popular works. 2. Geriatrics—popular
works. WT 120 O93]
HV1461.O95   1985   362.6'3   85–13941
ISBN 0–8248–0997–1

*This book is dedicated to those individuals
who lovingly care for elder family members
and to our own parents for their love and support.*

Contents

Foreword

The number of older people in our society has increased significantly. Individuals sixty-five years and older constituted 4 percent of the U.S. population and approximately 3 million persons in 1900 compared to the 11 percent and over 25 million people today. This book focuses on the old-old, the fastest growing segment of our population. The impact of these demographic changes is profound and affects our personal lives. Most of us can expect to live longer than our ancestors. More of us will be involved in the care of an elderly person. This is because frailty is positively associated with age. Of course, there is tremendous variability in functioning, and there are many elders in their eighties and older who are healthy, vigorous, and active in their intellectual and leisure pursuits. There are also individuals in their fifties and younger who have been incapacitated by a stroke, an accident, or Alzheimer's disease. As a general rule, however, physical and mental disabilities increase with age, necessitating more supportive services.

The editors and contributors of this book have performed a valuable service for people whose lives are intimately affected by the aging phenomenon. They have gathered an important set of gerontological information and packaged it in a way that is easy to understand. This information is useful whether we apply it to our own lives or utilize it in the care of others. Each chapter includes vignettes which illustrate the concepts discussed. Together, the chapters enable us to understand the aging process and how to deal with a possible decline in health.

The information is timely. Reforms in the health system are redirecting the flow of the aged from formal, more expensive providers of health care to community based services. Hospital stays are shorter and referrals to long-term care facilities are avoided whenever possible. As a consequence, families and friends find that the major responsibility for meeting the needs of very old relatives and loved ones is in their hands. These caregivers represent a range of people. Spouses tend to provide the most help with the least stress and are the most important factor in preventing institutionalization. Children, particularly those who live with or near parents, and daughters more than sons, supply emotional support and services in various forms— transportation, personal care, and housecleaning, to name a few. Sometimes grandchildren, nieces, neighbors, and friends serve as the major source of assistance. Unlike the past when life expectancy was shorter, the care of an aged person, for most of us, will not be limited to a single incident, but, rather, it will involve several experiences—first with grandparents, then with parents, and finally with spouse as we ourselves get older.

Caregivers are not without competing responsibilities. More women, who assume the major burden of care, are in the labor force than ever before. Younger caregivers may have children who must be provided for, and older caregivers may be faced with their own declining health. Caring for the aged is reward- ing, but it is difficult and exhausting as well. The care provided at home today requires greater sophistication and technical knowledge, and because of the prevalence of chronic condi- tions, takes place over a longer period of time. It also entails personal sacrifices. Because we are human, anger, resentment, and frustration may well within us. Aggressive behaviors which are generally suppressed may surface. All caregivers experience such feelings and behaviors. It is important that we recognize our limitations and find ways to relieve our burden and stress. An increasingly important task that caregivers should assume is to serve as the locaters and linkers of services provided by vari- ous agencies and individuals for both the elderly and them- selves. *Our Aging Parents* is a resource which caregivers will find immensely valuable.

Sylvia Yuen
Professor of Human Development
University of Hawaii

Preface

We all face the prospect of growing old one day. When we do, we hope that we will not have to do so alone. Aging requires accommodations and adjustments. Coping with these changes can be difficult, not only for the aging but for those closest to them as well. This book is intended primarily for families in need of guidance in caring for a dependent relative. It will also be useful to the aging person who, overwhelmed by the changes associated with aging, finds it difficult to manage alone.

In these times of shrinking resources and costly institutional care, more families are faced with caring for a dependent elder at home. In writing this guide to eldercare, the contributors and editors hope to support families in this role by providing practical, no-nonsense suggestions. The information is presented in such a way that you may read the book in its entirety or select specific chapters according to your need. Because your family, your situation, and your resources are unique, the information offered may not always apply to your specific case. Nevertheless, the following chapters will provide you with an overview of eldercare and, we hope, information that will spark new ideas and present options previously unknown to you. Please remember that any medical treatments or therapies suggested in this book should be discussed with your physician. One of the major points we make throughout is that aging is a normal life process. While not all of the changes associated with growing old will be to our liking, most of us can adapt to them quite successfully.

Caring for an older adult is a formidable task for the family, just as the loss of independence is a painful adjustment to the elder. The decision to provide home care will depend, among other things, on past familial relations and feelings of responsibility for older family members. Those taking on the responsibility of eldercare need to learn how to help—and how much help is enough. The dependent elder needs to know how to contribute to the effort. You can expect disagreements and struggles as well as the joys of sharing and giving. The situation will be demanding, but not without reward.

Whether or not to care for an elder at home is a family decision, one that should include the elder as much as possible. Do not hesitate to seek the opinions of others in making it. Reading about aging can help you prepare for what is in store. Most of us are afraid of the unknown. By studying aging we can hope to alleviate these fears.

Gerontology examines the process of aging. It attempts to prevent problems associated with growing older by understanding normal, healthy development. Because gerontology is a relatively new field, we have made every effort to present information we believe to be the most recent. However, we recommend that the information, especially that dealing with illness and community resources, be discussed with your physician and local specialist on aging. There is much that is being learned today about aging. We know, for example, that many of the symptoms attributed to aging actually have other causes. Confusion is not necessarily a "sign of aging" but may result from a stroke or from improper nutrition resulting from financial problems or depression. Such symptoms and their possible causes as well as the inevitable characteristics that do occur with age are discussed in the following pages.

Although convention favors the use of the masculine pronoun when both sexes are intended, we have elected to use the feminine pronoun. This was a conscious editorial decision made in recognition of two significant facts about aging: first, that the majority of caretakers are women and second, that in the sixty-five and over age group women outnumber men nearly two to one. Robert Butler, the distinguished gerontologist and author, has pointed out that the problems of the aged are actually the problems of women. In acknowledging this, however, we in no way wish to imply the slightest disregard or diminution of the cares and concerns of the older man or his family.

We wish to express our special gratitude to the contributors to this volume, many of whom labored four years on this project. As editors, we gained a great deal from their expertise and experience in their respective fields. We must also thank the many families who inspired this book. We are grateful, too, to the staff and clients of the Kuakini Medical Center in Honolulu for their support. We would like to acknowledge our publishers for their help with the final editing process. And finally, to our husbands, who provided us with love, encouragement, and belief in this project, thank you.

Colette Browne
Roberta Onzuka-Anderson

PART ONE
AGING AND THE FAMILY

1

Aging

COLETTE BROWNE

I have known Maggie for three years now. Inside her is a woman much like me who remembers her first dance, her first date, her first kiss. She can recall winning the eighth grade spelling bee as if it were yesterday, and she can remember the first day she met Tom, the man she married. She remembers her parents growing old—is it possible she is old now herself? "How quickly time passes," she often tells me. Maggie is eighty-two years old.

Maggie tells me she felt her own aging most when she was in her thirties. "It seems funny now," she laughs, "to think that I actually thought I was old at thirty. It wasn't that I felt suffocated by my home and family, you know, there was always so much to do. I had dreams of my own, but things were different then." She vaguely remembers wanting to be a nurse when she was young, but then she met Tom. By the time she was twenty-eight, she had four children. "It's different today," she says. "Years ago women didn't have the choices they do now. I wasn't unhappy, although I think I would enjoy being young now. It wasn't until the children left home to get married that I felt lonely. What was I to do? But Tom and I still had each other."

When I ask her what it feels like to be old, Maggie always responds the same way: "I don't know—I don't really feel old, but others say I am, so I guess it is true." "Did you ever question yourself, your life?" I inquire. "After Tom's death," she answers me, "I thought I was old then. I was fifty-five and he was sixty-one. I felt so lost—so empty and frightened. It took me a while to rejoin the world, but I did." She had moved to Hawaii from Iowa to live with her daughter and her daughter's family. When she was sixty-two, she had become a volunteer for a foster grandparent program and was active in an advocacy club for older adults. She felt healthy and happy.

But today, at age eighty-two, Maggie is not well. She has trouble walking because of her arthritis and poor circulation. She forgets where she puts things like her house keys, her money, and her purse, and she can't seem to remember whether a bill has been paid or not. When the florist recently returned her check noting she had already paid her bill, she wasn't surprised. She was worried, though. "What's happening to me?" she asks.

I met Maggie three years ago and now I try to be a counselor and friend. She is beginning to have problems living with her daughter and family. She would be the first to tell you that at times she makes unfair demands on her daughter. But her daughter doesn't spend much time with her anymore. "I know she's busy with work and her family," she says. "But what about me? Aren't I family, too? She seems to get so irritated with me lately."

Elaine, Maggie's daughter, is experiencing her own problems. "There are days when I realize I don't have that much time left to be with her," she tells me. "It scares me so. Then I take her out shopping or out for lunch. I try, I really do. But I usually end up feeling angry with her. I feel angry at her dependency and I feel angry when she walks so slowly and can't hear what I'm saying. I know these things aren't her fault, but it doesn't make my anger any more tolerable. I usually end up yelling at her for some stupid reason like watching her try to go up on the down escalator. Before I know it, I'm angry at myself for getting angry at her, and we both go home depressed. I don't know what's worse," she says sadly.

"Sometimes," Elaine continues, "I feel Mom is deliberately trying to harass me by making me repeat questions and directions over and over again. I swear her hearing loss is selective. Whenever Allan, my husband, and I are discussing anything personal, Mom could be in the next room but she'll repeat whatever it was we talked about to someone else." Elaine laughs at this, but her laughter subsides quickly. "I just don't have enough patience and understanding with Mom. I guess I really can't imagine what it's like to be old. Both Allan and I want Mom to live with us, but it's me who gets so annoyed all the time. I really do love her." What has happened to Maggie and her daughter? Is this what happens as we grow old? Is this what we can expect for our family members and ourselves?

"What About *My* Needs?"

This book is for people caring for frail elders. We believe that most families *want* to care for an older mother, father, or other elder in their homes and can resolve their problems through education, sensitivity, communication, and an awareness of what aging is and what it is not.

Most older adults retain close relationships with their children and other family members. But families have questions. A friend recently asked, "Why are there dozens of books on caring for infants but none to help me look after my 85-year-old mother? I don't need someone to explain to me the pros and cons of home care as opposed to institutional care. I just need to know how to change my mother when she has wet herself, and I need to know what to do with my feelings of guilt whenever I leave her alone in the house." Professionals who must deal with the challenges of aging are aware of the need for more information on aging and family relationships. They have seen middle-aged children come to them angry and distraught because they did not know what to do with Mother or Dad. Most never dreamed that they would one day be caring for an older relative. Often referred to as the Sandwich Generation, middle-aged children find themselves caring for teenage children as well as aging parents. "What about me and *my* needs?" is the cry counselors most often hear.

Honor Thy Father and Thy Mother. But *how*, asks the middle-aged child? Often problems simply become worse due to confusion about the older person's needs and what the family feels it can provide. How this lack of knowledge can undermine the well-being of a family was recently disclosed in an interview with a husband and wife who came to my office inquiring about nursing home care. This interview revealed quite soon that the husband and wife were not seeking to admit the wife's father to a nursing home but rather were crying for help to alleviate some of the emotional and financial burdens of round-the-clock care.

Counselor: How can I help you?
Wife: It's my father. He's been living with my husband and me for the past two years, ever since he had his stroke. I just don't know what to do or where to turn.
Husband: She's exhausted. . . . We are all exhausted.
Counselor: It sounds like you're feeling tired because of the demands placed on you to ensure your father's well-being and happiness.
Wife: Yes. Not that he's all that demanding. It's just that I have three children, two of them still young. . . . [Her voice trails off.]
Counselor: It's hard to find time for everyone when it seems everyone needs you.
Wife: I just can't seem to win.
Husband: We were thinking about placing Dad in your facility. Can you tell us about it? We've never done this type of thing before.

I explained the differences in facilities and levels of care and, more important, tried to obtain more information on the entire family situation and the woman's father. Was he independent? Could he walk by himself and bathe himself? Did he need round-the-clock supervision? Following a tour of the facility, we sat down again.

Wife: He really likes his own room.
Counselor: Well, we have private rooms.
Husband: He really likes to be with children.
Counselor: We encourage families to bring children when they visit.
Wife: He likes barbecue chicken on Sundays.
Counselor: I can't promise *that*. But I'd be happy to talk to our dietitian about chicken on Sundays.

There was a silence for a few minutes and then finally came the response I knew they were wrestling with. "We don't want Dad to live here," the husband said slowly. "We need something else. We need someone or something to help us help him. Can you advise us?"

Fortunately I could. In the facility I was directing at the time, there was an adult day-care program that offered its services Monday through Friday. We enrolled her father immediately in the program and after an initial adjustment period he was soon enjoying the therapeutic activities, the exercises, and the opportunities for socializing. A few months later, I received a call from the woman who had originally come into my office for information. "I just want you to know," she said, "that Dad died in his sleep last night." Before I could tell her how sorry I was, she went on to tell me why she had called, since we had only met once. "You know," she said, "he died with a smile on his face. That program helped make his last days very happy. I'll never forget that, and now my family's memory of Dad will be a joyful one. I had to call and tell you that."

In working with families caring for an older relative, I often ask: "Can you imagine yourself old? Do you picture yourself as a happy older person or a sad one? What do you think you'll be like at age seventy or eighty?" I often ask families these questions because most have no conception of what it is like to be old. Some, perhaps equating aging with deterioration in emotional and physical well-being, declare, "I don't want to think about it." Sometimes I receive a flippant comment, such as "Oh, I'll just kill myself at sixty so I won't have to go through it." A few anticipate the changes that come with old age and are planning for them. "We have quite a few real estate holdings," one couple told me, "because we don't want to have to depend on our children financially when we're old."

What exactly is aging? What is aging like for our mothers and fathers? What will it be like for ourselves? Let's take a quick look at the facts.

The Process We Call Aging

Unless we ourselves are old, aging remains a mystery to us. It is perplexing to some; many deny its very existence. It can be a source of anxiety for a young model who looks with dread at the mirror, wondering how much longer she can play the ingenue. But aging can also be a source of inspiration and strength.

The young guitarist who watches the 88-year-old Andres Segovia in concert hopes that each year will bring him closer to the master's level of musicianship.

Aging is a process of growth and change that affects us mentally, physically, emotionally, and socially. A brochure from the Gerontology Center at Pennsylvania State University defines aging as a lifelong process involving the complex interrelationship of the individual with his or her environment. Webster's New World Dictionary defines the verb "to age" as: to grow old or show signs of growing old; to ripen or become mature. These definitions, however, do not give us any clues about the real meaning of aging and, more important sometimes, how we feel about it.

For most of us, aging is defined as an *event*—our sixty-fifth birthday, retirement, the first gray hair, or the first time someone gives us their seat on a bus. These are common experiences we share with others. Although there is much that scientists do not know about aging, we do know that, notwithstanding an early death, we will all grow old with time. We also know, of course, that aging is nothing new; people have been growing older since men and women first appeared on the planet. And, despite individual differences in the way we think and look, we will all share the same general effects of aging if we live long enough.

Although society has its myths about aging—older people are "grouchy," "senile," "old-fashioned," "rigid," "unable to learn new ways"—research has found none of these so-called characteristics of age to be true. While we tend to think of certain changes such as wrinkles or the need for hearing aids as signs of aging, these are actually only age-related changes. Although many older people require glasses to read, we all know older people who do not. We do not necessarily decline with age. What we can expect in growing older is that we will most likely move around our world a little more slowly and carefully and that adaptive equipment (eyeglasses, hearing aids, pacemakers, and the like) will become part of our lives.

Robert Butler, in his Pulitzer Prize winning book *Why Survive: Being Old in America,* says that old age in America is often a tragedy. Few of us like to think about aging, he observes, because it reminds us of our own mortality. Butler goes on to say that it is not aging per se that is the tragedy;

rather, it is society's insensitivity and ignorance that have made the process of aging painful and humiliating. If we believe aging to be synonymous with poor health and unattractiveness, then it is not surprising that aging is viewed as undesirable.

Aging itself is not a problem; nor is it a time in life to be feared. Aging is actually a success story—a result of fewer women dying in childbirth, improved health conditions and public health measures, and the decrease in death from infectious diseases. Aging is a triumph, but it also carries with it many challenges due to the increasing numbers of the elderly in our population.

Aging in America holds a different meaning to us today than it did years ago. According to a recent census report, the life expectancy of persons born in the United States has increased twenty-five years since 1900.[1] In the early 1900s, life expectancy in this country was forty-seven years of age and older adults made up only 4 percent of the entire population. In contrast, in 1980 one out of every nine Americans was sixty-five or over, roughly 11 percent of the population. The 25 million persons sixty-five years of age and over in 1980 will grow to 55 million by the year 2030. Moreover, the fastest-growing age segment in this population is the group aged eighty-five and over.

Although the process we call aging will happen to most of us, it retains a *personal* definition: What is old to me is not necessarily old to someone else. The definition of aging is therefore relative. It is often difficult to say when, for example, middle age ends and old age begins. Consider these diverse definitions of aging:

- A little boy in first grade runs home from his last day of school prior to summer vacation and shouts to his mother enthusiastically, "Mommy, I'm so glad I'm old now—I'm a second grader!"
- Joan, a teenager, confides to her sister that she recently turned down a date from a very handsome man because of his age. "I just couldn't go," she whispers, "he's so old—he's thirty-two!"
- Jack, a postman in his early fifties, becomes furious when he meets his new supervisor. "You won't believe that new whippersnapper who's now my boss," he tells his wife. "He's twenty-four years old!"

• The 91-year-old nursing home resident shares a surprise with
his son: "My new roommate is so young—only seventy years
old!"

Each person has defined aging in his or her own way. Their
perceptions of aging were not wrong, however. Aging is a *process*, not something that occurs overnight or on a sixty-fifth
birthday. If anything, these examples show us that what we per-
ceived to be old will change as we ourselves age. One definition
of aging declares that it is always "fifteen years older than I
am," reflecting that aging itself changes our definitions.

Yes, aging is a process. But who is the older adult? And what
does it feel like to be old? Older adults are, as one government
publication so succinctly puts it, our future selves. But isn't
there an average older person, you might ask? No more than
there is an average teenager or middle-aged adult. But for many
reasons, we still tend to think of all older adults as a group
called Old People. Although most older people may be experiencing similar physical changes, not everyone with white hair
thinks and acts exactly alike. Remember: There are vast differences in older people just as there are in all age groups. We all
grow old in our own unique way.

Myths and Misconceptions

Society holds many different myths and misconceptions about
aging and older adults. One misconception tells us all older persons are lonely and isolated from their families and are perhaps
even dumped in a nursing home on their seventieth birthday
for no other reason but age. This myth would have us believe
that all older adults are sad, lonely creatures with no reason to
live. The other view would have us believe that all older people
are happy, successful, and financially without a care, living
their remaining years in a golden autumnal splendor.

Neither belief is, for the most part, true. The myth that all
older people are sad and abandoned by their families is just
that: a myth. Though the family has undergone many changes,
research repeatedly points to the fact that families, neighbors,
and friends continue to support the older person throughout
the life cycle. A study by the gerontologist Ethel Shanas reveals
that nearly 95 percent of the nation's population aged sixty-five

and over live in the community, and most live close to at least one family member they see at least weekly.[2] The vast majority of older persons are very much part of a family or kinship system.

As for the second myth, some older people are in fact financially well off. They are not, unfortunately, in the majority. Most adults plan for their later years, but increased health needs, high costs of medical care, and rising food and shelter costs can erode savings quickly. Those who planned to live on Social Security are finding that getting by is becoming more and more of a struggle each month. Even if the older adult wants to work, many employers will not hire a senior even though studies show older persons to be hardworking, dependable, and loyal employees. With savings spent and employment an impossibility, many older adults find themselves living in poverty, or close to it. For most, this comes as a shock with few solutions in sight.

There are other myths, too, that need to be discarded. One says that Social Security is more than adequate for retirement. Another says that Medicare will pay for all of one's health care costs. They are both, sadly, untrue. Social Security refers to a public retirement pension administered by the federal government. Social Security is not adequate to live on, even though eight out of every ten older adults list Social Security as their only income. As for Medicare, our national health insurance program for the elderly and disabled, it currently pays for roughly 38 percent of the average older adult's yearly health costs, a fact few realize.[3]

Another myth would have us believe that older adults have no housing worries upon retirement because mortgages are paid. Many older adults do own their own homes, it is true, yet many are burdened with high property taxes and costs of upkeep. Some are forced to sell and move into a rental unit. If they are lucky, the rental unit will not be converted into a condominium, since they probably could not afford to buy it. Others are not poor enough to qualify for public housing. For those who are poor enough, most housing projects for elderly citizens have long waiting lists. (Check with your local housing authority to find out more about financial requirements and waiting lists for available housing.) Housing can be a serious problem for aging persons.

Still another myth that all of us need to reject is the common belief that all older people are senile—or becoming so. There are actually minimal changes in our intelligence and memory as we age. Our speed of response may slow somewhat, but any real change in mental functioning is a symptom of a disease state or process, not old age, and affects only a small percentage of those sixty-five and older.

Who Is the Older Adult?

We now have a better idea of who the older person is not. But we still have not answered the question: Who is the older adult? Let's examine the facts once again. First, anyone who has reached the age of sixty-five in our culture is considered by many to be old. Many "old age" benefits begin with this chronological benchmark—for example, Medicare, retirement pensions, and Social Security. Aging, however, is a process that affects each person differently. "You are only as old as you feel," like all platitudes, has some truth to it. Second, the older adult in America is most likely a woman. Older women outnumber older men by 160 women to 100 men in the sixty-five and over age group. According to the Census Bureau, a man born today can expect to live approximately seventy years. A woman born today can expect to live approximately seventy-eight years. Maritally, more older women than men outlive their spouses; two thirds of all older women are widows. Their plight is compounded by a society that encourages older men to marry younger women while discouraging older women to do the same. The end result is fewer widowers than widows.

The Economic Picture

Financially, how does the older adult fare? The bright side shows us that many own their own homes and have acquired a certain number of possessions. The dark side warns us that older persons have, on the average, about half the income of nonretired people. Retirement often means loss of income and economic dependency on others. The average retirement income, including Social Security and other sources, was $6,600 for older women and $11,000 for older men in 1981.[4] One out of every seven aged persons is poor by government definition.[5]

Of the nation's poor, 71 percent are older women—quite contrary to the myth of the wealthy widow traveling around the world on her late husband's life insurance money.[6] Many older adults become poor after retirement because they believed Social Security would take care of them. Many find, instead, that Social Security is far too meager to live on due to the unplanned effects of inflation and the rising costs of health care, food, and housing. Unfortunately, eight out of every ten older adults live on Social Security alone.

Income is often tied to employment, yet age discrimination makes it difficult to get (and retain) a job. The Census Bureau did find recently that earnings accounted for 25 percent of the total income of adults sixty-five years of age and over in 1981. Those lucky enough to have a job must take care not to earn more than $6,960 annually to avoid a Social Security penalty. (This figure is for 1984. Check with your Social Security Office for yearly changes. Also, after the age of seventy there are no dollar limits placed on earning potential that will affect one's Social Security benefits.) Laws to limit mandatory retirement may make it easier for older adults to seek and retain jobs.

Living Arrangements

As a group, older adults reside in all states, although there is a certain migration to warmer areas such as Florida. Older adults are similar to adults of all ages in that they prefer to have their own residence, alone or with a spouse. Most do just this. Five out of every ten older adults live as couples. Approximately one out of six shares a residence with a middle-aged child. But for those in their own residences, either their own home or renting, many live in substandard housing. A house that may have once been their pride and joy is costly and difficult to maintain and often in need of expensive repairs. In today's mobile society, elders living in a three or four-generation family are not all that common. There is even some disagreement among researchers over exactly how common they ever were. Other places of residence for older adults include senior citizen housing projects, retirement villages, group housing, and various institutional and supportive care environments. Some 95 percent of older adults remain in the community, however, only 5 percent live in institutions at any given time.

Health

The health of the majority of older adults is generally good. Although certain parts of our body do change with age, the changes are not always negative. Aging does not mean sickness, although it can mean a greater chance of becoming ill or disabled. While most older adults have at least one chronic ailment, most retain their ability to function independently. With proper diagnosis, precautionary measures, and preventive treatments, changes associated with the aging process can often be controlled and the older adult can continue to live a productive life. Physical or mental changes should always be investigated with a physician to determine the cause. It is unfortunate that many of the preventive health care measures are not covered under Medicare at this time. Older adults find they must pay for most drugs, hearing aids, eyeglasses, dental care, or foot care (podiatry) themselves.

Some older adults, however, have been overwhelmed by the many changes we often associate with aging and find it difficult to manage alone. These older adults, frail and vulnerable, require assistance from family, neighbors, and community resources to function. It is the frail older adult who, without such resources, usually ends his or her later years in an institution. In the past ten years, however, the community has begun to respond to the needs of these people by establishing support services to help frail older adults remain in their own home. Shortages of services still exist, but changes are being made to support elders in a home environment.

Now for the Good News

Statistics and averages can never tell us what our personal experiences will be as we age; nor can statistics tell us how we will adapt. What we do know about aging is that most elders adapt well to the changes in health, social status, family relationships, financial security, and so forth. The process we call aging is very much an individual experience. One's inner strengths and past coping patterns will be called upon to meet the challenges of age and to grow with them.

What, then, is so good about growing older? Plenty. As a friend of mine, a 78-year-old physician, says with obvious relish: "At my age, I just don't give a damn what anyone thinks of me—and I do exactly as I please." With aging comes very often a genuine acceptance of life. It means being in touch with the real you and not simply the expectations of others. It requires taking a good look at who you are, what you do, and what you know you want to do without the self-imposed ifs and buts of life. It also means taking pride in a lifetime of accomplishments—valued friendships, children leading responsible and happy lives, and one's contributions to society.

What are the rewards of helping your parents as they age? There is self-exploration, self-discipline, and joy to be experienced. Your efforts to understand and support your aging relative will be comforting and reassuring to both of you. Supporting your relative to grow old gracefully with dignity will also help ease your own anxieties about aging. Treating your older relative with respect and love will serve as a positive role model for you and your own children. It can be a time to help—a time to assist your parents emotionally (and perhaps financially) when they need you. It can be a time to say thank you for all you have done for me.

When you care for an elder and watch the person grow old, you will see someone manage feelings of joy and sorrow and develop a stronger sense of self because of these experiences. Time doesn't have the same meaning for older people as it does for us, and we can learn to be less future-oriented. Your parent can teach you the importance of solving problems and handling life's irritations, as well as appreciating life's gifts. Aging relatives can also help you find what is really important in your own life by readjusting your priorities. Perhaps most important is the joy of giving when you know you are needed. Recognizing that most of the challenges that occur with aging can be dealt with will not only comfort your aging relative but will also relieve you of fears about your own aging.

Notes

1. U.S. Bureau of the Census, *Census of the Population, Detailed Characteristics*, final report (Washington, D.C.: Government Printing Office, 1981).

2. E. Shanas, "Older People and Their Families: The New Pioneers," *Journal of Marriage and the Family*, 42 (1) (1980).

3. R. Butler and M. Lewis, *Aging and Mental Health*, 3rd ed. (St. Louis: C. V. Mosby, 1982), p. 179.

4. Social Security Administration, quoted in *Aging*, February–March 1984 (N. 343) (Washington, D.C.: U.S. Department of Health and Human Services, Administration on Aging, Human Development Services), p. 3.

5. D. Fowles, "The Changing Older Population," *Aging,* May–June 1983 (N. 339), p. 10.

6. U.S. Bureau of the Census, "Money Income and Poverty Status of Families and Persons Living in the United States, 1982," in *Aging*, December 1983–January 1984 (N. 342), p. 39.

2

The Family's Role in Eldercare

COLETTE BROWNE
ROBERTA ONZUKA-ANDERSON

At first visit, it seems like the perfect Sunday dinner in the lovely colonial-style home. Mom is busy in the kitchen, Dad is carving the turkey, and the children are doing their part setting the table and feeding the dogs. There is a hum of activity and a feeling of warmth and love in this home. But something else is present in the air. We see another member of the family, the grandmother. She is sitting alone in the living room, waiting to be called in for dinner. She is eighty-one years old and still an attractive woman. She sits quietly, a member of this family, yet somehow apart from them. Dinner is called, but she does not move and we realize she must be hard of hearing. The grandson runs into the living room and talks into her good ear. "It's dinner!" he yells at her. We watch her then move slowly toward the table. She walks with the aid of a walker and her steps are slow but certain. The grandson runs ahead, too impatient to wait. The wife, the daughter-in-law of the older woman, finally sits down and joins the rest of her family who have begun eating.

"We didn't say grace," says the grandmother tensely.

"We'll say it tomorrow, Mom," says the father. "It's all right." "This is great turkey, Liz," he says to his wife. "Here, Mom, give me your plate." The grandmother doesn't respond. "Here, Mom," he says again loudly, "give me your plate for some turkey!"

"No, thank you," she replies. "You *know* turkey is bad for my indigestion." She glares at her daughter-in-law.

The daughter-in-law sits in silence. She is smoldering inside.

"Why is it nothing I do pleases her? I've been cooking almost the entire day, and besides," she thinks angrily to herself, "Tom and the kids love turkey. Does she think I only cook for her?"

As we thank them for the evening and begin to walk toward my car, the daughter-in-law calls us over. "You've got to help me," she says. "She's driving me crazy. When my father-in-law died, we all thought it would be a good idea for her to live with us. She seemed so lonely. But since she moved here, she either sits by herself looking depressed or complains. I just can't take it anymore."

✳ What in the world has happened to this perfect family? Perhaps we should take a closer look at the typical American family.

We are all born into families, and most of us grow up in them. As children and then as young adults, we are cared for by our family members. We mature and leave home, yet our family ties remain. What exactly is the definition of a family? It is a group of individuals with close ties related through blood or the law who share common goals and hopes for the future. Its purpose is not only to procreate for society but to meet the emotional and physical needs of its members. And who are the members of the family? Who do we refer to when we talk about the families of the elderly? We refer to husbands and wives, children, brothers and sisters, grandchildren, cousins, and other relatives who share a common bond with the older person. When there are no descendants or when the older adult is geographically and emotionally isolated from family members, friends and neighbors can assume the role of the family. But is there such a thing as an average American family? Family life in the United States is undergoing so many changes that it has become nearly impossible to describe the "average" American family. The nuclear family, which until recently most typified our society, is composed of a mother, father, and their children. In the nuclear family there may be close relationships with grandparents, aunts, and uncles, but these and other family members do not reside in the same house with the nuclear family. If the nuclear family did share a household with other relatives—for example, with grandparents, aunts, and uncles—then it would be called an extended family. There are obviously many other types of families in our society, including single-parent families, communal families, and blended families. Single-parent families are becoming more common with the increasing divorce rate and the number of single persons raising children. When these divorced parents remarry, the families become "blended"— hence the latter term.

As the world changes, so do our institutions. The family as an institution is not immune to these shifts in values and beliefs. Despite unceasing social change and technological advances, the family remains the major source by which we fulfill our basic needs for love and well-being. There are many aspects of family life that are undergoing change. Today we often find both parents working, for example, and families are smaller in size. One characteristic that has not changed, however, is the American family's view toward caring for older parents.

Contrary to popular opinion, most American families are very much involved with the lives of their older adults and care about what they do and where they live. While we may think that most older adults live in institutions, the facts tell us that the majority, approximately 95 percent, remain in the community. Some live alone; others live with spouses, with children, or in alternative living arrangements such as group homes or foster families. The proportion of older men versus older women living with families, however, differs dramatically. Approximately eight out of every ten men sixty-five years and over live in families. Among women, only five out of every ten of this age group live in families.[1] About half of the men approaching eight-five years of age are still married. On the other hand, only half of the women seventy years of age are still married and living with their husbands.[2]

In terms of family contact, we see that most older adults keep in fairly close communication with their children. National surveys have found that approximately 80 percent of all older adults have seen at least one child or grandchild within the last week whether they live with them or not.[3] The myth of the alienated older adult appears to be just that—a myth—and ready to be discarded. With the increasing longevity of the population, the issue of caring for aging family members will no doubt confront more and more individuals. Families who are presently providing most of the care to the disabled and frail have come face to face with a host of challenges and dilemmas

over this responsibility. Is this generation's approach to eldercare different from that of past generations? Let's take a look.

The Changing Family

America's history is that of an immigrant country. Many of our
parents and grandparents came to America in the nineteenth
century as immigrants, leaving their own families and way of
life behind. For many of our parents and even for some of us,
grandparents are merely names across the sea—"old people living in the old country." Most of us, therefore, were not raised
watching our own parents care for older family members.
There were no role models to prepare us for the aging of our
relatives . . . and of ourselves.

In the past, moreover, very few children saw their parents
and grandparents live to be old as we define the word today.
The average life expectancy in 1900 was only 47 years of age in
contrast to roughly seventy-two years of age today. We must
remember, too, that the nuclear family is a relatively new family style. Prior to 1900 it was not uncommon for families to be
made up of two and even three generations. In fact, an entire
family consisting of grandmother and grandfather, mother and
dad, and their children often lived under the same roof. The
care and welfare of older persons—eldercare—was the family's
total responsibility. There were no such programs as adult day
care, senior centers, or nursing homes to assist families in
caring for frail older adults.

Recent trends throughout the country are causing further
changes to the American family. These trends include the rising
divorce rate, the increased mobility of families, and the return
of women to the work force. Divorce, as we all know, is at an
all-time high. For every two marriages today, one ends in
divorce. Many children are being raised in families with multiple sets of parents and grandparents. It remains to be seen what
effect this trend will have on family relationships, responsibilities toward older family members, and the role of grandparents.

Families are also more mobile than in the past. Between 1975
and 1978, more than 34 percent of the total U.S. population
moved to a different residence.[4] Older people, compared to the
other age groups, are the least migratory. Among those between

sixty-five and seventy-four years of age, moving was at a rate of 15 percent; for those seventy-five and over, it was slightly more than 12 percent.[5] The amount of contact between elders and their children can be affected by geographical distance. It may be difficult to visit your mother more than once a year if she lives in New York and you reside in California. This is not an uncommon dilemma.

The number of women in the work force is also on the rise. Women's roles have traditionally included responsibilities for the family and care of the aged. Other than in wartime when women were needed in the work force, women have usually remained in the home caring for their husbands and children. When parents get old it has traditionally been the daughter or daughter-in-law who takes care of their needs. There is little question that this care is an important family and societal function. As women enter the work force in increased numbers, however, who will take over the function of eldercare? Shared responsibility between all members of the family may be one answer that will lead to a far more equitable and satisfying arrangement for the older individual as well as the family.

These changes in twentieth-century America have resulted in more middle-aged children caring for more older parents but without the knowledge or resources to do so. This is why families have turned to community programs and the federal government for assistance in caring for elders. One way to help is to understand clearly the family's role in eldercare.

The Family's Role

The family is not alone with its changing roles. Older persons begin to experience their own changes and losses. Some of these losses result in ongoing disabilities such as chronic diabetes, hypertension, arthritis, and poor eyesight and hearing. All this can add up to increased vulnerability and need for the family's support. Studies have shown that family members generally accept this responsibility. Their reasons for doing so are many: fulfilling an expectation or understanding between family members, religious belief, sense of duty, and respect or love. Now let us look at some of the factors that shape the family's role in eldercare.

Attitudes Toward Aging

Seeing a family member grow old can force you to think about your own inevitable aging. Parents can become constant reminders of what the future holds for each of us. If your parents are experiencing aging as a new opportunity for growth and are coping well with the aging process as most older people do, chances are you will not look with dread upon your own aging. If your parents face poverty, ill health, and loneliness, however, it is natural that your feelings will not be positive toward their aging (or your own) and may interfere with your involvement with them.

Health Status of Elders

Aging is not synonymous with ill health and disease. Nevertheless, aging may mean that your chances of becoming ill are greater than when you are younger and that your recuperative powers are not what they used to be. Families caring for older relatives who are mentally or physically disabled have no easy task before them. Caring for their health and personal needs may at times be burdensome and even overwhelming. It may be necessary, therefore, to take a break and seek additional services.

Watching a parent's health deteriorate is a trying experience. Some families, even those that are very loving, find the decline too dispiriting to accept. Families often pull away from their loved ones with a seeming lack of devotion when in fact they simply cannot bear to see the damages of irreversible chronic ailments. Professional help is recommended in such cases.

Economic Resources

As Social Security and private pensions become increasingly difficult to live on, some older adults may need financial assistance from their children. Depending on your resources and those of your older family members, financial needs may dictate your involvement with older relatives. Middle-aged children who can afford to help their parents are in a very different situation from those who cannot. Feelings of resentment may follow one who helps but cannot afford it; guilt may follow if a parent's request cannot be fulfilled. In either case, middle-aged children may feel in a bind and begin to seek reasons for reducing their commitment to the older family member.

Living Arrangements

The majority of older people want to remain in separate dwellings from their children for as long as possible. For the older couple whose health starts to decline, independence can be maintained by nursing one another and sharing household duties. The husband, for example, who was never expected to prepare breakfast now does so because of his wife's arthritic condition. If there is no spouse, it is often the adult child that an older person turns to in times of stress. And when disability develops to the point that care is needed, usually only two alternatives are considered: moving into the child's home or institutional care. Research has already shown us that it is the older adult without a family who is most likely to be placed in an institution. Moreover, divorce, migration, and residence in an apartment or condominium have all made it more difficult to offer a home to an aging parent. There is, however, a third alternative. The growth of community services for older adults now makes it possible for many elders to live alone successfully. Chapter 15 will provide you with more information on community services.

Quality of Past Relationships

When parents are emotionally stable and responsive to the needs of their growing child, the child is likely to be raised in a warm, nurturing environment. The child's positive feelings for her parents, moreover, will usually continue into their old age despite physical and personality changes. If the adult child believes her parents neither loved nor helped during the formative years, however, the relationship between aging parents and child may be cold and distant.

A past relationship filled with such negative emotions rarely develops into a close relationship when the parent ages. In working with older adults and their families, we have found that it is the quality of the past relationship that most often determines the children's degree of involvement with the older family member.

Misunderstood Feelings

We can understand when someone is grieving for a loved one or the loss of good health, and we sympathize. But how many of us can sympathize with someone's loss of the right to drive a car, the loss of a social role such as president of the PTA, or the loss of a pet cat or dog? These situations are more difficult for families to comprehend. A lack of communication of needs, wants, and feelings can also affect your involvement with your family member. A parent asking you to visit may be lonely; you may misinterpret this request as "putting a guilt trip on me."

Women's Return to the Work Force

It is estimated that most of the home care given to frail older adults today is provided by wives, daughters, and daughters-in-law. And as we have noted, more and more women today are working. This trend has obvious implications for the care of the elderly. What will happen when these women are not at home and are thus unable to offer this care? Will middle-aged men begin to take up this responsibility?

As older parents become more dependent, it is often the family that provides assistance and support. The support can come in varying degrees—from weekly phone calls to round-the-clock care. It can encompass assistance with income, housing, transportation, nutrition, and health care. Another form of support the family can provide is active advocacy on behalf of the older person. We all know how confusing the present health care system, Social Security, and senior citizen benefits can be, and the older adult can benefit from the family's assistance in dealing with government and other bureaucratic agencies.

Talking with Your Elder

Communication between the grown child and the parent is very important. Effective communication can make a great difference in the parent's acceptance of increasing dependence upon others. Above all, one must be realistic about the situation. If your aging mother lives alone in the family's big two-story home and is experiencing increasing health problems and difficulty managing the stairs, it may be time to discuss the alternatives—perhaps selling the family home and moving into a safer housing arrangement, finding someone to be a live-in companion, or moving her bedroom to the first floor and renting out the second floor.

Effective communication also involves discussing the matter with other family members. Consider the following situation: When Martha's husband Sam died, she and her four children and their spouses held a family meeting. It was agreed that Martha would sell the family home and the money would be put in savings for her use. She would live with her eldest daughter, son-in-law, and two grandchildren. Every weekend would be spent with her other children and their families who lived in the same town. Once a year, she would fly to California to spend two months at her fourth child's home. The arrangement was workable for almost seven years.

Then Martha began experiencing health problems. Another family meeting was held with all members present. It was decided that Martha would discontinue her yearly trips to California and instead spend all her time living with the eldest daughter and her family. It was agreed, however, that the daughter in California would call at least twice a month to speak with Martha and try to visit at least once a year. The other two children would visit their mother regularly and relieve the eldest daughter of caring for her on a weekend night. Since by this time Martha's savings were almost depleted, each child except the eldest daughter contributed a monthly allowance toward their mother's care.

Martha was actively involved in the family meetings. At first she was reluctant to give up her visits with each of her children and their families—she wished to see her grandchildren grow and to know what everyone was doing. She realized, however, that she was usually exhausted by the car or plane ride. Thus an arrangement was made for the grandchildren to visit at least once every two years. Martha was beginning to realize, moreover, that she was developing memory problems—sometimes she didn't know where she was or how to find her way around the different houses. Therefore, she was agreeable to remaining at one home. The one decision that upset Martha was the money she was receiving from her children. Everyone, including the older grandchildren, insisted that they wanted to give her something. They were so convincing, in fact, that she could not refuse them and felt loved more than ever before.

This account of Martha and her children does not discuss the disagreements that may occur from day to day. It is likely, however, that since the family has found an effective means of handling problems, their disputes will be settled through the same open discussion and joint decision-making. This is the important point. Unless all members of the family—including the older person—are involved in a decision, unnecessary resistance or bad feelings can get in the way of assisting the dependent older person.

The process of decision-making also involves examining the consequences of a decision. In the case of Martha, the children could have ignored their mother's desire to keep in touch with other family members. They might also have ignored the demands that could have resulted if the eldest daughter were solely responsible for their mother's care. Their decision to meet their mother's needs as she became more dependent demonstrates their concern for their mother as well as for each other.

Understanding the Needs of Older Adults

Martha had a need to remain independent and still see her grandchildren. What about other older adults? What are their needs? The needs of most older persons do not differ much from those of other generations. Alex Comfort, author of *A Good Age*, writes that the older adult needs four things: money, access to good health care, meaningful work, and dignity.[6] He adds that these are needed at any age to have a happy life. We all desire close, loving relationships with friends and family and value our independence and well-being.

A recent study conducted by the American Association of Retired Persons found that adults are most concerned over the need to remain independent—financially, physically, emotionally, and socially—as long as possible. This study also found that older people very much want to continue close relationships with family and friends.[7]

One way to determine the needs of your family member is to talk to your doctor. Your doctor is important to the older person's acceptance of the changes that occur in her life as well as your understanding of her needs. Consider the following example:

Thelma, age seventy-two, raised her four children on her own. Her husband died when their fourth child was still an infant. She has always been proud that she was able to earn a living as a beautician. When Thelma was sixty-nine she suffered a stroke that left her angry and depressed and feeling her life was over. Her children were concerned about her progress since she had little interest in the physical, occupational, and speech therapy sessions. It was the hospital social worker who observed that the relationship between mother and children could be influencing Thelma's acceptance of her condition. The children's discussion with Thelma on how she had coped with other hardships turned out to be instrumental in changing her attitude toward life and the therapy sessions. If her children had not been able to cope with their mother's feelings of depression and inadequacy or felt that they could not discuss things with her, they probably would not have been able to provide the encouragement she needed. Fortunately the relationship was always a strong one and Thelma eventually came to cope with her disabilities through her children's support.

As dependency grows, there are decisions that must be reached which are painful to all involved. These decisions are not easy to discuss and are made even more difficult if the relationship between parent and child is strained. An older person's need for assistance may be due to a gradual decline which can be prepared for, or it may stem from an unexpected crisis. In either case, many factors must be considered in deciding where your parent will live, what hospital she should receive treatment at, and whether or not she should liquidate her financial assets. Perhaps most important to consider are her desires. Her wishes, however, must be weighed against her needs. There are far too many older people who are unhappy because decisions were made for them. An older parent may move into her child's home in a new neighborhood and be assured of balanced meals, for example, but she may have given up the security of a familiar environment and an irreplaceable circle of friends. You'll have to consider these factors and many others in making decisions with your older family member.

The wish for independence is sometimes hard to encourage if

your older family member has a chronic ailment and is handicapped. This does not necessarily mean that the person needs
total support, however. Try to remember that the needs of Mom
and Aunt Minnie are not exactly the same just because they are
both seventy years of age. Do you have exactly the same needs
as your neighbor just because you're both the same age? One of
the best ways to understand the needs of your older family
member is simply to talk with her. Find out her hopes for the
future. Her future may be limited in time, but it's a future none-
theless. Above all, remember that few want to be considered
the "family problem."

Facing the Reality of Home Care

The prospect of seeing parents grow into old age is much more
likely today than it was fifty years ago. Middle-aged children,
often caught between caring for an older parent and their own
children, face a multitude of issues.

Chronic illness and chronic care are two major concerns of
aging persons and their families. Chronic illness refers to a disease that has no known cure. It can mean an end to an independent way of life, and no one wants to feel dependent on others.
While most of us boast of our independent nature as opposed to
our dependent one, we tend to forget that we all rely on our
families and society for love and self-confirmation. Although
many older people need some assistance, this does not imply
total dependency. Neither does it imply the older adult's second
childhood or a role reversal for the middle-aged child. It is
strictly a change in dependency needs.

Another issue facing families is the difficulty of providing
round-the-clock care. While it has been documented that 80
percent of frail older adults are cared for by a spouse or other
family member, there is little information on how families are
coping and whether they are in fact doing so with a great deal
of stress. After all, providing care can be extremely demanding
and stressful to the entire family. A person who is frail, for
example, may not be able to bathe, feed, or dress without assistance. Even taking someone to the doctor can be a laborious
task. Moreover, caring for a confused elder often makes the
caregiver as well as the elder homebound. Other considerations
are the *age* of the caregiver and whether he or she has any assis-

tance. Many spouses who are themselves in their seventies and eighties are caring for a frail husband or wife. This responsibility can have a harmful effect on the health of the caregivers if they neglect their own well-being.

For the adult child, there are still other issues involved in the care of older family members. A study done at the University of Southern California found that the most common issue facing families caring for an older adult was guilt.[8] Middle-aged children who feel responsible for their parents' well-being can feel guilty if the parent is lonely, depressed, or ill. Faced with problems of juggling careers, children, and their homes, middle-aged children often feel guilty if they do not have sufficient time to spend with Mom and Dad. And placing a parent in a nursing home can add to these feelings of guilt if you didn't do all you could to prevent it.

You can assist your older parent by acknowledging three very simple points:

- *Dependency is human!* Help only when it is appropriate—not too much and not too little. If you're not sure what is too much or too little, ask.
- *Mutual dependency is good!* You both have something of value to give to each other and to other members of the family. Enjoy each other.
- *Communicate!* Talk to each other and recognize the fact that we all grow and change. Everyone is worth knowing and we all have our own story to tell.

Benefits of Eldercare

While there may be problems associated with caring for a dependent older person at home, there are also benefits. As the oldest living members of the family, grandparents can provide a sense of beginning and continuity to the family system. Their knowledge of the past can lend greater meaning to the present and future; their wisdom from years of experience can offer guidance for the younger generation. Their multitude of life's experiences, both personal and political (World Wars I and II, the Depression), have given older adults a broad perspective that is valuable when critical family decisions need to be made.

Families benefit themselves when there is a reciprocal

arrangement with their aging relative. Often teenagers can go
to a grandparent for advice when a parent reacts too strongly to
the adolescent's need for independence. The older person, on
the other hand, through her contribution to the family, can gain
a sense of worth and fulfillment. The family's acceptance of the
elder's contributions reaffirms her position within the family
system. Nor should we forget that the older person's role in the
family and the degree of respect she receives will influence the
younger family members' view of the older adult as well as
their own aging process. The older adult, whether physically or
mentally impaired, also benefits from living with her family as
they are more sensitive to her personal, emotional, and medical
needs. The following case illustrates how both parties can benefit in the elder/child relationship.

Nancy returned to her hometown after fifteen years of living
in another state. Her husband, Roy, was in the military and
recently retired. Their decision to move back to her hometown
was prompted by the death of Nancy's father—she feared that
her mother would go downhill rapidly if she lived alone in the
family home. Because of Roy's transient career in the military,
Nancy and the children had never had a real home of their own.
Prior to returning to her hometown, Nancy and Roy met with
her mother, Ella, and decided on an arrangement that would
benefit all. Nancy, Roy, and their two sons would move into the
large family home Ella was presently living in alone. An extension was built to allow for privacy, but they would share the
kitchen. In exchange for a reasonable rent, Nancy and Roy
agreed to care for Ella in her old age. Ella, on her part, agreed to
help Nancy with the boys. When both Nancy and Roy found
jobs, they relied heavily on Ella to share in the responsibility of
raising their two sons. Ella enjoyed her grandchildren and they,
in turn, loved and respected their grandmother. The arrangement has continued to be rewarding for all.

We see, then, that aging is a process which begins at birth and
ends with death. For the most part, families remain actively
concerned about their older family members. Certainly there
are problems associated with aging that may lead to an emotional or physical separation between you and your older family member. But separating the elderly from families and the
mainstream of society may cause even greater problems. By
viewing aging as a continuous process we all go through, we

preserve a sense of our roots and the true meaning of "family." By separating the aging individual from society, we lose touch with aging as a process we will all experience—and thus we lose touch with ourselves.

Notes

1. U.S. Bureau of the Census, *Census of the Population: 1970 Detailed Characteristics*, Final Report PC(1)D1, table 204 (Washington, D.C.: Government Printing Office, 1972).

2. Ibid., table 203.

3. E. Shanas and P. Hauser, "Zero Population Growth and the Family Life of Older People," *Journal of Social Sciences* 30 (4) (1974): 79–92; Harns and Associates, *The Myth and Reality of Aging in America* (Washington, D.C.: National Council on Aging, 1975), p. 223.

4. *Public Policy and the Frail and Elderly* (Washington, D.C.: Federal Council on Aging, 1976).

5. Ibid.

6. Alex Comfort, *A Good Age* (New York: Crown Publishers, 1976).

7. I. Hirschfield and H. Dennis, "Perspectives," in Pauline Ragan (ed.), *Aging Parents* (Los Angeles: University of Southern California Press, 1979), pp. 6–8.

8. Ibid.

3

Caring for Disabled Elders

RITA VANDIVORT

Alice is a 40-year-old woman whose father and mother have become progressively dependent upon her for assistance. Her mother has had rheumatoid arthritis for the past fifteen years—her right elbow is frozen, and she has very limited use of her right hand, both knees, and ankles. She has suffered from two strokes, resulting in damage to her speech and kidney, and is bedridden most of the time. In some ways, though, Alice is fortunate. Although her mother lives with her, her father chose to live in a residential care home to lessen the burdens on his daughter and son-in-law.

Alice had been raised in a family which provided total care for an invalid grandmother and elderly friend. Her decision to care for her own mother was therefore influenced by her past experience as well as her desire to help her mother remain at home as long as possible.

Alice and her husband reside in their own home; they have no children and work full time. Alice's mother lives in her own cottage next to their house. Her personal needs are provided by her daughter and son-in-law. Breakfast and lunch are left in thermos bottles next to her bed. On especially difficult or painful days, her son-in-law returns home during his lunch break to help feed her. Dinners are spent together as a family. Alice and her husband have made several adjustments to meet the needs of her mother. An automatic dialer phone was installed in the bedroom. A whistle around her mother's neck can be used whenever help is needed—neighbors, relatives, and friends have been alerted, too. Weekends are busy with household chores, mother's Saturday appointment at the doctor, and visits with her father. If Alice and her husband must change this schedule, a relative is called in to help. Although Alice feels her brothers and sisters assist her, she recognizes that the primary responsibility of her mother's care remains with her and her husband.

National health statistics show that families like Alice and her husband provide approximately 80 percent of all home health care to ill and frail elders.[1] This finding certainly contradicts a common belief that families are indifferent to older family members or desert them as they grow older. It also contradicts the popular notion that only health professionals can provide care once an older person's functions reach a certain level of dependence. Recent studies have discovered that the absence of a caregiver at home is the critical factor in nursing home placement as opposed to what elders can or cannot do for themselves.[2] Who are the caregivers? They are people like Alice who provide care at home to an ill or frail older person, usually a family member.

Caregivers at home often deal with the same burdens as do professionally trained staff employed at hospitals and nursing homes—but without the education and training. Often the services available to facility staff are not available to families caring for elders at home. Families also are "on call" twenty-four hours a day, 365 days a year, unlike professionals. Another problem is that our health and social care system is biased toward paying for institutional care rather than assisting families with the same functions. In other words, institutional care may be paid for by Medicare and Medicaid, but Medicare will not reimburse a family member who must stay home to provide the same care. Studies have shown that a certain percentage of elders residing in nursing homes could function outside these facilities if only social and physical services were available.[3] Caregivers are doing a physically and psychologically demanding job with negligible assistance from either the government or their community. How are they doing this? And why?

When asked in a recent study why they continue to provide home care despite the lack of community and financial assistance, most family members say they do so because of love and affection for their elder.[4] They also wish to avoid the alternative of nursing home placement. Caregivers often speak of the rewards of caring for an elder at home: the overall benefits to the family, the funny incidents, the affection given and received from the elder, and the pride in doing a tough job. But the sacrifices and stresses are also real. What are the problems these caregivers face? And are there solutions?

Stress on Family Caregivers

During the last decade of hospital care there has been increasing pressure from government and insurance companies to keep the patient's stay in the hospital as short as possible. This trend is not surprising in light of rising hospital costs. As a result, families usually have little time to prepare for caring for an older relative at home upon discharge from a hospital. Often the family is still in crisis at this point, especially after a catastrophic health loss by the elder. Family conferences to sort out the problems are all too rare. If one family member assumes the responsibility for care, family resentments can develop over the question of a fair distribution of the burden. These feelings may further divide the family and make cooperation difficult.

After a catastrophic episode of illness, it may be impossible to leave the older adult alone for any length of time. Visits to a friend may be accomplished only with great physical effort and the use of a wheelchair or walker. Consequently, the older person may become more and more withdrawn. The result is not only a homebound elder but a homebound caregiver. Routine responsibilities such as grocery shopping and banking become major campaigns involving relief from another family member or sympathetic neighbor. Recreation for the caregiver becomes a luxury, perhaps taking more energy to arrange than the relief it might provide.

Growing Demands, Shrinking Resources

Families providing round-the-clock care often find that one family member, usually a wife, daughter, or daughter-in-law, must give up a job to care for Grandma or Grandpa—often representing a severe financial loss to the family. Seeking relief in day care or hired help can further tax the family's financial situation, as these services usually must be paid for with private funds. The homebound caregiver often pays the price in social isolation, too. Most activities are scheduled around the elder's needs. Most conversation is with the elder. The cumulative result is often a type of cabin fever, or role fatigue, with no end in sight other than the death of the older person—a thought that only brings feelings of guilt to the caregiver who thought them.[5]

For younger caregivers, competing demands may be more of a problem than role fatigue. Exhaustion may ensue when different family members begin making demands on the caregiver. The following case illustrates this situation. Jane, a young woman with a husband and three children, recently took her mother into her home to provide convalescent care after surgery. Responding to her increased tasks, Jane focused on doing essential services as quickly as possible, sometimes forgetting in her hurry to spend time talking with her mother. Jane's husband and children, missing the time they used to have with Jane, began to make more demands on her to gain her companionship. Jane's mother also made demands on her and felt neglected because Jane didn't take time to sit and talk. As a result Jane found everyone escalating their demands on her. She ended up exhausted, but satisfying no one.

This case came to the attention of a social worker at a community care program of a medical center. It was clear that Jane needed to reduce the pressures on her and her family. The social worker suggested that if Jane tried to involve her spouse and children in caring for her mother rather than trying to shield them, the family might then understand her burdens as well as lend a hand. Since Jane also needed to spend time with her mother just talking and listening, she decided to sit down with her on a regular basis whether or not she needed help. Jane also found it helpful to give everyone in the family a special time—lunch with mother, after school with children, evening with her husband—to avoid their feelings of competition with one another.

Changes in Life-Style

Another common stress is brought on by a change in the family's life-style. What does it mean for a family to care for an aging relative at home? The daily household routine may be disrupted when the parent needs the family for emotional support. A room may have to be arranged as a sickroom. The family may need to prepare special meals, assist in cleaning, and monitor medications. All of these tasks are demanding by themselves. But they cause further stress when they are combined with anxiety over the older person's failing health as well as the caregiver's fears about discharging these duties.

New Relationships

Yet another stress on caregivers is caused by the need to redefine the relationship for both persons. The older family member now becomes more dependent upon her child, the principal caregiver. The child that the older adult once took care of is now the person providing food, housing, and assistance with personal hygiene. Conflicts can occur especially when the caregiver must take care of the elder's finances and personal hygiene. The woman caring for her disabled husband may be managing their financial life for the first time—a common situation as women often outlive their spouses. Apart from the physical help she may give her ill husband, she must now take a new role in family decision-making. It may be hard to discuss the relationship openly if both sides have trouble adjusting to new disabilities and new responsibilities. And often there is no one to whom the caregiver can turn for support with these changes.

Chronic Illness

Caregivers often experience stress just observing the irreversible nature of the chronic illnesses afflicting their older family member. Although modern medicine has increasingly extended life expectancy, there is another side of the coin: Those who do live long will probably have more chronic conditions such as arthritis, heart disease, or diabetes. Rehabilitation and medical treatment may offer gains but no cures. A woman caring for her ill mother as well as her own children put the dilemma clearly: "When my children need help, I teach them how to do for themselves and they later become independent. With my mother, there is no hope she will ever become independent again; she will only become more dependent." Some illnesses may also change the behavior of the ill elder, thereby necessitating further adjustments in the relationship.

Fatigue

Fatigue is the most common complaint of family caregivers. It is the cumulative cost of caregiving at home unless efforts are made to protect oneself and set realistic limits. Older caregivers may be hindered by failing health, decreasing energy, and strained finances. Younger caregivers may be healthy and energetic and yet have numerous competing demands from family, friends, or career.[6] All caregivers must be careful to avoid chronic fatigue and its harmful consequences.

Survival Strategies for Caregivers

Like all humans dealing with the process of living, you may have a variety of feelings about being a caregiver. It is common to feel anger at the responsibilities, frustration with the burdens, and fear for the future. These are natural feelings and should be expressed without guilt. Try to bear in mind, however, *when* and *who* you are sharing them with. Some of the critical questions of caregiving—"How long will she need me as caregiver?" and "Will she become more dependent?"—are unanswerable. Some caregivers succeed simply by taking one day at a time.

The following suggestions are offered to help families that are caring for an elder relative at home. There are countless other strategies, of course, as many as there are situations. The most important idea behind these suggestions is that caregivers should not feel guilty about setting their own limits. Implicit in providing care to another person is taking care of yourself. Otherwise, the caregiving cannot continue without harming all family members.

Set Limits

Determine whether a particular aspect of caregiving is especially stressful to you, and then seek relief in that area. In this way a significant amount of stress can be reduced. Linda, for instance, was very uncomfortable bathing her father. In fact, her anxiety about this issue was draining her. When her husband agreed to bathe him instead, Linda was quite relieved and had more energy left for her other caregiving tasks.

Deal with Problems Immediately

It is important to deal with a problem before it becomes a crisis.
If your older family member is causing you to feel resentment,
try to talk openly about it before tempers become hot and sides
are drawn. In Alice's situation, for example, her parents had
previously lived with each of their four children and their families for three-month periods. This was a workable arrangement
for two years until Alice's parents had trouble negotiating the
stairs in some homes and her father became confused by the
constant moving. Her parents were also losing touch with
friends and relatives who could not keep up with their movements.

Although the parents were welcomed in each of their children's homes, it became evident that this was not the best
arrangement. Alice, her brothers and sister, and her parents
held a family meeting to discuss the situation and decide on a
satisfactory solution. They decided to build a small cottage on
Alice's property. Alice and her husband financed the home; a
cousin built it; the other sister furnished the home; and the
brothers helped with the upkeep and insurance. Her parents
were then able to live in a permanent location while still being
near the family and having their own privacy. Alice, her sister,
and her brothers were able to resolve their problem through
open discussion and by making their decision a family project.

Build a Support Network

Build a network of persons to provide you with relief. Many
find it difficult to ask others for help, yet sometimes it is crucial
to get relief in order to be able to continue caregiving. Perhaps
other brothers or sisters or even children can take regularly
scheduled turns at relieving you. Friends and neighbors may
also be willing to help if asked. Caregivers must learn to be
resourceful to find the support they need. Community programs can also provide assistance.

Minimize Special Efforts

You can also lessen certain burdens by minimizing special
efforts for the elder. Even though your older family member is

on a low-salt diet, there are still ways to cook only one meal for the whole family—thus avoiding making multiple dinners at each meal. Adaptive equipment, especially in the bathroom, can sometimes lessen the physical burdens of caregiving by allowing the frail person to move independently.

Maximize Independence

Maximizing the elder's independence can lighten the burdens on you and also make the elder feel more useful. Have your elder help in any way she can. Folding clothes can be done from a wheelchair, for example, and is good exercise while allowing her to contribute to the family. The elder should make as many decisions as possible, even if they are small ones. The manner in which a question is raised can help even a mentally confused person make decisions. Offer definite choices. Avoid open-ended questions. Instead of asking "What shirt do you want to wear today?" ask "Would you like to wear the green or red shirt?" Be resourceful about new ways to do old hobbies. Weeding the outside garden may not be possible anymore, but what about watering houseplants? Crocheting can be done using larger hooks. Being well groomed and dressed in street clothes is important even if the elder is not leaving the house. And eating is a major social event that should be shared with the family whenever possible.

Don't Forget the Community

While many families are presently caring for an older disabled family member at home, there are certain demographic and societal changes that may alter this trend. There is, for example, the present and anticipated increase in the number of older adults. Projections state that 20 percent of our population will be sixty and over by the year 2020—one out of five people. Moreover, the majority of services provided to the old are done by daughters and daughters-in-law; clearly, women's reentry into the work force will affect their roles as caregivers. Changes in family life-style and traditional responsibilities toward the older family member may exacerbate family conflicts. Few supportive services are presently offered to families as round-the-clock caregivers, thus increasing the multiple stresses on their lives. But there are services available in the community to help with home care. Many are tax-supported and do not cost the older person anything so long as certain geographical, financial, or other eligibility criteria are met. The local agency on aging or state office on aging will be able to refer you to the appropriate agency for assistance. You may encounter waiting lists for services, but don't get discouraged. If you are placed on such a list, call periodically to make sure your name is still on it. Check with Chapter 15 for additional information on community resources.

Not all are able (or willing) to share in the commitment to caring for an ill and disabled family member. It is a tough decision with no rules to follow and no right answers. It is a decision to be made by the entire family, most certainly including the older adult, and the physician as well. It may come down to what you are willing to do and how much you are willing to give. The needs and desires of your elder, the needs of your family, your own feelings, the reality of the situation—all must be taken into account to reach the best decision for all involved.

Notes

1. P. Uhlenberg, "Cohort Variations in Family Life Cycle Experiences of United States Females," *Journal of Marriage and the Family* 36 (1974).

2. J. L. Barney, "The Prerogative of Choice in Long-Term Care," *Gerontologist* 17 (1977); Stanley Brody, Walter Puulshock, and Carla Maschiochhi, "The Family Caring Unit: A Major Consideration in the Long-Term Care Support System," *Gerontologist* 18 (1978).

3. M. Powell Lawton, "Institutions and Alternatives for Older People," *Health and Social Work* 3 (2) (1978); Maureen Balthay, *Long-Term Care for the Elderly and Disabled* (Washington, D.C.: Congressional Budget Office, Government Printing Office, 1977).

4. Vida Goldstein, Gretchen Regnery, and Edward Wellen, "Caregiver Role Fatigue," *Nursing Outlook* (January 1981).

5. Ibid.

6. Ibid.

PART TWO
HEALTH CONCERNS

4

Exercise and Aging

MARY BRENEMAN
OTTO NEURATH
COLETTE BROWNE

Marian's husband died of cancer six months ago. Even though he had been ill for quite some time, his death came as a shock to her. Since his death, Marian has been unable to shake her feelings of depression and appears to have lost interest in her surroundings. She lives alone and is visited almost daily by at least one of her four children, but this has not helped to brighten her spirits. She spends most of her time sitting in her favorite chair, either watching television or doing nothing. One of her daughters recently asked Marian to join her family on a vacation; but Marian refused, claiming she was too weak and too tired to go. Four weeks ago, however, something wonderful happened to Marian. A visit from an old friend entirely changed her life. She began to step out into the world on her own again. She accompanied friends on walks and visited the museums and parks she had never had the time for. Marian seemed, miraculously to her family, like her former old self. She now takes regular walks, has joined a yoga class, and even went on a recent trip with her children to Las Vegas.

What was this miraculous secret Marian's friend shared with her? It wasn't a new medication or the name of a new doctor. It was a revived interest in life through *movement*. The magic was exercise.

As older Americans increase in numbers, there is a concomitant increase in attention given to exercise as a way of ridding people of surplus weight and sustaining a healthy mind and body. Exercise is being touted as a cure-all for physical ailments, as a necessity for preventing poor health, even as a fountain of youth. Newspapers bombard readers with reports about older persons jogging and running in marathons. Are these claims true or exaggerations? The value of exercise is recognized by most professionals, but what about most older persons? Is exercise necessary, useful, and suitable for older people? Is there such a thing as too much exercise? Is exercise ever *not* recommended; and, if so, when?

The Benefits of Exercise

After a brisk walk, a game of tennis, or other form of exercise, most people look and feel better. Exercise is the systematic practice of parts of the body with the goal of strengthening them and improving general body functions. Exercise can strengthen bones and slow down the process of osteoporosis, a bone thinning disorder especially common in older women. Exercise can establish and maintain muscle tone, assist in digestion, strengthen respiration, and help keep weight down when combined with a sensible, balanced diet. There is also evidence that regular exercise helps to strengthen the heart, increase circulation of the blood, control blood pressure, and reduce the incidence of phlebitis. And, as in Marian's case, exercise can also help people feel better about themselves.

Science is just beginning to research what people have known for a long time—that sitting leads to more sitting; inactivity leads to lethargy; and boredom may even lead to illness. Thus many health professionals are beginning to recommend exercise as a treatment to their patients. Dr. James Fries, director of the Stanford University Arthritis Center, tells his patients to exercise and to use the body or lose its strength. Run, not rest, is his advice.[1] "The way to keep lively is to be lively," says the President's Council on Physical Fitness.[2] But *why* is exercise good for older adults?

Proper exercise, when organized on a regular basis, is beneficial to body and mind. The heart becomes stronger with exercise since it can accomplish its work with fewer beats than the nonexercised heart. Exercise may reduce the risk of heart attack and promotes recovery following an attack. Although the heart as a muscle pumps blood to all parts of the body, it does not pump blood back to itself. This task is mainly accomplished through muscular activity. Muscles that are not exercised by walking, swimming, or some other means can cause the blood to stagnate, especially in the legs, and result in varicose veins and blood clotting. Exercise assists the heart by improving circulation.

Besides benefiting the heart, exercise is beneficial to the respiratory system. We breathe by expanding the chest and lowering the diaphragm—thus air is virtually sucked into the lungs. When your chest muscles are not exercised, however, it is easier for your lungs to get "out of breath." Stagnation of the blood in the lower part of the lungs can easily lead to infections such as bronchitis and pneumonia. People who are not physically active tire easily and can accumulate fat more readily than those who exercise regularly. A person who exercises regularly feels generally stronger, healthier, and happier than the person who does not exercise.

But What About Older People?

Generally speaking, people of all ages should exercise. Most older people, even those with illnesses or disabilities, can participate in some form of exercise. Exercise, for example, is often a prescribed treatment for stroke victims. People with heart disease are usually encouraged to do breathing exercises. President Franklin Delano Roosevelt, whose legs were totally paralyzed from polio, went swimming almost daily as part of his exercise program.

Children rarely need to be encouraged to exercise—their high energy levels inevitably promote their engagement in all kinds of activities. But with age there is sometimes less incentive to exercise. We are often "too busy" to spend the time. The only exercise many working middle-aged and older adults engage in, unfortunately, is walking from the house to their car in the morning and back to the house at night. Time will tell if the recent thrust into physical exercise of many Americans is merely a fad or a true change in life-style that will result in healthier older Americans.

It is true that there are physical changes in later life that can make one question the ability to exercise. Joints may stiffen and be painful from arthritis. Tiredness is common. Eyesight is not

quite as sharp as it once was. Exercising is only too easy to post-
pone to another day. And yet it is extremely important for older
people to exercise. As we have already noted, certain body
functions—muscular strength, blood circulation, and breathing
capacities, for example—can be improved and maintained
through proper exercise. People of all ages, especially older
people, should become aware of the importance of regular
exercise for the promotion of good health and the enjoyment
of life.

What types of exercise are best? There is no such thing as a
ready-made exercise program for an individual. If an older person has not exercised for a long time, it is best to see a physician
for advice. A physician can be of great assistance in planning an
exercise program to suit individual needs and health considerations. If the physician does not object to exercise, the choice
of what to do is up to the individual.

The best form of exercise involves the entire body and is
above all fun. Walking, for example, is good for all ages and can
be done to the point of moderate fatigue. (You should *feel* you
have done it.) Walking is also enjoyable, and neighborhoods can
be rediscovered through a walk around town. Other forms of
exercise, such as swimming, bicycling (even on a stationary
bike), and running for short distances, are also valuable. Older
adults may find, however, that they need to limit the amount of
exercising they do. Instead of jogging twelve miles a day, for
example, three may be enough. Again, *experiment*—but only
after seeing a physician. Isolated exercises such as lifting
weights at the YWCA, or certain forms of dancing and yoga, are
also beneficial and fun. Whatever form of exercise is chosen, it
should be enjoyable. Once the point of fatigue is reached, stop
the activity. If unusual symptoms such as aches or shortness of
breath develop, stop the activity and see your doctor.

Most people will be able to increase their exercise time the
longer they keep at it. Many marathon runners, for example,
will tell you that they started running two, three, and four
miles, and slowly, very slowly, worked their way up to twenty-
six miles. It is best to do some sort of exercise daily, even for
short periods, for maximum benefit. Competitive exercise may
or may not be advisable—check with a physician for advice.
Remember that sports need not be competitive to be enjoyable.
The main purpose in finding an enjoyable activity program is

that the person will continue exercising regularly and reap the full benefits of keeping active.

What about getting started? Some older people, especially those who have led sedentary lives for most of their years, may find the thought of exercising frightening. They may fear that exercise will do them more harm than good. The opposite is usually the case. It is true that many older persons have chronic health conditions that can interfere with exercising. Because of this, they may tire easily and experience discomfort, especially when starting an exercise program. Certain chronic ailments common with older adults, such as osteoarthritis, can cause stiffness and joint pain. But on the whole, exercise, if started slowly, can gradually strengthen muscles and alleviate pain and stiffness in joints and muscles. Nor is a chronic heart condition usually a reason to stop exercising. It may be necessary to limit the extent of physical activity, but heart specialists today stress the importance of exercise for a healthy heart. Again, as a general rule of thumb, any new exercise program should be started slowly and gradually and after a visit to a trusted physician. Once in an exercise program, the person can judge for herself how much and how often the activity can then be enjoyed.

What About Those Who Can't Exercise Alone?

What happens when the family physician does not recommend starting a new exercise program for you or your older relative? What if the physician recommends the services of a physical therapist? Do not be discouraged. The goals of independent exercise and a prescribed exercise therapy program are the same—to promote and maintain an active, independent lifestyle. Physical therapy is a form of therapeutic care with an emphasis on restoring lost function in a physically impaired person. If this is not possible, the person is taught to function *with* the disability. Physical therapists strive to restore a level of function that will permit the person to be as independent as possible. Ambulation, or getting the person up and about, is a common goal. Registered physical therapists are trained in the application of therapeutic exercise, heat, and many other forms of treatment to restore lost or poor function due to accident or illness. Supportive mechanical devices such as walkers, canes, and prosthetic equipment can restore much functional capacity to a great number of people. Physical therapy can also restore a person's will to live and self-esteem by enabling her to continue to be a lively member of society.

An older adult is usually referred to a physical therapist by a physician. People with many different diagnoses—cerebrovascular accident (stroke), hip fracture, Parkinson's disease, dementia, and generalized weakness due to bedrest—are seen by physical therapists. What can be expected from a physical therapy session? When first visiting a physical therapist, a person is evaluated in seven areas: joint range of motion, muscle strength, activities of daily living, gait, posture, and sensory and psychological evaluations. Let's take a closer look at these areas:

- *Joint range of motion:* This refers to the amount of movement present in a joint. The range of motion in a joint is evaluated to determine whether there is a specific joint problem. A physical therapist may follow a general evaluation or may use a goniometer, which measures joint motion in degrees.
- *Muscle strength:* How strong are the muscles? This area is evaluated by a graded muscle test and a general assessment.
- *Activities of daily living:* Can the person accomplish tasks such as getting in and out of a bed or chair, getting up and down stairs, or transferring to a commode or toilet from a wheelchair? Can these tasks be done independently or is assistance required?
- *Gait:* This refers to the way a person walks. Evaluation includes examination for any instability as well as its cause, such as weakness, dizziness, or vision and hearing problems. The need for a cane or walker is also assessed.
- *Posture:* Is the person able to stand upright? Is she hunched over? Does she favor one side over the other?
- *Sensory and perceptual evaluation:* It is important to assess for a loss of touch, pain, and temperature sensation since the loss of these sensory functions affects a person's recovery. Sensory losses are often found in stroke victims, especially those with left-sided weakness. As a result, the individual often ignores sensory input from the involved side. In fact, the extremity may not be used even if the muscle is working. A loss of vertical and horizontal space perception is also com-

mon in hemiplegic (half-paralyzed) persons. In other words, the individual may not know if she is standing erect, bent over, or leaning heavily to one side. This problem will, obviously, make learning how to walk again difficult, but by no means impossible.

- *Psychological evaluation:* Alertness, orientation, ability to follow instructions, and motivation are evaluated in this part of the examination. These characteristics are often a key to a successful rehabilitation program. A person confused due to severe dementia will not be able to follow directions. (Chapter 8 will provide you with further suggestions.) Many older adults become depressed and lose motivation after a serious illness or disability. This is understandable. But, in most cases, the first signs of progress and success will bring a return of enthusiasm toward the exercise program.

Physical Therapy Programs

After you or your family member has been evaluated by a physical therapist, a treatment plan will be developed. The physical therapist may decide that the older person does not require his or her services and will instead recommend an exercise program. Or the therapist may decide, following an assessment, that an active or passive, preventive, or bed-bound type of therapy program would be most beneficial.

An exercise program may be classified as active or passive. In an active program, the exercise or motion is performed *by* the older person; in a passive program, the therapist performs the action *on* the person. In either case, the physical therapist should be asked about following such a program at home.

If you or your family member has been placed on a preventive exercise program planned by a physical therapist, the program may be as simple as providing encouragement to walk or a general strengthening or range of motion program. Or it may be more specific, such as increasing the range of motion of an individual joint, say a knee or shoulder. A loss of adequate knee flexion, for example, can make going up and down stairs difficult, which, in turn, will begin to limit activity. Specific exercises can correct this problem.

Muscular strength must be preserved. It is unfortunate that so little attention is paid to overall strength until the person begins to notice she is not quite as strong as she once was. The normal—but incorrect—response is to reduce the amount of activity. This tendency unfortunately begins a cycle of decreased activity which often leads to even less muscle strength. Rather than reduce or stop an activity, consult a physician and physical therapist. The best exercise anyone can do is to walk. Walking not only maintains strength, but improves circulation and endurance. In conjunction with the walking, it is wise to follow through with a short program of exercises at least one or two times a day. A joint that is carried through its range ten times a day will retain its mobility. And since mobility, once lost, is difficult to restore, prevention is definitely worth the time and effort.

One of the worst things that can happen to a reasonably healthy person is to spend most of her time in bed. Some of the negative side effects of bed rest include loss of muscle strength and endurance, atrophy from disuse (muscle shrinkage), joint stiffness, osteoporosis, and thrombophlebitis. There may be times, however, when your family member is bed-bound. What can be done to prevent a loss of strength and muscle tone?

While the person who is bed-bound cannot be expected to play basketball or a set of tennis, there are exercises that can be done to strengthen muscle tone and flexibility. If your aging relative is confined to bed for a few days or for an indefinite period of time, bed exercises can be carried out to prevent further complications. It is best to check with your physician and a licensed physical therapist for a demonstration of such exercises.

Initially, an exercise program for the bed-bound should concentrate on keeping all available motions intact. As your relative advances beyond this point, it is good to use weights in the program to increase her strength. Weights can either be purchased or made by filling bags with sand. These bags can be weighed on a bathroom scale to ensure the correct amount.

Isometric exercises may or may not be recommended by a physician or physical therapist. These exercises consist simply of tightening a muscle around a joint without actually moving the joint. Isometric exercises can increase the blood flow around a joint and help to maintain muscle tone and are, at times, recommended when a joint is too sore to move. Some physicians believe these exercises may not be beneficial to those with heart disease, however, so consult your doctor.

The exercises described in Table 1 can be done by a person in bed at home with the approval of a physician. They can be performed twice a day, ten times each. If they are painful or your relative becomes very tired, check with your physician before continuing the activity. Be sure to break the exercise time down into several short periods throughout the day. These exercises should be done *actively*—without assistance. They can also be performed while sitting in a wheelchair, as most of them require the person to be in a sitting position.

Motivating Older Adults

Whether your older family member is independent, in need of some assistance, or bed-bound, you may run into a roadblock when you recommend exercising. If this happens, try to understand your relative's feelings. After years of getting around independently—driving a car or walking to the bus stop—an older person's loss of ambulation and movement can lead to feelings of inadequacy and a poor self-image. Tasks that once were done with great ease now seem laborious. The older person, faced with handicaps, can feel frustrated and lose enthusiasm for accomplishing anything involving physical activity. What can be done? Older people are like younger ones in that no one wants to feel dependent on others. Those with physical handicaps need encouragement. They also need specific information showing them how to use and retain their exisiting abilities. Certain devices and techniques can improve their functioning or help them adapt to their changed body image.

What about an older family member who is physically and mentally able to exercise but has lost the desire to do so? Because exercise is so important to people of all ages, it is worth the effort to encourage your family member to begin an exercise program. First, talk to your relative and try to find out *why* she does not want to exercise. Does she believe it will be dangerous? Does she equate exercise with boredom? Does she know where to start? Does she think she'll look foolish exercising at her age? Does she feel the neighborhood is no longer safe to go on walks? Would she exercise if someone accompanied

Table 1. Active Range of Motion Exercises
(to be done in a sitting position)

UPPER EXTREMITIES

Shoulder Exercises

- Lift the arm slowly forward and upward. Keep the arm straight. Return it slowly to the starting position.
- Move the arm away from the side and raise it sideways and upward. Keep the arm straight. Return it slowly to the starting position.
- Place the palm of the hand on or near the back of the neck. Then rotate the arm downward and place the hand in the small of the back.
- Move the arm from the side of the body to a 90° angle. Make circles with the arms, keeping the elbows straight.

Elbow Exercise

- Bend the elbow until the fingertips touch the shoulder (if possible). Then fully straighten the arm.

Wrist and Hand Exercises

- Bend the wrist back and forth as far as possible.
- Bend the fingers, making a fist. Then fully straighten the fingers.

LOWER EXTREMITIES

Hip Exercises

- Sit with hip and knee bent and the lower part of the leg hanging over the edge of a bed or chair. Bend up at the hip, bringing the knee up in the air.
- Sit with the lower part of the leg hanging over the edge of a chair or bed. Move one foot inward in front of the other leg, rotating the thigh outward.
- Sit with the lower part of the leg hanging over the edge of a chair or bed. Move one foot outward, rotating the thigh inward.

Knee Exercise

- Sit on a chair. Bend the knee as far as possible and then straighten it.

Ankle Exercises

- Raise the toes and foot forward as far as possible.
- Bend the toes and foot downward as far as possible.

her? Whatever the reasons, listen carefully and try to offer specific solutions to her problems. One woman, for example, wanted her mother to join a health club with her. Her mother's refusal left her daughter puzzled and concerned. It turned out that the mother no longer felt comfortable driving at night. When the daughter volunteered to pick her mother up and drop her at home, her mother readily agreed to join the club.

Talk to your family member about her hopes and fears regarding her body. Adjusting to the idea that one's strength is declining can be a trying time. One woman recently complained that her mother seemed to talk only about the way she *used* to be. The daughter found herself being less patient with her mother than she would have liked. But with her daughter's encouragement and the support of others, her mother did adjust. How did she help? The daughter didn't tell her to stop talking about her loss—the mother had a need to let it out. Repressing negative emotions can lead to very real physical ailments, so she encouraged her mother to talk. But she also arranged special events such as going to a restaurant or movie or arranging a visit from an old friend. In these ways, she helped her mother to adjust emotionally to a change in her physical image. If your family member does not believe exercise is for her, encourage her involvement in other activities such as arts and crafts, fishing, gardening, or community projects. While they're not as beneficial as physical exercise, they will help her to remain an active participant in life.

Notes

1. James Fries, *Bedside Care* 5 (2) (Spring 1981).
2. *Fitness Challenge in Later Years* (Washington, D.C.: President's Council on Physical Fitness, 1979).

5

Vision and Hearing Problems

ROBERTA ONZUKA-ANDERSON

Flora, a 76-year-old widow, lives alone in her own apartment. Always an active woman, Flora is finding that recent changes in her eyesight are preventing her from continuing some of her favorite activities. Her daughter has tried to persuade her to use her glasses, but Flora says they haven't been of much use for the past year and a half. Sadly, she has packed away her unfinished quilts and given away her books. She found some enjoyment in listening to the radio until the apartment manager informed her that the volume of her radio at half-past four in the morning bothered her neighbors. Now Flora is upset. It's so unfair, she thinks, that growing old means a loss of her vision and hearing.

Most people expect their senses of sight and hearing to deteriorate as they grow older. Most adapt to these changes and are able to continue rich and full lives despite their sensory limitations. In some cases, however, the older person may not be so fortunate in learning to cope with these changes. Other problems may interfere. It may be that friends and family members assume she is just getting old or "senile" rather than experiencing hearing and vision problems that can in fact be corrected. Or perhaps the older person herself chooses not to cope with the changes and just gives up.

Jack moved into his daughter's home after his wife's death. When he started to complain that the neighbor's children were peering into his bedroom window at night, his daughter feared that he was becoming "senile." At first she tried to convince him that the children were not allowed outside at night. Then she tried to humor him. Finally she just gave up and ignored his complaints. Unfortunately, Jack's daughter was unwilling to look for other reasons for her father's complaint. If she could have looked through *his* eyes, she might have surprised herself with the vision—the gradual changes in his eyesight, the poor lighting at dusk, and the clothes hanging on the outdoor line certainly gave the impression of someone moving near the window. Thus a misunderstanding resulted in frustration and strained feelings between father and daughter. And, even more unfortunate, Jack was now labeled and treated as a "senile" old man.

How can you avoid placing yourself and your older family member in Jack's predicament? This chapter provides some answers to the leading questions: What vision and hearing changes are normal for the elderly? And what can I do to help my parent cope with these changes?

Vision

There is no question that your vision changes as you get older. For some, it may be a matter of blurred vision, seeing double, difficulty distinguishing colors, or total blindness. Many of these changes may result from problems with circulation and the nervous system. Here are some of the common causes of vision problems or blindness in the elderly:[1]

- *Cataracts:* This disorder is characterized by opaque spots that form in the lens of the eye. Since this clouding prevents light from reaching the back of the eye, vision is blurred. Surgery may be successful in treating cataracts. In some cases, the affected lens is removed and replaced with an artificial lens.
- *Diabetic retinopathy:* This disorder is a complication of diabetes and one of the leading causes of blindness. Simply stated, it is caused when blood vessels burst in the eye and leave scar tissue. Blurred vision or the complete loss of sight may result from this disease.
- *Glaucoma:* This problem is caused by increased pressure in the eye due to buildup of fluid. The disease develops slowly and painlessly and is a major cause of blindness in the elderly. The first symptom of glaucoma is the loss of peripheral or side vision. Glaucoma is a controllable disease if detected

early. Treatment can consist of special eyedrops, medicine, and in some cases surgery.

- *Macular disease:* This disorder is a degeneration or wearing out of the area of the retina that permits perception of fine detail. It may be caused by inflammation or poor circulation to the eye. Diet, medication, and vision aids such as magnifying devices may help the older person with this disease.

Vision may be impaired by disease; it may be a symptom of other problems such as a stroke; or it may be due to actual physical changes such as the loss of elasticity in the lens—a condition known as presbyopia or farsightedness. Whatever the reason, changes to this vital organ may leave a person frustrated and sometimes frightened. Sensitivity to the needs of visually impaired elders is therefore a must. It becomes even more important when the person also must cope with other impairments such as hearing or memory loss. Using touch, identifying yourself, describing the environment and who is in the area, and following set routines are simple but often overlooked methods to help your older relative feel secure and in touch with everyday activities. Here are a few other suggestions for assisting loved ones with vision problems:

- *Lighting:* Rooms should be well lit with a minimum amount of glare.
- *Contrasting colors:* Dark objects on light ones or vice versa will help a person distinguish between them.
- *Large print:* Calendars, clocks, books, telephone dials, and similar items used daily should have large print for easier recognition.
- *Vision aids:* Magnifiers, telescopes, and other devices in addition to prescription glasses may help the person to continue daily tasks and leisure activities independently.
- *Professional care:* Seek the care of a professional eye doctor on a regular basis. This preventive measure could save your aging relative's vision.
- *Encouragement:* A positive attitude should be the rule. Encourage the person to assume daily tasks such as personal grooming, housekeeping, and shopping.
- *Imagination:* Make adjustments in the physical environment to keep the person as independent as possible. George, for

example, painted bold black numbers next to each burner on the stove and the corresponding heat panel so that his wife could continue cooking.

For the older person who loses her sight completely, a great deal of time, assistance, and encouragement may be necessary to help her adjust. Community agencies that specialize in working with the blind may be especially helpful in providing the training and support. Check your telephone directory for an agency in your community or contact the American Foundation for the Blind.

Roger was seventy-six years old when he completely lost his sight. Mary, his daughter, anxious about her dad living alone, insisted that he move to her home. One day following her father's appointment with the doctor, Mary moved her dad, a suitcase of clothes, and a few of his favorite belongings into her extra bedroom. Overwhelmed by his blindness and the sudden move to an unfamiliar home, Roger became profoundly depressed and moody. His angry outbursts and silent withdrawals, so unlike him, confused his daughter and grandchildren. And the mess created at the dinner table when Roger knocked over his glass of water or spilled his food upset and embarrassed everyone.

Mary's reaction to her father's blindness was prompted by concern and good intentions. Unfortunately, it caused more distress than relief. If Mary had been able to look objectively at her father's situation, the problem might not have become so complicated. Perhaps Roger could have remained in his own home. With a few simple modifications—such as moving sharp-edged furniture out of the way for safety and organizing his belongings so he could locate them easily—Roger might have been able to remain independent in his own home.

If Mary had shared her concerns with her father, he might have agreed to modify his own home rather than moving into hers. In any case, Roger's adjustment to his new home might have been hastened if Mary had taken the time to describe the layout and provided markers to let her father know where he was in the house. At mealtime, Roger could have been told what was being served and where it was located. It helps to describe the location of food on the plate according to the face of a clock—for example, the potatoes are at three o'clock, on the right side of the plate; the main dish is at six o'clock, directly in front of the person; and the vegetables are at nine o'clock, on the left side of the plate. It's also helpful to serve the same type of food in the same place on the plate—green vegetables always at nine o'clock, for example. This method may also be used to orient your parent to the location of objects in a room—for example, informing her that when she's standing at the door, the bed is at three o'clock and the dresser at nine. These simple cues help the blind or visually impaired older person to remain as independent as possible.

Hearing

Some degree of hearing loss is experienced by most older adults. Studies have shown that older men may have more difficulty hearing high tones and older women low tones. There may also be greater difficulty in distinguishing sounds. Here are some other problems that may cause hearing impairment:[2]

- *Conductive losses:* Problems in the external or middle ear affect the way sound is conducted to the inner ear. Impacted earwax, swelling of tissue due to inflammation, fluid accumulation, and infection are problems which may cause conductive losses. These problems may be treated by a physician; moreover, the person may be helped by the use of hearing aids and similar devices.
- *Sensorineural losses or nerve deafness:* This problem occurs in the inner ear which houses the nerve that transmits sound waves to the brain. Damage to the inner ear may cause permanent damage, even deafness.

Problems with hearing may lead to other problems. Some people are embarrassed or choose to deny the impairment; some withdraw and isolate themselves; some may become suspicious, even paranoid, of others because they are unable to hear everything that is said and imagine the rest. Joseph, for example, was confused by his aging mother's recent behavior. She had always been cheerful and loving but now seemed depressed. His attempts to find out what was bothering her usually ended in a frustrating one-sided or nonsensical conversation. When he tried to have her come live with him so he could care for her, she accused him of trying to take away her home and independence. He could do nothing to please her.

It wasn't until Joseph's sister suggested that their mother should have her ears checked that the impacted earwax was discovered. The doctor spent two hours flushing the wax from both ears, and the results showed in the smile on her face. She could hear clearly again! Joseph's mother was fortunate that her hearing problem was treated so successfully. Not all hearing impairments in the elderly can be treated, however, so here are some suggestions for communicating with one whose hearing is impaired:

- *Be patient.* If the person has trouble understanding you, repeat yourself and try to rephrase the sentence.
- *Speak slowly and clearly.* Don't shout—this may only distort the sound.
- *Keep a quiet environment.* Reduce the amount of background noise—radios, televisions, air conditioners, or fans may be distracting
- *Use aids in communicating.* Facial expressions, gestures, demonstrations, writing, or drawing pictures may help you convey your message.
- *Be sure the person understood what was communicated.* This guideline is especially important to prevent misunderstandings.
- *Make arrangements in case of emergencies.* If your aging relative cannot hear, she may miss the sirens, shouts, or car horns that alert her to possible danger.
- *Encourage the use of hearing aids or devices.* With the examination and advice of a qualified professional, the use of an aid may alleviate some of the problems of hearing impairment. Be sensitive, however, to her reaction to using a hearing aid. She may refuse to use it because it would be an admission of a physical problem or growing older. More complex and costly hearing devices are being developed—for example, an infrared hearing system which enables a person to enjoy a speech or sermon clearly without the room noises that intrude with a simple hearing aid. Keep abreast of technological developments that may be useful to your elder.
- *Use touch to get her attention, not shouting.*

Your Role as an Advocate

You can play a vital role in helping your elder cope with a vision or hearing loss. Through observation, questioning, and follow-up with the physician or appropriate specialist, you may help her avoid the isolation and frustration of living with a sensory impairment. Here's a simple list of what to look for, what to ask, and who to seek in helping the older adult with vision problems:

1. Do you notice frequent spilling, misjudging of distances, squinting, uncontrollable eye motion, use of touch to identify objects, or lack of recognition of friends or family members? If so, these could be signs of a vision problem.
2. Ask your elder:
   * Do your eyes hurt? Do you see rainbows, halos, blind spots?
   * Are you able to see? Do your glasses help you see clearly?
   * When was your last eye exam? The last change in prescription for your glasses?
3. Seek the services of an optometrist, a specialist who is trained to prescribe and fit glasses, or an ophthalmologist, a physician who specializes in the study and treatment of eye diseases.

Here's a similar checklist for hearing problems:

1. Do you notice a shorter attention span, inappropriate responses, talking louder than necessary, increased television or radio volume, or constantly asking you to repeat yourself? These could be signs of a hearing impairment.
2. Ask your elder:
   * Do you experience ringing or buzzing in your ear? Dizziness?
   * Can you hear me when I speak?
   * Can you hear me with your hearing aid? When was the last time the battery was changed?
   * When was the date of your last ear exam?
3. Seek the services of an audiologist, a specialist who is trained to evaluate and advise on aids for hearing disorders, or an otologist, a physician who specializes in the study and treatment of ear diseases.

Your awareness of the changes occurring with the older person and your willingness to pursue the cause and treatment of the problem will certainly pay off. Don't accept age or "senility" as the reason for behavior changes or problems. Your persistence can make a difference.

Notes

1. American Foundation for the Blind, "Who is the Aging Blind Person and How Can You Help Him?", in *An Introduction to Working with the Aging Person Who Is Visually Impaired* (New York: 1972), pp. 1–2.

2. American Speech-Language-Hearing Association, *Communication Problems and Behaviors of the Older American* (Rockville: 1979).

6

Common Diseases: Diabetes, Cancer, and Parkinson's Disease

COLETTE BROWNE

Certain diseases become more common with age; dementia due to Alzheimer's disease (discussed in Chapter 8) and arthritis (discussed in Chapter 9) are two examples. Diabetes, cancer, and Parkinson's disease are three other diseases that become more prevalent as we grow older. These last three diseases will now be discussed in more detail with special attention given to what families can do to help.

Diabetes

Few diseases are more misunderstood than diabetes. Diabetes mellitus is the name for a chronic, noncontagious disease that affects the way the body utilizes food. In the normal, healthy body, starches, sugars, and other foods are changed to glucose, a form of sugar. Most people are able to metabolize an almost unlimited amount of carbohydrates—sugars and starches—in their bodies. The blood then carries this glucose through the veins to the cells where it is converted into energy with the assistance of insulin. The pancreas is the producer of insulin, the body's natural hormone which regulates the amount of sugar in the body. When the body's insulin is not sufficient to burn the sugar, or glucose, it accumulates in the body and eventually spills out in the urine. It is this high level of sugar in the blood and body that can lead to damage to the eyes, kidneys, nervous system, and the heart. Because of these potential complications, many diabetics face the possibility of a shorter life.

Diabetes, then, is a disease that affects the way the body

digests food and burns sugar. Nearly 10 million Americans have this disease, roughly 5 percent of the population, and its incidence is on the rise.[1] Three times as many people over the age of sixty have diabetes as opposed to those in the middle years.[2] It is not really known why this is so. Research is being conducted to determine whether the increased blood sugar levels in the older population are actually a sign of diabetes or just part of the natural aging process.[3] Diabetes is America's third leading cause of death and the second leading cause of new cases of blindness.[4] Contrary to public opinion, diabetes *is* a serious disease when not diagnosed or treated.

There are two types of diabetes. Type I is insulin-dependent diabetes (formerly called juvenile-onset diabetes). Type II is non-insulin-dependent diabetes (formerly called adult-onset diabetes).[5] Type I results when the pancreas is unable to produce natural insulin. Older adults primarily develop Type II—the pancreas produces natural insulin but not in sufficient amounts to do a good job of converting the sugar into energy.

It is always up to a physician to diagnose this condition. There are, however, certain symptoms that can alert you to the existence of diabetes:

- Weight loss or obesity
- Excessive thirst and drinking of fluids
- Weakness, nausea
- Irritability, tiredness
- Itching of skin
- Frequent infections in skin, gums, urinary system
- Slow healing of cuts and bruises
- Cramps in legs

Some older people visit their physician with the complaint of just not feeling well. It is only after a variety of tests are given that the diagnosis may be diabetes. And since symptoms may also occur over a period of time, individuals may even forget they are not feeling as well as they once did. In addition to symptoms, there are also risk factors that predispose certain people to this disease. The American Diabetes Association lists the following people as being at risk: those over forty years of age, those who are overweight, and those with a diabetic relative.[6]

Diabetes is a chronic disease—it is lifelong and has no known cure. It is also hereditary, meaning it is genetically transmitted from parent to child. Neither its cause nor its cure are known at this time, but it can be controlled with proper treatment following a correct diagnosis.

Treatment

Treatment, of course, depends on the type and severity of the disease. While diabetes cannot really be prevented, controlling one's weight can help. Diabetes control depends on proper adherence to instruction from a physican or other health professional regarding diet, medication, exercise, proper rest, and timing. Timing refers to the importance of a *routine* in eating, sleeping, and other activities.

- *Diet:* Type II diabetes can often be controlled with diet and exercise. A dietitian can be invaluable in planning a special diet. In general, the diet will limit sugars and starches and emphasize proteins. A predetermined number of calories must be ingested daily. It also helps for overweight people to lose those extra pounds. With today's diet-conscious Americans, many grocery stores carry sugar-free products that are good for diabetics. Many older people who are diagnosed with diabetes late in life can control the disease with diet alone. When this regimen does not work, medications may be prescribed.
- *Medication:* Insulin is prescribed according to a physician's orders and must be taken by injection. Oral medications are called oral diabetic agents or oral hypoglycemic agents. There is some dispute today over the value and safety of oral medications.[7] It is best to discuss this question with your doctor. As with any other medication, the instructions must be followed exactly as they are written. Most people are able to inject themselves with insulin after being taught the correct procedure. Family members can also be taught. For those with vision problems, a home health agency or public health nursing service can help.
- *Exercise:* Exercise is beneficial because it burns food quickly. This relieves the pancreas, the producer of insulin, from doing all the work by itself.
- *Rest:* The right amount of rest helps the body to work efficiently and maximize its strengths.

- *Timing:* The body needs to eat, rest, and sleep at approximately the same time daily. Talk to a health professional about the best schedule to follow.

Problems

Two serious problems can develop if diabetes is not under control. One is hypoglycemia—when the blood sugar level is too low. The other is hyperglycemia—when the blood sugar level is too high. Hypoglycemia is caused when too much insulin or oral medication has been taken and the body's sugar level gets too low. Hyperglycemia occurs when the diabetic neglects to take insulin or follow a diet. Excess sugar is the result and can lead to diabetic coma, or ketoacidosis. If left untreated, death can occur. Table 2 can help you recognize which reaction is taking place.[8]

What should you do if you detect these warning signals? In

Table 2. Warning Signals for Hypoglycemia and Hyperglycemia

Hypoglycemic Reaction (Insulin Reaction)	WARNING SIGNS	Ketoacidosis (Diabetic Coma)
Sudden	ONSET	Gradual
Pale, moist	SKIN	Flushed, dry
Excited, nervous irritable, confused	BEHAVIOR	Drowsy
Normal	BREATH	Fruity odor (acetone)
Normal to rapid shallow	BREATHING	Deep, labored
Absent	VOMITING	Present
Moist, numb, tingling	TONGUE	Dry
Present	HUNGER	Absent
Absent	THIRST	Present
Headache	PAIN	Abdominal
Absent or slight	SUGAR IN URINE	Large amounts

Source: Reprinted with permission from the American Diabetes Association. © 1976.

the case of hypoglycemia, or insulin reaction, get the person to eat or drink a fast-acting sugar such as orange juice or a soft drink (non-dietary), or candy or a cookie if she can swallow. Call your physician at once. With hyperglycemia, the safest course is to call your doctor without delay. If you're aware of the right amount of insulin previously ordered for this condition, give it immediately.

What to Watch Out For

There are certain problem areas that those with a diabetic relative should watch out for. These include:

- *Impotence:* Impotence is often the first sign of diabetes in males. Discuss the problem with your doctor.
- *Hunger:* It is common for the diabetic person to feel hungry, since not enough sugar is being eaten. Ask a dietitian or your physician for special dietary suggestions to combat these hunger pangs.
- *Denial:* Some people simply will not take diabetes seriously. Diabetes has been correlated with serious diseases, however, so it is crucial that the person be helped to accept the realities of the disease.
- *Depression:* No one is truly prepared for disease, especially one with no cure. There can also be anger—anger for having a disease that implies disability. Encourage the discussion of such feelings.
- *Foot care:* Diabetes often results in impaired circulation of the arteries that lead to the brain, the heart, and the legs. Neuropathy, the destruction of nerves, results in loss of sensation. Poor circulation, coupled with neuropathy, can cause an older adult not to feel any sensation in the hands and legs. To prevent infections, diabetics need to avoid ill-fitting shoes and socks and walking barefoot; to prevent frostbite, they must wear warm footwear in cold weather. The diabetic who is wheelchair-bound or bed-bound must be especially careful about preventing infections and should try alternating positions to encourage good blood circulation. The advice of a podiatrist, a health professional trained in the special care of the feet, can be extremely helpful in promoting good foot care.

- *Nonadherence to diet:* Most diabetics learn to adjust to a changed diet quickly. But some find the restrictions of a diabetic diet too hard to follow, and end up ignoring them. Talk to the person if you note such behavior. It may also be necessary to discuss the situation with your doctor.
- *Compulsion to diet:* Others may take a martyr attitude toward their dietary restrictions. Again, you may have to help the person accept the realities of diabetes. If the compulsion is due to fear, help the person learn as much as possible about diabetes in order to alleviate some of her anxiety.
- *Infections:* Personal cleanliness is important in the prevention of infections. Since diabetics are especially susceptible to infections that can lead to serious complications, it is smart to prevent their occurrence. Those who have colds or the flu should not be in close contact with diabetics. A sore throat should be tested for infection, and any problems involving the feet need to be taken care of at once.
- *Signs of insulin reaction:* If you note any symptoms of insulin reaction, such as sweating, hunger, pale skin, or the appearance of drunkenness, follow the directions for hypoglycemia.
- *Signs of hyperglycemia:* If you note heavy breathing, flushed skin, vomiting, coma, and similar signs, call your doctor at once.

What Your Elder Should Do

Here are some things the elder with diabetes can do:

- Feel good in general if the disease is under control. If, instead, the person feels poorly, consult a doctor, especially one who has knowledge of diabetes.
- Avoid muscle atrophy by changing the site of the insulin injection daily.
- Be tested for control on a regular basis.
- See a doctor immediately for any foot problems.
- Follow the physician's instructions regarding diet, medication, exercise, and rest.
- Avoid excess weight.
- Maintain personal cleanliness to avoid infection.
- Visit the eye doctor to test for any signs of eye damage.

- Wear an identification bracelet so others will know this condition exists in case of an accident.
- Break in new shoes slowly and carefully, and cut toenails straight across to prevent foot problems.
- Take responsibility for following the doctor's orders unless it is absolutely impossible to do so independently.
- Maintain her love of life. By following recommendations and orders from a physician, a diabetic can feel good and lead a normal life.

Cancer

Few words elicit as much fear as the diagnosis of cancer. It is the second most common cause of death in the United States, behind diseases of the heart and vascular system.[9] Cancer can affect every part of the body. Today, however, even with a diagnosis of cancer, there is hope. One out of three persons diagnosed with cancer is saved. Cancer is, however, more common among the elderly, and the overall incidence rate increases with age.[10]

What is cancer? It is cellular dysfunction; in other words, certain cells in the body somehow become abnormal and begin to grow uncontrollably. There are many different types of cancer. A cancer may be localized in the organ or organs where it started. The cure rate for this type is better than if it has spread to an entire region such as the lymph node. Or the cancer may metastasize to distant parts of the body, causing new tumors to develop. When this happens, the prognosis is generally not good.

Some cancers are curable, some are not. Some can be treated with radiation or chemotherapy and arrested. Others require surgery, and, sadly, others kill. The American Cancer Society lists the following symptoms as the warning signals of cancer.[11] Any suspicion of cancer should be immediately checked out with a physician.

- Unusual bleeding or discharge
- A lump or thickening in the breast
- A sore that does not heal
- A change in bowel or bladder habits

- Hoarseness or coughing
- Indigestion or difficulty in swallowing
- A change in a wart or mole

Can cancers be prevented? Generally, a person can minimize the chances of cancer by not smoking, by drinking in moderation, by avoiding fatty foods (including beef), by avoiding sun exposure, by sleeping seven to eight hours a day, by reducing stress in the work and home environment, and by avoiding pollutants.[12] There are no guarantees, however, that following these suggestions will ensure a cancer-free life. Cancer remains the last major disease for which we do not know the cure.

Treatment

Treatments for cancer generally fall into three categories: surgery, radiation therapy, and chemotherapy.

- *Surgery:* Once a cancer is diagnosed, surgery is a widely used method to remove it if it is localized. Surgery can also be recommended to alleviate pain.
- *Radiation:* This method makes use of ionizing radiation to kill off or melt the cancer cells. There are side effects to radiation therapy, however; discuss this possibility with a doctor.
- *Chemotherapy:* This treatment uses anticancer drugs to rid the body of this disease. The basic premise is that cancer cells are different from normal cells. In reality, though, chemotherapy affects both cancerous and normal cells, often leading to toxicity of the drug in the person's system. In other words, the drug cannot selectively destroy the cancer cells because it cannot tell the difference between normal cells and cancer cells. Certain leukemia cancers, though, are exceptions to this rule.

Health care costs are a real concern to the person with the diagnosis of cancer and her family. Improved cancer treatments are prolonging life but also often increasing the person's health costs as a result. Moreover, cancer victims are generally hospitalized more often throughout the illness than persons with other diseases.[13]

Living with the Diagnosis

A diagnosis of cancer is a diagnosis for the entire family. Some will take this diagnosis as a death sentence. Some will cope successfully; others will not. Dr. Barbara Giacquinta, a practitioner in oncology, has studied how families function once a diagnosis of cancer has been made.[14] From working with families, she has noted four distinct stages of dealing with this disease: living with cancer; the living/dying interval; bereavement; and reestablishment.

Living with cancer is the first stage. Families attempt to go on with their lives as they deal with their emotions, inform relatives, and so forth. In this stage, it is important for the family not to fill their moments with so much busywork that the person with cancer ends up being isolated. Rather, it is a time for family cohesion; a time to come together for mutual support and love. The ill person may feel helpless and vulnerable. Now is the time for the family or caregivers to cooperate as a team and foster the security of every member. And, yes, it is also a time for courage and for humor.

The second stage is a time for reliving and framing memories and for recognizing the uniqueness of that person's life. It is not maudlin to show those old home movies, nor is it necessarily depressing to pull out the old photo albums. By doing these things, you are allowing the ill person to reflect upon her life. You are also strengthening the image you hold of your loved one. This will help you realize that the physical presence is not a prerequisite for love.

In the third stage, bereavement, the family experiences death, separation, and mourning. Be with the person who is dying and support all the members of the family once death has come. Mourning involves grief, possibly the strongest human feeling. Grief is a personal experience shaped by the relationship one had with the deceased.

The last stage is reestablishment. Overcoming alienation and accepting the death of a loved one is the primary challenge. Families report that communities in which they have lived their entire lives become strange for a while after the death of a loved one. One man I know told me that, following the funeral of his wife, he returned to his home and became furious with the neighbor's children for playing ball in the street and laughing. This is a common reaction to feelings of grief; it will pass.

What to Watch Out For

There are certain problems that those with a relative suffering from cancer should be especially alert to:

- *Pain:* Cancer often causes pain. Speak to your physician about alleviating it.
- *Weight loss:* A sudden weight loss can tell you something is wrong. Even if your relative has already been diagnosed with cancer, a weight loss is a symptom that should still be brought to the attention of the physician.
- *Despair:* Any disease for which there is no known cure can elicit feelings of hopelessness. While it is important to be honest, there is nothing wrong in sharing feelings of hope.
- *Isolation:* Make sure that isolation is not a result of fears concerning the disease. The person is still very much alive and part of a family; don't exclude her from family affairs or discussions. To do so will only increase her feelings of isolation and abandonment.
- *Fear:* Cancer victims often express fear of pain, mutilation from the treatment, or loss of body functions. Encourage them to share such feelings and try to counter their fears with factual information that may alleviate them. *Be there.* Sometimes this is enough.
- *Abandonment:* Don't do it!

What You Can Do

The adjustment to a diagnosis of cancer is an especially difficult one. Your elder will need your support and encouragement.

- Give your love, honesty, and support. "Should I tell her the diagnosis?" is a question often heard. Ask yourself: Is this my decision to make? Who will have to live with the consequences of this decision? And who am I protecting by withholding such information?
- Speak freely and openly. Respect the feelings and wishes that are expressed to you by your elder. Is it a wish to prolong life?

What about the choices of treatment? Many communities have support groups for those diagnosed with cancer. Such groups can be very successful in supporting the cancer patient and the family. Contact your local cancer society for more information.

- If rehabilitation can alleviate suffering, encourage participation in it.
- Encourage her to eat nutritiously. The body responds better to certain treatments when it is well nourished.
- Help her deal with feelings of anger. "Why Me?" is a common expression of disbelief, sorrow, and anger. If you cannot discuss such feelings with your elder, perhaps your local cancer society can assist you.
- Report any new problems to your physician.
- Encourage her to be as active as possible, and rest when tired.
- Stay involved in her personal cleanliness. Wearing regular clothes rather than bedclothes can help a person's spirits.

Parkinson's Disease

Parkinson's disease affects the central nervous system and strikes one out of every thousand persons in the United States. It becomes more prevalent with age: One out of every hundred men and women over the age of sixty has been diagnosed as having this disease. Parkinson's disease is progressive—in other words, the person with this disease can expect it to worsen with time. Parkinson's disease affects the part of the brain that controls posture and orderly movement. Rigidity and involuntary tremors and general body weakness are the hallmarks of this disease.

Symptoms vary according to stages of the disease. At first, the person moves more slowly than before and may experience tremors. The legs and arms may become stiff and difficult to move. The face takes on a strange, unemotional affect, almost as if the person were a robot. In the later stages, tremors and rigidity increase. Walking becomes shuffling and may be hard to stop without help. Keeping one's balance and sitting straight also become difficult. As the disease progresses, speech becomes slurred and, eventually, the person has trouble swallowing.

The cause of Parkinson's disease is not known at this time. Science is researching the connections between sets of twins when one or both have the disease, but there is no concrete evidence that points to this disease being hereditary.[15] There is some evidence, however, that Parkinson's disease is associated with the death of certain brain cells, perhaps due to the thickening of the blood vessels in the brain. What *is* known is that this disease is more prevalent among men than women and with older people. We also know that certain drugs of the phenothiazine group (chlorpromazine, perphenazine, and others) can induce Parkinsonism as one of their side effects.[16] As more and more people are prescribed these drugs for treatment of mental health problems, we may see a rise in the incidence of Parkinson's disease. While treatment is limited at this time, neurosurgery and certain medications have had some success in alleviating some of the symptoms of Parkinson's disease.

The husband of a woman I knew had been diagnosed with this disease when he was fifty-two years old. He is now sixty-one and in the later stages of Parkinsonism. His wife, a loving woman, worked diligently to keep him at home with her. They had two adult daughters who were both married and lived in the same town. She resisted their offers for help and relief because she did not want to bother them. When I first met her, she was exhausted from the demands of round-the-clock care. I then recommended a plan of action.

First we enrolled her husband in a community adult day-care program. A combination of activity and rest is nearly always beneficial, and the day-care program provided it. He was able to adjust fairly well, although he remained somewhat of a loner. He attended the program three days a week, allowing his wife time to be by herself, visit friends, and do chores and run errands. Eventually there came a time when his needs were beyond the scope of this program. The staff then recommended a nursing home admission, but she would not hear of it. Instead, we found a senior companion from a community program that trains the elderly to help others less healthy than they. This senior companion came to the home seven hours a week, again giving this woman time to be by herself and do things she needed to do. Public health nurses also helped with his care, which by this time was becoming more difficult. Eventually, home care services were required. Meanwhile, I tried to make her see that her daughters very much wanted to help her care for their father. When the day came that he could no longer be cared for at home, she was able to admit her husband to a nursing home without guilt. She knew she had done all she could for him. Even with this change in their living arrangement, she continues to visit him daily.

What to Watch Out For

There are problem areas that those with a Parkinson's disease relative should watch out for. These include:

- *Incontinence:* Often the muscles around the bladder become lax, resulting in slow urination.[17] Rigidity can also make getting to the bathroom in time somewhat difficult. A commode (portable toilet) in the bedroom can help. And allowing more time to get to the bathroom may prevent embarrassing accidents from occurring.
- *Muscle cramps:* Levedopa, a medication often prescribed, may produce a side effect of muscle cramps. There are other drugs that, taken at night, can prevent this condition.
- *Facial movements:* A robotlike expression is common in Parkinsonism because the disease affects the muscles that control facial movement. The American Parkinson's Disease Association suggests that exercises using different facial expressions (anger, fear, confusion, love, and so forth) be done in front of a mirror to increase facial mobility and maintain movement.[18]
- *Depression:* Try to remember that dealing with a chronic disease is frightening to the person and can be depressing. Be supportive and encouraging.
- *Home safety:* Establish the same home safety rules as you would follow for any frail elder. Get rid of those scatter rugs, remove clutter, and so forth. See Chapter 14 for additional suggestions.
- *Nutrition:* Since diet may be a factor in maintaining strength, make sure that the elder's food is wholesome and nutritious.
- *Dry skin:* Use creams and lotions generously if skin becomes dry and itchy.
- *Choking:* Eating can be a source of worry due to the possibility of choking. Be there when the person is eating, or assign another family member to be there. Learn what to do if chok-

ing occurs. The Red Cross or Public Health Nursing Service in your area can teach proper procedures to follow in case of choking.

What Your Elder Should Do

Your elder with Parkinson's disease should:

- Take her time when walking or talking. Don't rush. When walking, take short, careful steps.
- Keep the body as a triangle when standing. Spread the feet approximately six inches apart to help retain a sense of balance.
- Practice facial exercises.
- Eat slowly and carefully.
- Avoid falls by picking her feet up when walking.
- Talk to close friends or members of the family about her feelings.

Notes

1. *What You Need to Know About Diabetes* (New York: American Diabetes Association, 1980), p. 2.

2. Harold Geist, *Psychological Aspects of Diabetes* (Springfield, Ill.: C. Thomas Publishers, 1964), p. 60.

3. National Institute on Aging, *Special Report on Aging, 1981* (NIH publication 81-2328, U.S. Public Health Service, U.S. Department of Health and Human Services) (Washington, D.C.: Government Printing Office, 1981), p. 10.

4. *Report of the National Commission on Diabetes to the Congress of the United States, vol. I, The Long Range Plan to Combat Diabetes* (DHEW publication NIH 76-1018) (Washington, D.C.: Government Printing Office, 1976).

5. *What Is Diabetes?* (New York: American Diabetes Association, 1979).

6. *What You Need to Know About Diabetes,* p. 9.

7. "Frank Talk about Oral Drugs," *Diabetes Forecast* (New York: American Diabetes Association, 1980).

8. *What You Need to Know About Diabetes,* p. 13.

9. Barrie R. Cassileth (ed.), *The Cancer Patient* (Philadelphia: Lea & Febiger, 1979), p. 1.

10. Ibid., p. 35.

11. *Facts About Cancer* (Honolulu: American Cancer Society, Hawaii Division, n.d.).

12. *The Cancer Patient,* p. 115.

13. Ibid., p. 47.

14. Barbara Giacquinta, "Living with Cancer," *American Journal of Nursing* (October 1977).

15. American Parkinson's Disease Association, *American Parkinson's Disease Newsletter* (Summer/Fall 1981): 3.

16. Gilbert Gnuaguluch, *Parkinsonism* (London: Butterworth, 1964), p. 1.

17. *American Parkinson's Disease Newsletter,* p. 1.

18. Ibid., p. 1.

7

Depression and
What to Do About It

HAZEL BEH

At a recent family education program for middle-aged children caring for their elderly parents, a woman stood up to speak. "I have an 81-year-old mother that lives with me," she said. "She moved in about a year ago because my sisters and I felt she needed to be with family. Of course she didn't want to move and leave the old neighborhood, but we convinced her it would be better. In my home, she has her own bedroom and bathroom, beautiful new furniture that I bought for her, and absolutely no responsibility for household chores. She should be having the time of her life, but all she does is sleep. In fact, she could sleep through her meals and never change from her nightgown if I let her. She should be going out and making new friends. She's in perfect health except for the cane she uses to walk. I can't understand why she's become so lazy and disinterested in people. You know, when she lived alone, she used to volunteer at a preschool for children and was even known as 'Grandma' to the neighborhood kids. I think she's unhappy, but my sisters and friends tell me not to worry. I just don't know. I think she has given up. What should I do? What's wrong with her?"

Is Depression Normal?

The later years can be characterized as years of great change and loss. Widowhood, deteriorating health, change in residence, diminished social role, and loss of status are but a few of the many and varied changes that confront the elderly. And any of them can trigger an incident of depression. Depression can be described as a feeling of helplessness or hopelessness, sadness, apathy toward life, or general lack of energy. It may range in severity from a momentary feeling of unhappiness to a crippling disinterest in life. It is epidemic among the elderly, but family members and professionals do the elderly a great disservice in assuming that depression is an inevitable aspect of aging.

Normal aging is a rewarding process characterized by wisdom, insight, and hope. Older adults who are depressed, however, find no purpose or pleasure in life and seem to be in constant misery. They are not "normal" and deserve proper care and compassion from friends and professionals. Concerned family or friends should consider depression as a potential problem when an older person cannot say:

- "I'm satisified with my life."
- "I think my mental health is good."
- "My daily routine satisfies me."
- "I like myself."

Many people are temporarily unable to feel quite so positive about themselves because of crisis, loss, or conflict in their lives. Most of us, however, are eventually able to respond positively to life's ups and downs through inner determination and spirit, along with the love and support of others or professional counseling. Unfortunately, older adults often face the greatest challenges of life—particularly the loss of loved ones and declining health—with the least resources. Their self-esteem and confidence are often undermined by social and physiological forces in old age. They are the least likely to have a strong circle of friends and family to bolster them. And, finally, professionals are often reluctant to treat an older adult's depression thoroughly because of preconceived notions of aging. Often professionals wrongly believe that efforts to treat the elderly are futile because it is "normal for the aged to be depressed" or useless "because the aged will die soon anyway." It is for these reasons that the depressed older adult often goes to her grave sorry ever to have lived and unable to affirm the usefulness of her life. The tragedy is that this elderly person might easily have been helped.

Sometimes depression resists even the best efforts at treatment. For some, overcoming depression is a lifelong struggle against causes unknown. Others, particularly those with brain injury, have a kind of depression that seems to defy treatment. The family must realize, though, that until reasonable treatment is at least attempted, no one can possibly know whether the person's depression can be lifted. It is crucial to seek competent assessment and treatment and not to assume the depression is untreatable. Even when the depression does not lift or recurs intermittently, the family and the older adult can benefit from professional support, education, and alleviation of symptoms.

Dan had a stroke two years ago that left him with left-side paralysis. Although his wife was deeply concerned and his children were nearby and very supportive, his depression seemed insurmountable. Despite the efforts of a psychologist, a support group of others with stroke, and the continued love and attention of his wife and children, he remained depressed and seemed to sense that he did not have the resources to pull himself out of it. He felt guilty because of the tremendous efforts of family and friends and missed the intensity of his former life. His wife and children were sometimes angry and frustrated that they could not lift him out of his depression no matter how hard they tried.

This family was eventually helped by understanding the changes which can occur with strokes. They attended sessions to talk about their anger, frustration, and guilt, and they learned some techniques that would help engage their father in family life to the best of his abilities. Dan was encouraged to recognize the *positive* aspects of himself and his achievements and to accept himself as he was. Although he continued to feel withdrawn for the most part, he and his family began to see the importance of their family relationships, to appreciate the small moments of joy and humor among them, and to accept the significance of the total person.

Caregivers of the elderly must learn to accept them as they are. Excessive demands or expectations beyond their capabilities undermine rather than strengthen them. Capitalize on their strengths. Seize opportunities to enhance their lives. Do not burden them with guilt simply because their lives do not meet *your* expectations.

Depression in the elderly deserves serious consideration

from family and requires professional assessment and treatment when personal efforts fail. Besides the obvious mental agony of depression and the very real risk of suicide, depression jeopardizes the physical health of the aged. There are indications that when we are depressed, for example, we are least immune to illness. Depression can also mimic common "senile" behavior such as forgetfulness and confusion. In most cases, with appropriate intervention by family members, friends, and professionals, the elderly can free themselves of depression. For others, understanding and emotional support can unburden the family member. But first you must learn how to recognize depression in the older adult, what to do about it, and how you can help.

What Does Depression Look Like?

Sometimes depression is easy to recognize. The older person may seem sad and perhaps cries frequently. She may admit her depression or make statements about her worthlessness. Often facial expressions and tone of voice indicate depression. But depression can masquerade in other forms as well. Often the complaints are physical, such as headaches, indigestion, lack of interest in sex, fatigue, or sleeplessness.

Depression that presents itself as physical complaints may go unrecognized by the family, the doctor, and even the person suffering. When a diagnosis is finally reached, often the reaction is disbelief and denial—most people prefer to believe that their body rather than their mind is acting up. Most of us do not really understand the relationship between our emotions and our physical health and cannot believe that one may be responsible for the other. A second reason is that most older people were brought up to believe that depression is a sign of self-pity and weakness. Seeking professional help therefore identifies them as "weak" and "crazy."

When depression causes physical problems it is important to look for clues as to diagnosis. If depression is the real root of the problem, physical illness may interfere to an unreasonable degree. Many people suffer from arthritis of varying severity, for example, but the depressed person finds the arthritis preventing her from making dinner, shopping, or doing other daily activities. It is not that she is "using" her arthritis; rather, her apathy toward life has become connected with her arthritis. Not all physical illness is caused by depression, of course. Thus professional help is needed to determine accurately whether depression is really at work. Let's look at a case in which a serious and treatable illness was mistaken for depression.

George, a "busy" man all of his life, was said to be suffering from severe emphysema and possible lung cancer. The cancer remained unconfirmed, however, since surgery for a biopsy might endanger him because of his emphysema. The family optimistically hoped that there was no cancer. When he visited his daughter, he seemed flat and expressionless and spent most of his time looking out of the window. When her efforts to engage him in activities failed, she assumed he was depressed about his illnesses. When he returned to the doctor after his visit, it was discovered that the cancer had metastasized or transferred from one part of his body to another, and was now in his brain. Treatment of his brain tumor with radiation helped relieve the lethargy and dullness he was experiencing, and he faced his impending death with the energy and courage he had shown throughout his life.

In this case, George was suffering from a treatable brain disease. The family doctor is often the person in the best position to diagnose depression. Family members can greatly assist professionals by letting them know what the older person was like *prior* to symptoms of depression. On the other hand, the following case study depicts a woman who cannot accept depression as a cause of her crippling physical symptoms and searches for relief from medical doctors.

When May's husband died two years ago, she was thrown into a deep depression and isolated herself at home for months. Her only contact with others was through visits to her family doctor. She never admitted that she missed her husband or that she was unhappy with herself. Instead she said she could no longer enjoy life because of vague aches and pains throughout her body. Her doctors were unable to find a cause or satisfactory treatment for her complaints, and she became angry if they suggested that depression might be an underlying cause. She switched doctors regularly and was never satisified with one longer than a few weeks.

When depression appears to be the cause of suffering and is

verified by a professional, the next step is to look for the *reason* for the depression. Depression can be triggered by an external event such as the loss of a spouse, friend, or job. It may be caused by medications prescribed for other illnesses. The cause might be more obscure as in feelings of low self-worth, unattractiveness, or helplessness in controlling one's life. Sometimes depression may be caused by chemical imbalances or brain changes. In many cases, a combination of factors is likely to be contributing to depression in the older adult. Take the case of Shirley, for example.

Shirley, an elderly woman, had been depressed off and on throughout her life. She had a devoted son who tried desperately to make her happy but to no avail. He even admitted a long-standing sense of inadequacy and failure with regard to his mother. Although she was encouraged to participate in family activities, she always refused. She rejected the church after a squabble with several other women. Whenever she was invited out, her arthritis or her heart was troubling her. Both her heart disease and her arthritis were verified illnesses which did in fact cause intermittent pain and discomfort. But both the family physician and the son suspected that depression was the true culprit because Shirley never seemed to adjust to her illnesses or overcome them. Instead she allowed them to make her reclusive. Moreover, she could never understand that she could actually provoke symptoms whenever she was faced with tasks she did not want to perform because of her depression.

Finding the reason for this depression was complicated. She and her family agreed that she was not still grieving for her husband; she had worked this out a number of years ago. They did, however, discover that she had always been vain, someone who took pride in being the most beautiful woman in the room. Although she was still quite attractive, her seventy-five years were evident. Significantly, she left the house only once a week—to go to the hairdresser. She also confided that she wore long sleeves to hide her wrinkled arms and used a variety of creams and cosmetics daily—even though she rarely saw anyone.

Shirley had moved to Hawaii in the last years of her husband's long illness and was unable to find time to make friends. Her disagreement with the women at church had driven her away from a strong force in her life. As she and her husband made their retirement plans, she had once thought that Hawaii was paradise, but she now found herself uncomfortable around the many ethnic groups. She thought her son would invite her to live with him after her husband died, but it was clear that he and his wife had no such intentions. Suddenly she found herself single, and being single was a characteristic she associated with unattractive women. About this time, her arthritis and heart disease were becoming troublesome and began to remind her of her old age.

Shirley was experiencing feelings of boredom, loneliness, helplessness, anger, and sadness. It was important to acknowledge those feelings because they could be rectified by changing her environment. In Shirley's case, a multitude of "if's" might have prevented her deep and tenacious depression. Perhaps she could have stayed in her old neighborhood among her aging friends. If her arthritis or angina symptoms had been relieved, she might not have felt her age so strongly. Likewise, if she had been able to make new friends or found strength in her church or if her son had been able to master his feelings which fed her depression, things might have been different. But the inescapable truth is that Shirley had a lifelong tendency toward depression and circumstances only fed her underlying problem.

How Can Family and Friends Help?

One way to help your family member is to reach out and spend time with them—to share your life and your own family with them. Family and friends underestimate the therapeutic value of their relationships with others. Most people who suffer severe losses or face depression often say in retrospect: "I don't know how I could have managed without my friends and family; they were so patient and supportive." Unfortunately, the elderly are more often lonely and isolated than other groups of people, due to a cruel combination of social and physiological factors. Sometimes it's the loss of family and friends they are mourning and there's no one around to help. I remember Jody, a friend of mine, telling me at her husband's funeral, "I could get through this if only *he* were here to talk to." What a sad irony! Depressed people often lack the confidence to seek out new friends and support. Children will often say, "There's a senior center just two blocks away, but she avoids it. She says it's for old people and too cliquish besides. I know she'd have a good time if she went."

One problem with trying to help your relative is that depressed people tend to drive others away. Even if they're not openly hostile (which they sometimes are), they often cause such uncomfortable feelings for their visitors that others begin to avoid them. Being around a depressed elderly person brings out a sense of failure. "My mother has always been able to make me feel better," confided a friend, "but now when she needs *me* I can't seem to help her." There can also be anger. "My mother has always been a fighter," the same woman said. "How can she just give up living? That's not a family trait!" Many families confess that they feel exhausted after visiting a depressed relative. Spontaneity may be absent, certain topics and words may have to be avoided, the elder may weep without consolation, and the relationship may seem all give and no take. One begins to dread the next visit when this is the situation. The guilt engendered by thinking about avoiding visiting a depressed relative completes the spectrum of negative feelings. Because of these feelings, families shy away and may finally refuse to visit a relative. One 86-year-old woman I know said, "I can't help the way I feel—my daughter doesn't come around much anymore, which is okay because all she ever did was scold me."

Bearing this in mind, family and friends can still offer the best source of strength, encouragement, and hope. But first you must accept the fact that you have not caused, nor are you responsible for, your elder's depression. Here are some guidelines for helping the elderly when they are depressed:

- *Accept her feelings.* If she describes her life as worthless and her mental condition as agony, believe her. Recognize that despair and anguish can be far worse than physical pain. Don't tell her that she "doesn't really feel that bad" or "doesn't really mean it."
- *Let her know she is cared for and can count on you.* When a depressed person sees herself as worthless, it is important for someone else to reaffirm her worth. Let her know that she has touched your life and has significance for you.
- *Remind her of her strengths.* While acknowledging that she is in a low state now, remind her of past accomplishments and

strength of character. Let her know that you have confidence in her ability to survive. Give her hope for the future.

- *Do not desert her.* Because being around the depressed person is emotionally draining, consider limiting the time you spend with her but do not abandon her entirely. It is important for her to know that you are her friend, now and always, and that your support is not based on her getting better or remaining ill.

- *Help her find purpose in life.* It may seem in the beginning that she is being dragged places almost against her will. She may even flatly refuse to participate in activities. Find things to do that are almost guaranteed to be successful and non-threatening, such as going to the hairdresser.

- *Be honest when you are frustrated or disappointed by continued depression.* Friends have the right to share their feelings, although it is best done without criticism or anger. It doesn't hurt to say, "Mom, you must be as discouraged as I am that you remain so down. But I still have hope, and I hope you do too." Showing the depth of your concern won't hurt and it might even help her. But avoid placing guilt on her. ("Everyone here is just about standing on their heads to make you happy, but you don't even thank us.") Let her know that you care about her whether or not she improves.

- *Learn when to make demands of her, and praise her for taking risks.* When she begins to show improvement, seize the opportunity to get her out and feeling even better. And recognize the courage it takes to venture out of her small world. A woman who had been alone and depressed for several years was invited next door for eggnog at Christmas. She went and seemed to have a good time. The next day, however, she complained that it has been an exhausting and uncomfortable evening. She was praised for being able to take such a risk anyway. And she was reassured that her social skills were still very much intact even though she was always afraid she would cry and tremble in public. In the end she continued to be depressed, but she had gotten through Christmas and now had a little more confidence in her social abilities.

- *Be careful not to fall into the trap of "rewarding" her for being depressed.* Don't give her special attention when she's low and ignore her when she's happy. Try to offer her a healthy role model in yourself by not curtailing your activities or neglecting your needs in sacrifice to her.

- *Be kind to yourself.* Loving and caring for a depressed older person is not easy and is to be admired. But your life needs to be nurtured as well, and you need the company of healthy and happy people in order to survive emotionally.
- *And, finally, don't look for trouble.* A dentist came to me and said that his mother was depressed and had lost the will to live. Something had to be done. The mother smiled when I asked if she was depressed. She said, "My son must have sent you. I am a tired old woman who has had a good life. I don't want to run five miles a day or take up yoga. I like to knit and read. My legs hurt if I walk long distances. I see my grandchildren enough but not too much, and I'm very proud of my children. I have a good life. My only problem is my youngest son's perpetual nagging that I should take up jogging!"

When Should You Seek Help?

Although the support provided by an older person's social network is very important, sometimes professional help is necessary. You may find, for example, that all your best efforts and good intentions do not seem to be helping. As a general rule, you should consider referring the elderly if:

- Depression is so intense that it limits daily activities.
- Depression lasts for several months or comes and goes with frequency.
- Suicidal thoughts are expressed or close friends and family have suspicions that suicide is being considered.
- The treating physician recommends outside help.

Begin the search for the right helper through social service agencies, family counseling centers, doctors, nursing homes, and rehabilitation hospitals that *work with the elderly.* In most cases, the elderly will need comprehensive social services to improve the quality of their life along with competent counseling. It is imperative that the counselor has an interest in continued and comprehensive care for older adults. It does the elderly little good to treat their depression if they continue to live in isolation and loneliness without opportunities for socialization.

Psychologists, psychiatrists, and psychiatric social workers are generally able to treat depression, although their treatment may vary a great deal in each case. A psychiatrist, as a licensed physician, may use medication to treat depression. But remember: Medication should be an adjunct to psychotherapy, never the sole treatment. In many difficult cases, the judicious use of medication can produce miraculous results. Be aware, however, that many medications used to treat psychiatric disorders have serious side effects. These medications may therefore complicate the course of existing illnesses in the elderly and often make the patient feel worse before she feels better. Some drugs are also addictive. The best advice is to discuss your concerns about drug use prior to treatment. And if you observe any side effects to the drug use, discuss them with the doctor.

Sometimes, in an effort to help, the family doctor prescribes antidepressant drugs. While this treatment may help, a thorough evaluation by a professional counselor is necessary if it fails. Molly's doctor had been prescribing drugs for several years because of his concern for her depression. These drugs seemed to help slightly. Her son finally persuaded her to see a psychiatrist who, in consultation with her family doctor, changed her high blood pressure medicine and tried her on a different antidepressant and finally none at all. The psychiatrist counseled both mother and son and helped them recognize certain patterns of behavior which contributed to her depressed state. As a result, she felt happier than she had for many years and enjoyed her relationship with her son much more.

Convincing the elderly person that she needs help may be difficult. She may dismiss your concerns as overreactions or she may become defensive. Getting professional help for emotional problems is often seen as evidence of weakness, insanity, or failure. Moreover, many people have a basic lack of confidence in psychotherapy. Incessant nagging by concerned parties only makes matters worse. Nagging destroys what might be a very positive relationship between you and your aging relative. Sometimes the rift can last forever. Don't destroy your relationship with your relative by harping at her to get help—even when professional help may seem the only answer. Presenting a sound case for seeking help and providing *specific* information on how to get it may be most effective. Let her think about your plea for a period of time and then approach her once more for her answer.

Some social service agencies are able to reach out to the elderly even before they ask for help. This is often the best solution. If professionals seek out the older person at the request of family members, they can often intervene before the elderly person hits rock bottom. In making a case for professional treatment, it is reassuring to the older person to know that it is offered because of the love and respect you feel and the hope for their future you hold.

Treatment can be nonthreatening and rewarding. Sometimes group sessions with professional staff and other elderly people are more supportive and make the depressed person feel "less sick." These sessions may also provide opportunities to socialize and find other activities to add meaning to their lives. Sometimes the group need not be focused on mental health problems but may be organized for widows, stroke victims, cancer patients, or the institutionalized. Many such groups list their services in newspapers, or check your local information and referral service.

Remember, the elderly are entitled to be free from depression and to find as much satisfaction in life as other age groups do. Symptoms of depression should be investigated, for depression is not a normal aspect of aging and is usually treatable. Treatment should be sought especially when depression is severe, when it lasts for several months, when suicide is a spoken or unspoken threat, or when the physician recommends it. Normal aging should be a rewarding life process.

8

Senility:
Putting an End to the Myth

ELAINE FIBER
OTTO NEURATH

Emily first began noticing changes in her mother's personality and behavior in seemingly nonrelated events. A birthday card her mother sent would never reach her because it was addressed incorrectly. Wedding anniversary gifts would arrive three and four times in a single year. Family gossip would be repeated and repeated again unwittingly. It was not until Emily's father called, informing Emily that her mother had left the gas on and almost burned the house down, that Emily asked her physician, "Is my mother senile?"

One of the most dreaded aspects of growing old is the loss of one's ability to think, learn, and remember—a condition often referred to as "senility." This word is popularly but erroneously used to describe symptoms of forgetfulness, confusion, and changes in behavior and personality in the elderly, but it is neither a normal sign of aging nor even a disease. The word *senility* literally means "pertaining to old age"; but it has gradually assumed the meaning of being weak and infirm and has come to imply that a person, just by being old, is also mentally deficient. This assumption is the myth of senility. Too ready an acceptance of this myth may prevent the timely diagnosis and treatment of a problem that may in fact be due to quite treatable physical and mental conditions.

All organs in the body follow a slowing-down course after maturity. The brain, as the central organ of functioning for most of the other systems in the body and the seat of all intellectual and emotional activities, follows the same decline as do these other organs. The brain consists of millions of nerve cells with some ten thousand processes linking them to other nerve cells. Throughout the course of aging, these brain cells gradually decrease in number. Brain function is not necessarily lost, however, due to the many linkages between cells and also the vast number of cells.

The striking fact about the brain is that its nerve cells do not regenerate as do the cells in other organs. The cells in damaged skin and internal organs such as the liver and kidneys are able to regenerate and continue functioning. The brain, unfortunately, cannot replace its cells. This means that a disease affecting the brain can lead to permanent damage. These changes, their effect on older adults, and the potential for treatment will be our concerns in this chapter.

The Diagnosis of Senility

There are many names for mental decline in old age: senile dementia, Alzheimer's disease, chronic brain syndrome, organic brain disorder, cerebral atrophy, and arteriosclerosis. The term *dementia* literally means "having lost the mind" and refers to progressive intellectual decline and memory loss. Because so many factors may be producing the symptoms, it is important that a complete diagnosis by a physician be given to determine whether the elderly person's problems are irreversible or reversible. The following cases illustrate the importance of a thorough diagnosis.

Shirley was sixty-seven years old when her husband died. Her two sons insisted that she sell the family home and move to the city to live with either of their families. She refused, however, and managed to live alone for twenty years. But Shirley, now eighty-seven, was recently found wandering the streets late at night. Although she was able to give her name to the police, she did not know her address or phone number. It took a search through her purse to discover the information needed for her safe return home. During a visit with his mother, the oldest son was told of the wandering incident by Shirley's neighbor. The neighbor also told him that she had observed even stranger things occurring at the house. She said Shirley had accused people of stealing her belongings and often wore several dresses over her nightgown when leaving the house. The neighbor suggested that Shirley be "put away" because she had become "senile."

Instead, Shirley's son took her to the family doctor. After administering a complete physical, neurological, and psychiatric examination, including a computerized tomographic X-ray of the head (a CAT scan), the doctor, in consultation with other specialists, learned that the stroke Shirley had suffered five years ago had been followed by a series of undiagnosed ministrokes. Shirley had permanent brain damage. The following weekend, Shirley moved into her oldest son's home where she could receive the assistance and support she now needed.

John's case was quite different. He and his wife had always been financially and socially independent. John was a strong-willed man from Scandinavian stock who had taken his wife's recent death quite well. At least, that is what Bill and his wife, Anne, thought. Bill was John's only child and lived 165 miles away with his wife and three children. John seemed to adapt to his new "singlehood" and continued to enjoy his favorite pastimes, fishing and gardening. And although he did not have many friends, he never appeared lonely. On his eighty-third birthday, Bill and his wife decided to surprise John with a visit. They were shocked by what they saw when they entered the house. They found John unshaven, disheveled, and in a state of utter confusion. The house, once so clean and neat, was filthy. Worse, the house had a foul odor and Bill found, to his embarrassment, that his father was soaked in his own urine and feces Bill was quick to call an ambulance for medical attention. The only way they could persuade Bill's father to step into the ambulance was by promising to accompany him to the hospital. The young physician who first examined John informed Bill and Anne that his father was senile. "After all," the physician said, "he's eighty-three years old!"

John was fortunate that his son and daughter-in-law refused to accept such a hasty diagnosis. When his father's private physician arrived at the hospital, he too was alarmed at John's fast deterioration. A careful piecing together of information between the physician, Bill, and what they could get from John led to the real causes of John's state of disorientation. John had fallen in his garden three weeks prior to the emergency hospitalization and had gone to see his physician for headaches. The medication prescribed was apparently too high a dose for John, and the side effects had made him weak and confused. As his confusion increased, cooking became a bother and he stopped eating. It was therefore the combination of head trauma, over-medication, and poor nutrition that had resulted in John's condition.

After a thorough reexamination, the medications were stopped and the head trauma was treated with a different medication at a lower dosage. Bill and Anne arranged for a Meals on Wheels program to deliver John's meals and spent the weekends with him to ensure that his diet was adequate. The house was given a complete cleaning and, in two weeks, John was back to his old self, celebrating a belated birthday with his family.

John's story has a happy ending. The life stories of many other older persons, however, do not. Without a determined physician and a supportive family, John may have been sent to a nursing home with the diagnosis of senility. Just what is the difference between irreversible and reversible mental impairment (often summarily referred to as senility)?

The Forms of Mental Impairment

There are numerous causes for memory problems and confusion in older adults—heart attacks and strokes, nutritional deficiencies, overmedication, arteriosclerosis, and psychiatric illness, to name a few. Mental impairment can be reversible or irreversible. In either case, a course of action can be followed by the family to help treat, or at least cope with, the problems of confusion and memory loss.

Irreversible mental impairment signifies that the problem may be treated but without the hope of restoring the lost brain function. In other words, there is no known cure at this time. The two most common incurable forms of brain failure, or dementia, are Alzheimer's disease and multi-infarct dementia. Only a qualified physician can determine whether the condition is irreversible or reversible. Alzheimer's disease can cause changes in a person's thinking and behavior from accustomed patterns to bizarre behavior and severe confusion. It is a specific disease that can occur at any adult age. Symptoms include confusion, memory loss, loss of control over emotions, and a decrease in control over physical functions. A shuffle-like walk, loss of bladder or bowel functions, and aimless wandering may also characterize the person with this disease.

The Burke Rehabilitation Center in New York describes the four phases of an individual suffering with Alzheimer's disease as follows.[1] The first phase may be difficult to determine. The older adult may seem slower to react, less discriminating, and quick to anger. She may shun the unfamiliar and seek the familiar. By the second phase, the family usually begins to notice something wrong with their family member but will not know what it is. The older adult may still be functioning, but she now requires supervision in certain activities. Increased difficulty in making decisions, a slower rate of speech and understanding, insensitivity to others—these are all symptoms of the second stage. The third phase leaves the family with no question that their relative is disabled. There is a marked change in behavior; little warmth; severe confusion and memory loss (although past memories may remain clear); and she will be hesitant how to act. The fourth phase usually results in the need for total care. The older adult will most likely show signs of apathy, will be incontinent, and will not recognize familiar people or places.

These phases may occur rapidly, or they may take years. In either case, watching a person develop this disease is painful and frustrating. The disease can develop so slowly that families, when asked, will not be able to say exactly when the symptoms first started. Research has yet to discover what causes Alzheimer's disease or how to cure it. It is estimated that approximately 50 to 60 percent of all elderly persons with irreversible mental impairment have Alzheimer's disease.

Multi-infarct dementia is another incurable type of mental impairment that, similar to Alzheimer's disease, results in the death of brain tissue. With multi-infarct dementia, however, repeated strokes are the cause. This was the reason for Shirley's confusion. Approximately 20 percent of the mentally impaired elderly have this form of dementia. Its symptoms are similar to those of Alzheimer's disease and can also include problems with speech and vision.

Reversible mental impairment is often confused with irreversible impairment because of the similarity in symptoms. With reversible mental impairment, however, there is something

medically wrong with the person's mental or physical condition that is showing up as confusion. The most common cause
may be infection. Pneumonia, for example, is often afebrile in
older adults, meaning there is no sign of fever, but it often
presents the symptom of confusion and disorientation. Infections in the urinary system and cerebrovascular occlusions can
also result in symptoms of confusion. These symptoms usually
disappear when the real cause, a very real physical disease, is
diagnosed and treated. Other reversible conditions that can
result in confusion include depression, boredom, poor diet,
overmedication, high fever, and minor head injuries. In the
case of John, we saw that the combinations of poor diet, head
trauma, and overmedication almost led to his diagnosis of
dementia. Remember that although many of these problems can
be successfully treated, they can lead to permanent brain damage if ignored.

The following acronym lists a number of disorders that can
lead to a condition of confusion that may actually be reversible—either treatable, curable, or both:[2]

- *D:* drug toxicity (sedatives, hypnotics, heart drugs, diuretics,
  digitalis)
- *E:* emotional disorders, depression, schizophrenia
- *M:* metabolic and endocrine disorders, thyroid and pulmo-
  nary diseases, diabetes, decompensated liver disease
- *E:* eye and ear disorders
- *N:* nutritional disorders, vitamin deficiencies, anemia
- *T:* tumors and trauma
- *I:* infections, pneumonia
- *A:* arteriosclerotic complications, heart failure, stroke

Although this list is by no means complete, it does provide a
handy reference to the many underlying problems causing confusion that can be treated. Drug toxicity—too much medication
in the body's system—is very common in older people for several reasons. A drug must be broken down (mainly by the liver)
and excreted by the kidneys and intestines. All of these bodily
functions are slower in older adults than in younger people.
This means, then, that the drug remains in the person's system
for a longer period of time. And each additional dose adds to
the amount of the medication already present in the body.
Another reason is that many older people have a number of

chronic conditions that can lead to a great number of drugs being prescribed. This pattern is further complicated by the fact that the older person is often under the care of several physicians and neglects to inform all of them of her various medications. It is usually best to choose one physician and keep this doctor informed of all medications taken so that their effects can be properly assessed.

Another cause of confusion in the elderly is depression. The loss of a spouse, family, friends, job, and income may lead to loneliness and the fear of one's approaching death. Cooking for one can be lonely, and poor nutrition can result in symptoms of confusion. Remember, however, that depression is not the same thing as dementia or mental illness. A thorough assessment, proper treatment, and care can often lead to dramatic improvement and prompt disappearance of the dementia or confusion.

Arteriosclerosis is still another reason an older person may appear confused. It is a common disorder in older people and refers to the thickening of the walls of the arteries. This condition can restrict the flow of the blood to the brain, affecting the person's mental capacity. It is a general diagnosis that can lead to other complications such as stroke and heart failure. The mere presence of arteriosclerosis without disabling complications needs no treatment.

The Role of the Physician

As demonstrated by the cases of Shirley and John, a thorough evaluation by a physician is crucial at the onset of symptoms of mental confusion. During the examination, the physician should be informed of any recent traumatic incidents experienced by the elder, such as the death of a spouse or friend, to rule out depression as a factor. The examination should also include an assessment of the person's diet, general life-style, and the number and types of current medications. Medical tests which may include the brain scan can provide information on the question of brain damage. At no time should the person's problems be dismissed simply because of old age. A complete assessment is necessary to determine whether the symptoms of confusion can be cured or at least held in check.

In the event of a diagnosis of irreversible mental impairment, disoriented behavior may persist even after medical treatment. For families and friends who care about their older relative, this is a sad time. It is often a difficult time as well if the family's schedule must be rearranged to care for the confused elder. Suggestions to families caring for a confused older adult will be discussed later. Understanding her behavior and finding methods to assist her are the first steps to coping.

Guidelines for Coping

The degree of the person's confusion depends on many things. Changes in mental status may range from simple forgetfulness to severe psychotic conditions such as hallucinations and delusions. Hallucinations refer to sounds and sights that are not really there. Verbal reminders, notes, and even the use of a calendar may help the person experiencing hallucinations keep in touch with reality. Prescribed medications may also be called for. Serious psychotic conditions such as delusions—untrue beliefs that are held by a person who has lost touch with reality —may require the attention of the family physician and, in some cases, a psychiatrist.

In general, the two most common losses of mental functioning in the older adult are termed confusion and disorientation. For the *confused* older adult, identity is jumbled—she may be able to tell you her name but not necessarily where she is or the approximate time of day. She may have trouble recognizing family members or friends at first glance. Her verbal responses also tend to be vague and not in the proper order. She probably knows she cannot recall information very well anymore and may even have trouble expressing herself. The *disoriented* person, on the other hand, has little or no perception of time, where she is, and who she is.

There is often a fine line of distinction between confusion and disorientation. Moreover, the degree to which a person is confused or disoriented may vary from day to day. The methods for coping to be described are directed more toward the confused older adult and are mainly the products of trial and error efforts in institutions and the community. Caregivers dealing with the disoriented adult must bear in mind that their efforts will require greater patience, intensity, and consistency.

Physical Aids

There are ways of helping the confused older adult maintain a certain level of awareness and orientation. Orientation refers to the ability to locate oneself in one's environment with respect to people, time, and place. Physical aids provide visual cues and remind the confused person about relevant information: who she is, where she is, and the time, day, and month. Since confusion can stem from vision and hearing problems, adapting such aids to these needs is important. The use of clocks and wristwatches with large faces and calendars with large numerals and spaces for notes are among the most common visual aids to help with time orientation. If an X is drawn through the date at the end of the day, the older adult will be able to orient herself to the next day with little effort.

The use of bright colors in the form of drapes, bedspreads, and other items in the home will assist the confused person in distinguishing one room from another. Use of a night light will also assist your older parent in orientation to time and place should she awaken in the night. For those who wander, use of an identification bracelet stating her name, address, and phone number may assist the older adult in getting home safely. At the very least, it may help someone else to direct her home.

Television, radio, newspapers, and other forms of media provide excellent sources of information to orient a confused person to time, people, place, and events. Encouraging her to pursue a hobby or tend to specified tasks in the home such as gardening also helps to preserve a sense of identity and belonging. Such aids can assist in her orientation but cannot take the place of human warmth. Outings to familiar places with relatives and friends provide much stimulation to the confused adult. It is the day-to-day socializing with you, the family, that contributes to keeping the confused older adult in touch with reality.

Observation and Interaction

For the family of a confused older adult, one of the most difficult tasks is developing skills in listening, observing, and responding in a way that is both reassuring and realistic—that is, in touch with one's feelings and surroundings. Often family members and professionals alike have found themselves ignoring or humoring the jumbled statements of a confused adult simply because they do not know what to say or how to approach a person who is clearly out of touch with reality. Families may also feel embarrassed about their older relatives and may try to hide them from company. Socializing with friends may also be discouraged. A newsletter devoted to Alzheimer's disease and related disorders offers five suggestions for families in handling social visits.[3] These suggestions, however, may be used with any confused older adult.

First, educate your friends about your relative's condition. It is nothing to be ashamed about, and your friends will appreciate knowing what is causing your discomfort. *Second,* don't try to educate your friends about the disability in front of the older person; she still has feelings. *Third,* show patience with your relative in front of your friends so they can model their behavior on yours. *Fourth,* include children in the explanation of the problem but remember to keep it simple. *Fifth,* use your own judgment in how much to confide with others. If the person has a very difficult time eating, perhaps it would be wiser to feed her before your guests arrive. These five points emphasize that social interaction remains crucial for the confused older adult. Severe confusion that is irreversible is sad, not shameful.

We turn now to several general points that should be considered when caring for a confused older relative or friend. Above all, a sense of humor goes a long way.

- *Maintain a calm environment.* There is nothing more distracting than a home where everyone is running about, the television is blaring, and no one seems to know what anyone else is doing. Such an environment only adds to the person's confusion. In a calm and orderly household, the older adult is better able to stay in touch with her surroundings.
- *Establish a daily routine.* This does not mean a strict schedule but rather a general daily format such as having meals or other activities at close to the same hour every day. When a schedule exists, the person knows what to expect. Routine can be a source of reassurance to the person whose world is overwhelming and filled with unfamiliar people, things, and events. A schedule can also be a helpful tool to maintain an awareness of time.

- *Ask questions clearly and concisely.* The confused person cannot process information quickly. Keep questions simple, but avoid the temptation of speaking to her as if she were a child. It may also be helpful to offer *specific* choices in your questions. For example: "Would you like eggs or pancakes for breakfast?" as opposed to "What would you like to eat?"
- *Allow for independence.* Encourage your family member to continue to do as much for herself as possible.
- *Allow sufficient time for response.* The time lapse between a question and the response may be longer for the confused older adult. Avoid rushing a response, as the person may become anxious and more confused.
- *Review instructions or other information.* Or ask the confused adult to repeat what is said. This will show you how much of the message was heard and understood. If necessary, repeat the instructions. If your mother has been forgetful lately about her medications, slowly and carefully repeat the time she is supposed to take them. Then ask her to repeat what you have just told her, and check on how well she understood your directions. If your mother is unable to repeat your instructions, you may have to seek other methods.
- *Don't shrug off incoherent ramblings.* Reorient. Reorient means to help someone adjust to her present situation by being in touch with those around her and her surroundings. Reorienting your family member requires gentleness as well as an appreciation of the feelings behind her statements. In visiting your 79-year-old confused mother who resides with your sister, for example, suppose she tells you that her mother (who died fifteen years ago) is coming to dinner. In frustration, you tell her that no one else is joining you for dinner and she knows quite well that Grandma has been dead for fifteen years. This response is direct and honest but somewhat cruel. Because you have ignored the emotions behind the message, you have hurt her feelings; you may also have angered her and compounded her confusion. You could have tried another response: "Well, Mom, I guess you've been thinking about Grandma today. It's been fifteen years since her death and it sounds like you still miss her very much. So do I. Tell me more about what it was like growing up with Grandma." Such a response is realistic, but it also provides an

opportunity for the confused person to reminisce and socialize, two aids in orientation.[4]

- *Be firm when necessary.* Sometimes it may not be possible or
  even desirable to give the person a choice in affairs that concern her—as in the matter of personal hygiene and eating—
  due to the severity of the confusion. In such cases, clear
  expectations for behavior and your guidance may produce
  the desired result.
- *Make your home safe.* Knobs may have to be taken off the
  stove and latches put on cupboards to ensure a safe home.
  Bathrails and hallway guardrails can also help. Remove clutter, footstools, and scatter rugs that can cause falls and accidents.
- *Look into legal protection.* Do so at the very onset of confusion, and include your relative to ease any anxiety and suspicion. You may have to seek power of attorney for your relative or, in serious cases, become her legal guardian. Seek legal
  counsel. If there is a legal aid society in your community,
  they may provide low-cost services.
- *Take steps to deal with wandering.* Wandering is a common
  but serious problem. See if someone in your family can go for
  walks with your relative to channel some of the energy.
  Check your house to see if there is a locked outdoor area
  where your relative can wander safely. If not, place locks
  in unfamiliar places on doors (toward the bottom, for example) or install alarms to prevent a runaway incident. Don't
  forget to have her name and address on a bracelet or sewn
  onto clothes so a safe return home is possible if she does wander off.
- *Use judgment.* If your father is very disoriented but still
  wants to drive the family car, you must intervene and take the
  keys away from him. This step is essential for his safety and
  the safety of others.
- *Be aware of feelings.* While your relative may have trouble
  organizing her thoughts, she is still aware of feelings transmitted to her by other people. Anger, frustration, love, and
  acceptance can still be felt. When you are tired or upset, it's
  hard to respond kindly to a confused person. Families must
  realize and accept the fact that there are limits to what they
  can achieve. Seek help from other family members or community programs when you're feeling exhausted.

Outside Helpers

When you're seeking assistance, other family members may be your primary resource. The confused adult will be more comfortable and relaxed with familiar people, and family members may find enjoyment in helping. Moreover, community resources are available. Home health agencies, friendly visitor programs, senior companion programs, and adult day-care centers provide services while giving the family time to rest and attend to other affairs. Local support groups or chapters of the Alzheimer's Disease and Related Disorders Association may also be helpful. In the event of a personal emergency, vacation, or extreme fatigue, some nursing homes may provide a temporary residence. A local agency on aging or other information and referral service can help families locate these services.

How long should the family be responsible for this type of round-the-clock care? It all depends on you. Professionals can assist families who are grappling with such a question. In cases of severe confusion, the person's physical needs may exceed the family's ability to care for her. It is wise at that point to seek professional advice to determine whether the situation is still manageable at home. Social service agencies and your physician can work with you to chart the course of action that can best assist you at this time.

Successful coping, then, involves a combination of your attitude as a caregiver, your skills in responding to the confused person, and the availability of a support system of other caregivers to provide periodic relief. With this combination, the chances of keeping the confused adult at home with some degree of orientation to reality are greatly improved.

Notes

1. Burke Rehabilitation Center, *Managing the Person with Intellectual Loss at Home* (White Plains, 1980).

2. Jerome Yesavage, "Dementia: Differential Diagnosis and Treatment," *Geriatrics* (September 1979): 52.

3. *The Alzheimer's Disease and Related Disorders Association's Newsletter,* Fall issue, 1981.

4. Robert Butler and Myrna Lewis, *Aging and Mental Health* (St. Louis: C. V. Mosby, 1977).

9

Arthritis and Aging

BILLIE DeMELLO
CAROLE FUJISHIGE
LINDA GERSON

Jeannette, age sixty-nine, had always been active and blessed with good health. Her life was both happy and busy: helping Saul, her husband of fifty years, with the family store, babysitting for any of her eleven grandchildren, and volunteering for many community affairs. But over the past year, she began to feel a growing discomfort and pain in her left knee that was preventing her from enjoying her gardening and other activities. Saul kept urging Jeannette to see their doctor, but she always refused, saying "Why should I go and spend money just to hear him tell me what I already know? I'm just growing old!"

But Jeannette was wrong. She is one of 35 million Americans who have a disease called arthritis.[1] Arthritis is a term used to describe nearly one hundred rheumatic diseases. It affects the muscles and skeletal system and causes inflammatory or degenerative damage to a joint. It is not synonymous with old age, for people of all ages can have this disease. (It is true, though, that more older people have this disease than younger ones.) Arthritis is a chronic disease—it is lifelong and has no known cure. It is also a serious disease—it causes pain and can cripple and disfigure hands and knees. Anyone experiencing the following symptoms should see a physician for diagnosis and, if necessary, treatment:

- Persistent pain and stiffness on rising in the morning
- Pain, tenderness, or swelling in one or more joints

- Recurrence of these symptoms, especially when they involve more than one joint
- Recurrent or persistent pain and stiffness in the neck, lower back, knees, and other joints
- Numbness or a tingling sensation in hands, feet, and fingertips[2]

Common Types of Arthritis

The three most common types of arthritis affecting the elderly are *osteoarthritis* (also called degenerative arthritis), *rheumatoid arthritis*, and *gout*. These, however, are just three of the more than one hundred different types of arthritis. Most people who suffer from a variety of aches and pains involving muscles, joints, and bones usually experience the pain only now and then. Many of these conditions resolve themselves after a short time following rest and proper medication. For those whose problems persist and even increase in severity, a physician should be consulted so that the condition can be properly diagnosed and a comprehensive treatment designed. Because arthritis is a chronic disease with no known cure, its diagnosis is usually depressing and often frightening to the individual. Try to be understanding. The person will experience good and bad days. Your love and support will help. Now let's consider in more detail the three most common types of arthritis.

Osteoarthritis

Osteoarthritis is the most common type of arthritis found in older adults. In fact, most of us will get arthritis if we live long enough.[3] With osteoarthritis, there is a breakdown of cartilage, the substance that cushions the ends of our bones. As the breakdown continues, the joints begin to rub each other, causing the joints to become stiff and painful to move. Shoulders, hips, knees, ankles, and spine are usually affected. The joint can also become bumpy due to an overgrowth of bone that is trying to heal itself. The enlarged joints can cause severe pain where they put pressure on nerves in the neck or spine.

The cause of osteoarthritis is not yet known. Some believe

hereditary factors play a part in its occurrence. Excessive wear and tear on the joints caused by certain occupations and past injuries that caused a joint to function improperly may also have a bearing on osteoarthritis, although the results may take years to see.

Pain and stiffness are the most common symptoms of osteoarthritis. The signs usually start so gradually that your family member will probably not be able to tell you when they first began. Osteoarthritis causes varying degrees of discomfort—from mild stiffness and aching of the fingers to severe pain and limitation of activity. In either case, there are specific measures that will help the person live and function with comfort and independence. While the handicaps from the disease cannot be cured or always prevented, they may be corrected. Your family member who is diagnosed as having osteoarthritis does not have to resign herself to becoming disabled.

Rheumatoid Arthritis

Another type of arthritis is rheumatoid arthritis. This disease may begin with general fatigue, stiffness, and pain in joints. A loss of appetite and weight is also common. Eventually, the pain becomes localized in the joints, resulting in tenderness, redness, and swelling. This disease affects all ages and occurs more frequently in women than men. It is not as common as osteoarthritis and yet it is far more disabling. In rheumatoid arthritis, the cells lining the joints, called synovial cells, increase in number and invade the cartilage and bone of the joints. The involved joints become swollen, warm, and painful and in time may become deformed. The person's ability to move may be seriously reduced. The symptoms of rheumatoid arthritis may occur suddenly, but most often they appear gradually over a period of time. Each case of the disease is different in presentation and course and must be treated as such.

Gout

Gout is still another form of arthritis. It is more common in men than in women and usually affects joints like the toes and ankles. Gouty arthritis occurs when excess uric acid forms salt crystals in joints resulting in inflammation, swelling, and joint pain. It is a painful disease but can be controlled with proper diagnosis and medication.

Diagnosis and Treatment

Michael had suffered from painful, swollen joints off and on for many years. These arthritis attacks would often develop after he had drunk too much alcohol. His last attack had been especially painful, however, prompting Michael to see his doctor. Following an examination and lab tests, he was told he had gout. The doctor explained that further attacks could be deterred by daily use of prescribed medications, a gradual reduction of weight, and avoidance of certain foods and all alcohol.

Not all types of arthritis can be so easily treated. It all depends on the individual case. A specific medication may be prescribed for one kind of arthritis, for example, and not another. Too often people feel that aches and pains are a natural part of growing old and thus ignore them or simply accept them. But prompt diagnosis and treatment by a qualified physician can often prevent needless suffering and crippling.

How arthritis will affect *your* family member depends on its type and its degree of severity. This is why your physician is so important in diagnosing the disease, determining its type, and trying to avoid crippling deformities. Since there is no cure, the goal is *control*. Early diagnosis is essential; neglect and delay are the worst enemies in treating arthritis.

There are no magic cures for arthritis. But certain treatments such as prescribed medications, proper diet, the right balance of rest and exercise, and heat therapy and cold treatments can help. Dealing with this disease requires combined efforts by the arthritis sufferer, her family, and her doctor.

Medications

Medications are often prescribed to relieve inflammation and pain in the joints. There are a variety of drugs which can perform this function, but aspirin is the one you are probably most familiar with. One can only derive the benefits from medications when they are taken in the amounts prescribed by a physician. Self-regulation of doses can result in inadequate blood levels of the drug and thus inadequate relief of the symptoms. Moreover, an older person may forget to take the medication, leading one to believe it is not working.

Aspirin, when taken in adequate dosage, is one of the most effective medications for arthritis sufferers. It reduces inflammation—the cause of stiffness—and swelling and pain in the joints. Aspirin is not the only medication for arthritis, however. Consult a physician to determine other alternatives. If your elder is taking other medications, be sure to inform your physician of this fact to avoid negative drug interactions. Your doctor should also be informed of any undesirable symptoms such as nausea, stomach pain, dizziness, or ringing in the ears—these may be side effects caused by aspirin. Tylenol and other medications which contain acetaminophen should not be substituted for aspirin because they do not control inflammation. Steroids are sometimes prescribed to treat arthritis, but they can cause confusion and disorientation in older adults, so watch for such side effects.[4]

Diet

When Kay told her friends that she had rheumatoid arthritis, she was offered all kinds of advice on what foods she should and should not eat. Kay tried whatever new remedies were suggested but soon learned that her arthritis did not improve with these suggestions. There is no scientific evidence that too much or too little of any particular food or vitamin can cause arthritis. Conversely, no particular food, vitamin, or mineral is known to cure arthritis. (There is some evidence, though, that excessive weight may cause osteoarthritis due to the extra pressure placed on the joints.) Gout is the only form of arthritis with dietary restrictions.

The best course is to eat adequate amounts of meat, fish, poultry, cereals, dairy products, vegetables, and fruits. Be aware that painful joints can make it hard to open containers and prepare meals. But don't let your elder skip meals on that account—fatigue and loss of appetite may result. These factors can lead to poor eating habits and inadequate nutritional intake. Very often, simple devices such as electric can openers or jar wrenches can be useful aids to a person with painful hands and wrists. For more complex problems, the advice of an occupational therapist, a skilled health care professional, can be sought.

Rest and Exercise

Apart from diet and medications, a doctor may prescribe a program of rest and exercise. The balance between the two will depend on the severity of the disease and the type of arthritis. Rest is beneficial in reducing joint inflammation. But too much rest can lead to stiffness and weakening of muscles. Is there a *right* balance of rest and exercise? Generally more rest and less exercise is prescribed during an acute stage—in other words, when the joint is painful, red, tender, or swollen. At these times the joint should be rested and protected from stress and overuse. As the inflammation subsides, exercise can be increased. The key word here is *balance*. Remember: An exercise program must be planned for each person's specific needs.

Whether your elder has osteoarthritis or rheumatoid arthritis, the hallmark of these diseases is a painful joint. And when a joint is painful, the tendency is to keep it in a position of comfort. Most of the time this means keeping the joint in a bent position. If the joint is kept in this position too long or too frequently, however, the muscles crossing the joint will shorten, resulting in a contracture and even more pain. Suppose, for example, a person with a swollen, painful knee keeps it in a bent position for comfort. In a few weeks to a month, she may find she cannot straighten it. Any attempts to do so will cause great pain. And walking with a bent knee will eventually disrupt posture in other parts of the body and cause pain in *those* joints.

Instructions on proper positioning can be given by a physical therapist to prevent a joint from becoming contracted. There are also specific exercises which can be done to improve or prevent contractures. Exercises can also be given for strengthening weak muscles. If your family member must walk with a cane in order to protect a swollen and painful knee, a therapist can fit the cane and instruct her in its proper use.

If a family member is bedridden or wheelchair-bound due to arthritis, special care must be taken to prevent the development of contractures and pressure sores. Get a firm mattress which provides strong support. Use pillows with care since they can contribute to joint contractures. A person who lies in bed all day with a pillow under both knees will soon find that she is unable to straighten her legs. A physical therapist or visiting nurse can advise on the proper lying position. Other family members should help the person to change positions frequently to prevent stiffness and pressure on bony parts, which can cause skin breakdown.

The ultimate responsibility for everyday therapy belongs to the arthritis sufferer and her family. Arthritis is a chronic disease. Government agencies and medical insurance companies will not finance physical therapy indefinitely. It is often up to the family and the elder person to learn the therapies so they may be continued at home. Exercise cannot *cure* arthritis, but it can help your family member remain as mobile and independent as possible.

It is not uncommon for people with arthritis to have questions on sexuality. Often it is the sufferer herself who initiates these questions, but a spouse or partner may also be in need of answers. Since arthritics usually have pain in several joints, it takes the love and understanding of both partners to solve any problems in this regard. There are several good booklets out today that discuss the various ways couples can continue to be intimate safely and comfortably for the person with arthritis. Contact your local arthritis foundation for further assistance or talk to a physician.

The proper mix of rest and exercise can do much to alleviate the pain and discomfort of arthritis. But exercise is often unpopular because of joint pain. What can be done if your relative refuses exercise as a treatment? Explain that the biggest advantage of participating in a prescribed exercise plan is that exercises will help her to maintain movement. While there is no magic formula for motivating people to exercise, look at your elder's personality and priorities and then set up an exercise program that will appeal to her.

Physical therapists can teach an arthritis sufferer proper sleeping, sitting, and walking postures to protect the joints. They can also teach your aging relative how to use assistive devices such as canes to help in movement and can instruct her in proper ways to lift objects while protecting the lower back.

Types of Exercise

People with arthritis are encouraged to do specific exercises for affected joints twice a day. The type of exercise will depend on the type of joint pain. Generally, a person with a sore swollen joint is instructed to do *isometric* exercises coupled with rest periods. (Isometric exercise is done by tensing the muscle that crosses a joint without moving the joint itself.) Gentle *passive* exercises, three or four repetitions at a time, can also be done by a family member when the joint is too sore for the person to move it alone. Once the joint swelling and pain have decreased, *active assistive* exercises can be started. In these exercises, the person gets a little help from a family member but tries to do as much of the activity as possible. The most important type of exercise for the arthritis patient is *active* exercise. In this case the person does the exercise independently throughout the full range of motion. Unless a person gets to this stage, maintaining muscle strength will be difficult. (*Resistive* exercise, consisting of using weights, should not be used on a sore swollen joint.)

Heat Therapy and Cold Therapy

Heat treatment can be done easily at home by taking a warm shower or bath in the morning or before exercise. Heat helps to reduce pain by relaxing muscles and making it easier to move them. Very hot temperatures should be avoided for longer than twenty minutes over a swollen joint, however, as high temperatures tend to increase circulation and swelling to that joint. For a particularly troublesome joint, a therapist can demonstrate other heat treatments that can be done at home, such as paraffin, hydrocollator, and heating pads.

Cold therapy is also very effective in the treatment of individual arthritic joints. Cold therapy is not very popular, though, as most people say that cold treatments make them more stiff. Nevertheless, research has shown that cold treatments can in fact produce more positive results than heat treatments at times. Cold therapy helps reduce pain and swelling and, when tried with the right attitude, can be beneficial prior to beginning an exercise program. Cold therapy is easily applied at home by using ice cubes rubbed continuously against the skin for five or ten minutes over a three-inch by four-inch area.

Promoting Independence

Families often ask, "How can I best help my mother who has arthritis?" One way is to learn about the disease. Another way is to show your mother, by listening to her concerns, that she is still important and capable and loved.

We all know, however, that listening and caring are sometimes not enough in helping the arthritis sufferer to feel good about herself. Promoting independence is another important way to prove to the person she is still a capable human being. Certain activities will need to be done with greater caution than before the disease was diagnosed, but most activities need not be discontinued. There are three basic techniques to help the person remain independent: protecting the joints of the hands, simplifying the work, and conserving energy.

Protecting the Joints of the Hands

Louise, in her mid-fifties, was sent to a therapist by her physician. She was recently widowed and all her grown children now live in other states. As a secretary in a large office, she noted there were days when pencils or pens would suddenly fall out of her hand. She also complained of her finger joints becoming either stiff or swollen when she did a lot of typing. She was having trouble with household chores, especially opening cans and jars and preparing meals. Eating out in restaurants had become a problem, too, as she found she was having trouble using utensils. She worried that she might not be able to continue with her job. What could she do? The therapist determined that Louise had rheumatoid arthritis and needed to protect the joints from damage. The best way to protect the joints of the hands is to enlarge the handles on the things we use. The tighter the grasp needed, the more pressure on the joints and, thus, the more damage to the joints.

The first way to cut down on the wear and tear of the finger joint is to use laborsaving devices—electric can openers, jars with wide lids, electric typewriters, shoulder holders for telephones, and electric pencil sharpeners. The second way is to buy ready-made devices—lightweight aluminum pots and pans, long-handled brooms and dustpans, silverware with large handles, and cooking utensils with thick handles.

Try building up the handles of common utensils to the thickness desired for an easier grasp—for example, the plastic inner tube from the paper rolls on adding machines are perfect for pens, pencils, and other small, round handles. Inexpensive black foam tubing can also be purchased for this purpose. The foam can be stretched to fit several shapes such as pot handles, knife handles, cooking utensils, toothbrush handles, working tools, and silverware. If the hole is too large for the handle, try putting a rubber band around the handle before fitting the tube. This tube can be easily carried in one's purse and can be used at work, at play, and at home. Flat foam, found in most department stores, can also be used. Cut it into a wide rectangular strip and wind it around the handle. Then cover it with plastic-coated tape.

Louise was able to function more easily after adapting the pens and pencils and using the thick black foam on her pots, cooking tools, and toothbrush. She also learned how to alternate writing, answering the telephone, and typing to give her hands an occasional rest. Housework too became easier, and she could do more with less trouble. She also used the foam when eating out and could cut her own meat. In summary, the following outline covers the various joint protection techniques she should use:

1. Keep all joints in extension (straight) as often as possible.
2. Avoid cramping a joint in one position for a period of time.
3. Make the grasp as big as possible.
   • Buy thicker handles.
   • Use the plastic tubes from adding machine tapes.
   • Use the stiff cardboard from knitting tapes.
   • Use foam rubber handles.
4. Use long bones—not joints—for holding things.
5. Use proper body mechanics—always bend at the knees to lift; don't bend at the waist. Push things, don't pull them. Carry things near to the body.

Work Simplification

To understand how work simplification can ease the plight of the arthritic older person, consider the case of a middle-aged person with rheumatoid arthritis who came to an arthritis center for help. He was fifty-one years old and worked in a family-owned gas station. The job often involved ten hours a day and sometimes seven days a week, but he had a wife and several children to support. He had to fix the cars, crawl under cars, pump gas, answer phones, and do paperwork. Although he was unable to keep up with his workload, he did not want to ask for special favors because he was the owner. In fact, he loved his work. He was always stiff first thing in the morning, however, and by midafternoon he had several hot, swollen joints further hampering his ability to work.

Since it was clear that he wouldn't change jobs, he needed to understand how to adapt his life to his present illness. At the arthritis center, he was taught how to protect his joints by building up the handles of his tools—the first step to making life easier for him. Then work simplification techniques were discussed. There are ways to make both the overall job and each individual task easier. There are four ways to do this.

First he was taught how to organize his day's work. Every workday he would list the things that needed to be done. He divided them into different groups depending on the amount of handwork needed, how much bending he had to do, and whether the task was done standing, sitting, or lying down.

Then he looked at the jobs individually. He decided which ones could be combined and done at one time, which ones called for enlarged handles or power tools and which ones could be tried in entirely new ways.

He then tried to determine the jobs that would cause him pain on that particular day. These jobs would be delegated to others while he took on the less troublesome tasks. He further set up his own work area with all the tools for the day close at hand.

Finally, he allotted a specific time for each task and planned breaks around each task. He would try to alternate tasks so that he would do some standing, some sitting, and some lying down. He would go from a job that made him use his hands often to one where he spent his time sitting and supervising.

By using these methods and adapting his job to his daily needs and his pain, he was able to keep working and keep feeling worthwhile. At the same time he was helping to keep his disease under control. The work simplification techniques are outlined as follows:

1. *Organize work.* This is best done by sitting down and planning the tasks on paper.
   - Analyze the task to be done.
   - Break it into as many steps as possible.
2. *Simplify tasks.* Use the information from step 1 to:
   - Make changes in the equipment.
   - Combine several steps into one simple task.
   - Change the order of the work.
   - Change the methods.
3. *Eliminate unnecessary steps.* Get others to do the painful or troublesome jobs. Arrange the work area ahead of time:
   - Set a special place for the job.
   - Make sure the work height is suitable for sitting or standing.
   - Keep supplies within easy reach.
   - Place things in the order to be used.
4. *Do activities in moderation.*
   - Plan work breaks according to the clock, *not* to the task at hand.
   - Use two hands to save time and motion.
   - Use other parts of the body if possible—put foot pedals on garbage cans, for example, or knee pedals on sewing machines.

Energy Conservation

Celia, a sixty-year-old woman, came to see the therapist when she learned from her physician that she had systemic lupus erythematosus (SLE), a form of arthritis. She had recently returned to a community college to earn a degree, something she had always dreamed of doing. Her husband's position with a large company made it necessary for her to attend parties, join social groups, and volunteer her time. Although she had problems with aching joints, these were relatively minor—her major concern was her constant lack of energy. She felt tired all the time but was unable to see any way to cut down on her activities. The thought that her fatigue was a reflection of her age depressed her even further.

The therapist recommended that Celia conserve her energy and suggested that she think of her body as a kind of battery. When a flashlight battery is fully charged, it gives out a strong beam of light. When the energy in the battery has been partially used up, the light grows dim. When all the energy has been used up (we call this a dead battery), there's no light at all. Our bodies work in somewhat the same way. At times we have fresh energy and can fill our days with many activities without feeling tired. When we've used up some of our energy, we can only do a few activities. And then there are days when we've used up all our energy and can do almost nothing.

Our bodies also have an internal fuel system made up of four components. These components either use up fuel or keep it balanced for a steady bright light. These components include:

- The *emotional system* concerns how we feel. This system can either drain our energy (when we're depressed or elated) or maintain a balance (when we're operating on an even keel).
- The *physiological system* controls our physical well-being. We drain this system when we're ill and keep it in balance when we're well. Those with chronic diseases like arthritis constantly drain this system.
- The *internal system* controls the normal functioning of our bodies. This system keeps our muscles in tone, makes our heart beat, and ensures that our liver, kidneys, and so forth function smoothly. When we're exhausted, we drain this system.
- The *joint system* concerns the energy we use in moving our joints. If certain joints are overused, we tire the muscles and drain the system. We need to alternate use of our joint and body positions so that all joints get moved and rested throughout each day.

These four systems work simultaneously to determine how we feel each day. When you do things during the day, you often draw out the energy from the entire day. Like a battery which has used up much of its energy and only gives off a dim light, your body will be using up too much energy if you're taxing these systems. When are these systems taxed? Let's see what happens:

- *Emotionally:* If you're very happy, very excited, very nervous, or very sad, you will use up energy.

- *Physiologically:* If you're ill, have a cold, the flu, or a systemic illness (rheumatoid arthritis, cancer, heart disease), you will use up energy.
- *Internally:* If you're exhausted from lack of sleep and yet try to continue working, you will use up energy.
- *Joints:* If you move around a lot and constantly bend or straighten your arms, legs, fingers, and other body parts—or if you remain in one position for a length of time—you will use up energy.

Just like a battery that gives off a steady light, our bodies can function at their best if we use up only what we have stored from the night before. Our systems are not overburdened when:

- *Emotionally:* We feel normal with good and bad times balanced throughout the day.
- *Physiologically:* We feel well all day long.
- *Internally:* We have had adequate sleep at night plus rest periods throughout the day.
- *Joints:* We have used all of our joints and have not abused them or stayed in one position for a length of time.

A battery plugged into an outlet can recharge itself. Our bodies, too, can recharge themselves daily and even hour by hour. How can we replenish our systems (recharge our batteries)? Here are three proven ways:

- *Pure rest:* You need eight to ten hours of sleep at night. You also need at least a half-hour rest at midday. This rest period should be spent lying on your back with your arms and legs out straight and a small pillow under your head. By stretching out straight, you'll help to prevent flexion contractures. Another position restful to the body is to lie prone. Lie on your stomach, feet off the edge of the bed, with a small pillow under your midsection. Keep your arms out straight, too.
- *Rest-work cycle:* Alternate between working and resting. In this manner you'll continually rebuild your energy supply hourly. The length of each part of this cycle can change both daily and hourly. Try following this schedule. Work for about half an hour and then take a rest break for fifteen minutes. If

you feel fully refreshed, you can try working for forty-five minutes before trying another fifteen-minute break. If after this break you are still not tired, then your next work period can last an hour. If you *still* feel tired after the first fifteen-minute rest, however, you need to rest for another fifteen minutes. When you begin to work again, work for only fifteen minutes and then take a fifteen-minute rest break. In this manner, you'll be able to judge both the amount of work and the amount of rest that you need every hour of the day.

• *Changing body positions:* By changing body positions, you'll prevent both contractures and joint stiffness. Not only will you be keeping your joints loose, but you'll also be using different sets of muscles which will keep them from getting weak. There are several body positions you can use. They can be used in any order so long as you go from one to another. For example:
  1. Standing
  2. Sitting in a chair, feet up on another chair
  3. Sitting in a chair, feet flat on the floor
  4. Sitting in a chair, legs stretched out in front of you
  5. Sitting on the floor, legs out straight
  6. Sitting on the floor, legs crossed in front of you
  7. Lying on your back
  8. Lying on your stomach
  9. Lying on either side

The main object here is to change from whatever position you're in to another every thirty minutes. Make sure you change from sitting to standing to lying down as well as changing your arms (at the shoulder, elbow, wrist, and fingers) and your legs (at hip, knee, and ankle) from bent to straight.

Putting the Techniques in Action

The following examples illustrate how these techniques can be applied to two common activities. First we'll see how they apply to **cooking:**

1. *Joint Protection*
   • Lightweight pots and pans
   • Electric can openers

- Large-handled silverware
- Plastic plates
- Two-handled ovenware
- Rubber gloves
- Dishwasher

2. *Work Simplification*
   - Plan ahead. Know all the steps of the job; don't forget to include setting the table, the work itself, and the cleanup.
   - Simplify the task. Get others to help set the table and clear it; carry objects in both hands; set up the work area (on the tabletop or on the counter near stove, sink, or refrigerator).
   - Eliminate unnecessary steps. Go to the refrigerator, sink, or stove only once. (Coordinate steps!) Place all supplies in one area. *Slide* materials on countertops. Sit and stand while working.
   - Use moderation. Take breaks if the cooking task is a long one. Prepare only *one* main meal a day.

3. *Energy Conservation*
   - Monitor your body energy. Do you feel fine? Then you can do as much as you feel able to. Do you feel upset? Then you will have to do less in the kitchen. Do you feel ill? Then you may need help in the kitchen. Do you feel completely out of sorts? Then you'll need help in the kitchen and will also have to cut down on the amount of work planned.
   - Use the techniques for energy conservation. Remember the rest and work cycle: Lie down in bed for at least half an hour before you begin working in the kitchen. Don't plan on doing another large task either before or right after cooking. Remember to change positions: Alternate sitting with standing while preparing and cooking your meal. Go lie down while food is in the oven.

Now let's see how these techniques can be applied to **gardening:**

1. *Joint Protection*
   - Use large-handled tools.
   - Plant in lightweight plastic pots.
   - Use large aluminum pans.

- Use potting soil (a lightweight material which looks like sand).
- Use long-handled hoes, rakes, spades.
- Use gardening gloves.
- Use *electric* hedge cutters.
- Use hose attachments to spray an area without having to hold the hose.

2. *Work Simplification*
   - Organize your work. Do small amounts several times a day rather than a large task once a day. Plan the garden to suit your abilities.
   - Simplify the tasks. Do all the tasks that need to be done in one area—seeding, watering, planting, and so forth. Combine tasks so that one task is completed before you begin another. (Do all the holes, put in the seeds, cover all the holes, water. Don't do one hole, put in the seed, cover the hole, and then do the next hole.)
   - Eliminate steps. Set up new, easily reached work areas. Put your garden up on benches at either chest or waist level. Get others to do the heavy work, dig holes, pull weeds, cut branches, set up your watering hose, and the like.
   - Work in moderation. Work for short periods. Take several breaks. Use a stool rather than sitting on the ground.

3. *Energy Conservation*
   - Monitor your energy. Do you feel fine? Then work within your limitations of time, pain, and fatigue. Do you feel upset? Then do less work. Do you feel ill? Then make use of help to do several of your planned tasks. Do you feel completely out of sorts? Then eliminate all of the work planned for that day or do only one easy task.
   - Use the techniques for energy conservation. Remember the rest and work cycle: Be sure to lie down and rest for at least half an hour before you begin gardening. Plan your gardening tasks so that you go from a finger task like seeding to a hand task like using a large-handled trowel to a body task like hoeing. Remember to change positions: Alternate sitting, standing, lying down, and walking so that you are not in any one position for more than fifteen to thirty minutes. Alternate working with your hands in the dirt (lying or sitting) to using a short-handled tool (sitting or kneeling) to using a long-handled rake (standing).

In both these examples—cooking and gardening—only general ideas have been suggested. If there are specific tasks you need help in planning, talk to a health professional such as an occupational therapist.

Notes

The authors wish to thank Dr. Michael Catalano, former director of the Arthritis Center of Hawaii, for his assistance.

1. The Arthritis Foundation, *Arthritis: The Basic Facts* (Atlanta: 1981), p. 2.
2. Ibid., p. 6.
3. Ibid., p. 14.
4. R. Butler, *Why Survive? Being Old in America* (New York: Harper & Row, 1975), p. 200.

10

Stroke and the Older Adult

OTTO NEURATH

HERBERT YEE

GRACE IHARA

COLETTE BROWNE

A loud thump startled Emma one evening as she was cooking dinner. When she rushed into the living room to find out what was the matter, she saw her husband, Frank, lying on the floor. Emma was alarmed but still she managed to prop Frank up on a chair. His right arm had no strength at all and he could barely speak. Both of them were frightened. Emma immediately called the ambulance and within minutes Frank was on his way to the local hospital. The physician in charge told Emma that Frank had suffered a stroke but, in his opinion, Emma could be optimistic about her husband's chances for at least partial recovery. After four months of treatment and exercise programs, along with the love and support of his family, Frank came home. His speech had returned and he could manage quite well with only a slight weakness on his right side.

Michael's situation was quite different from Frank's. Michael learned that the weakness in his left arm and leg he first noticed a month ago was the result of a stroke. During his hospitalization, he seemed to regain some movement on his left side. In the physical therapy gym of the hospital, there were other people who were described as stroke victims. One woman constantly drooled and Michael found it difficult to look at her. Another woman, who looked only about forty years old, was also said to have suffered a stroke. She was able to walk with a cane but seemed hesitant and unsteady. Still another stroke patient, an elderly man, never made any sense when he talked and had a hard time writing.

Michael was confused. He asked his therapist, "If I had the same thing as these other people, why do we all have different problems? Why am I unable to do some of the things others can do? How much better will I be getting? And what more can I do when I leave here?"

What *Is* a Stroke?

It has been said that the fear of a stroke haunts older adults, but no age group is entirely immune from stroke. It is true, however, that risk increases with age. Stroke can leave a person paralyzed or unable to speak and think clearly. Exactly what is a stroke? A stroke, or a cerebral vascular accident (CVA), is a localized damage to the brain caused by a sudden reduction in the brain's blood supply. In simple terms, a stroke means something has gone haywire with the circulation of the blood to the brain cells resulting in damage to the brain. This damage may be in the form of a rupture resulting in bleeding or in the form of a blockage caused by a number of substances. A stroke can result in physical, intellectual, behavioral, and emotional changes in the person's functions.

Recovery from a stroke can be difficult and frustrating. As Michael found out, there is no single pattern of disability. A stroke victim who masters a task in the morning may not be able to repeat it in the afternoon or the following day. She may be optimistic about what she can do, but her physical strength will belie her statements. She may sob at good news and laugh at sad news. This behavior can be very confusing to family members as well as the stroke victim. Before we discuss exactly what happens to a person who has suffered a stroke, let's be sure we have a clear understanding of the brain's importance to the functions of the body. This knowledge will help us understand how damage to the brain can suddenly make one lose the abilities to walk or talk.

The brain consists of millions of cells interconnected with one another. The brain depends on the nervous system to connect it to the other organs and body parts such as the heart, kidneys, and muscles. It is the brain that regulates the functions of these organs, and it is also the seat of memory, intelligence, and emotions. In part because of its many functions, the brain requires a great amount of nourishment in the form of oxygen and nutrients to do its work. The brain receives its "food"—

blood and oxygen—through the arteries. Damage to these blood vessels interrupts the brain's oxygen and blood supply with the result that brain cells die and consequently are lost. The damage to the brain causes malfunctions of the involved organs and body functions. Unlike the skin and other organs which can regenerate, brain tissue lost remains lost. If the injured area is limited in size, however, the surrounding areas can be trained to perform functions that were lost. (We'll come back to this topic later.)

What Are the Symptoms of Stroke?

Stroke can occur suddenly with or without warning. Warning signs can include frequent headaches, especially in the morning, that gradually increase in frequency and intensity; dizziness; passing out; weakness in an arm or leg; temporary difficulty in speaking; and short periods of memory loss and confusion. These incidents—known as transient ischemic attacks but sometimes referred to as "little strokes"—require immediate attention by a doctor. These little strokes are actually warning signs of a serious stroke.[1] The occurrence of a major stroke is so dramatic there can be no question that medical attention must be given at once. Frank's stroke, described in the beginning of this chapter, was such an example.

What Causes Stroke?

Because stroke is a serious health problem, prevention is extremely important. One way to prevent a stroke is to understand what causes it. Properly functioning blood vessels are essential to provide an adequate blood supply to the brain. If any abnormality in the blood vessels cuts off this supply of blood to the brain, it will also interfere with the normal delivery of oxygen and nutrients to the brain—and damage to the brain's structure and function will result. Physicians may blame one or several factors as causing stroke. An artery can be narrowed, ruptured, or closed by a blood clot. The first condition, narrowed arteries, is usually caused by arteriosclerosis (often called hardening of the arteries). Ruptures in the arteries prevent normal blood flow and occur frequently in people who have very high blood pressure (hypertension). A blood clot (thrombus), sometimes the result of arteriosclerosis and complications from other diseases, may block an artery in the brain or neck.

The American Heart Association has listed sixteen factors associated with an increased risk of stroke. These factors include arteriosclerosis, hypertension, being a male, belonging to a nonwhite race, heredity, geographic area of residence, population density, use of oral contraceptives, obesity, inactivity, cigarette smoking, stress, heart disease, diabetes, and transient ischemic attacks.[2] Some of these risks can be minimized— for example, by cutting down or quitting smoking. Others cannot. One can do little about being born a male, for example. It is best to share your concerns about any of these factors with a physician.

Can Stroke Be Prevented?

It is a tragedy that strokes have become such a frequent occurrence in the United States. Approximately 500,000 cases of stroke are diagnosed every year in this country. Of these, 150,000 are fatal.[3] Although certain predisposing factors associated with stroke cannot be dealt with, certain diseases should obviously be closely monitored and controlled by the older person and her physician to reduce the danger of stroke. High blood pressure is one disease that can now be controlled with proper medication and treatment. Diabetes, another disorder that is thought to be associated with strokes, can be kept under control by diet and often with insulin as well. Medical researchers have not been so successful in controlling the development of arteriosclerosis; but replacement of diseased arteries with synthetic grafts can relieve some symptoms of this disease while possibly reducing the danger of stroke. Stroke-preventing drugs or surgery may also be considered.

In general, a well-balanced way of life, both emotionally and physically, strengthens resistance to such potentially debilitating diseases as stroke. A person who is active, doesn't smoke, is not obese, and handles stress well may be helping to prevent the occurrence of stroke.

How Does Stroke Affect a Person?

We have already noted that the brain controls all parts of the body as well as the mind and emotions. What many people are not aware of is that different parts of the body are controlled by different parts of the brain. Our speech center, for example, lies in the left side of the brain. Movement of our arms and legs is controlled by areas located in the upper and frontal parts in the brain. Damage to either the right or left side of the brain therefore results in different disabilities. Paralysis on one side of the body is the most common sign of stroke. Injury to the right brain results in paralysis of the left side of the body (left hemiplegia). Injury to the left brain hemisphere, on the other hand, can result in paralysis on the right side of the body (right hemiplegia). This is because each half of the brain is mainly responsible for movement on the *opposite* side of the body, although there is some overlap. Let's take a closer look at the differences between right-brain and left-brain injury.

Right-Brain Injury

The person with right-brain injury may have left-side paralysis and problems with self-care skills such as brushing her hair and getting dressed. Speech, however, is not affected. The person with right-brain injury will have trouble judging distances, forms, and the speed of movement. She may also show poor judgment with regard to her own abilities. She may become impulsive and careless, and memory is often impaired. Figure 1 shows what right-brain damage can do to the person.[4]

Left-Brain Injury

A person who has suffered a stroke affecting the left side of the brain is likely to have right-sided paralysis and problems with speech and language. A problem with speech, called aphasia, is discussed in greater detail in the section on communication problems. The person with aphasia has trouble with speaking and comprehension—clearly a frustrating disability. Instead of being impulsive like the individual with right-brain injury, the person with left-brain injury is cautious and slow. Figure 2 shows how left-brain damage affects an individual recovering

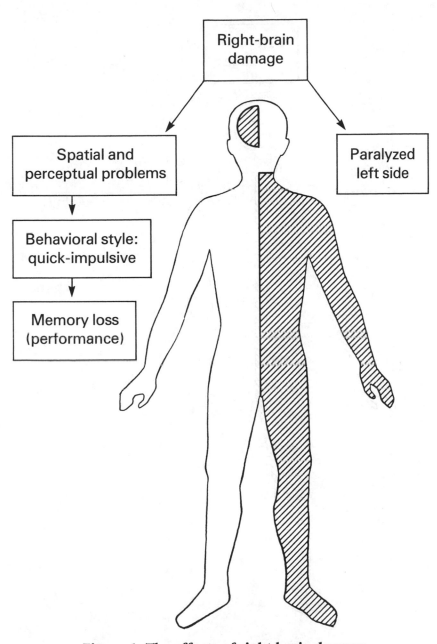

Figure 1. The effects of right-brain damage

Adapted from *Stroke: Why Do They Behave That Way?* by Roy S. Fowler and W. E. Fordyce, American Heart Association, 1974, p. 10. © Reprinted with permission.

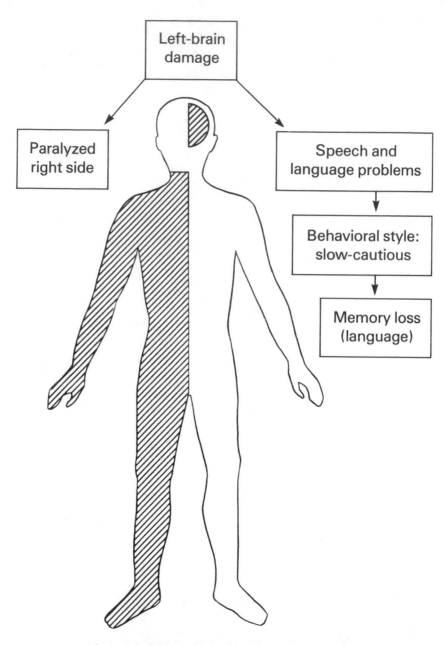

Figure 2. The effects of left-brain damage
Adapted from *Stroke: Why Do They Behave That Way?* by Roy S. Fowler and W. E. Fordyce, American Heart Association, 1974, p. 4. © Reprinted with permission.

from a stroke.⁵ Check with your physician to find out what side of the brain was affected by the stroke. Then you will have a better idea how to care for your family member.

Movement

The brain is not only a magnificent storehouse of information; it is also our control center for muscle movement. As we walk down a street, we rarely think about what our body is doing. But our movements involve a complex series of events that must occur in the proper sequence and at the proper rate for smooth movement to take place. In bringing your hand to your mouth, for instance, those muscles that extend the elbow must relax before the muscles that bend your elbow begin to move. As the hand starts coming up, the muscles of the forearm keep the wrist in position so the hand does not go limp. The movement becomes more complex as the hand needs to be guided through space to your mouth. All of this motion is coordinated by and involves—what else?—the brain.

Stroke can damage the part of the brain that controls movement. When this happens, losses can range from a total absence of muscle tone and uncontrolled cramplike spasms to mild weakness and loss of coordination to a barely noticeable limp. In all but a few cases, the symptoms are on either the left side or the right side.

Unlike most of the other organs of the body, the brain and spinal cord do not replace their lost cells. How, then, does movement return? One theory proposes that cells formerly unused take over the lost functions. Another reason is that a stroke is followed by a certain amount of swelling which places pressure on the brain and suppresses its function. As the pressure is reduced, either on its own or by medical intervention, movement usually returns. Such was probably the case in the early stages of Michael's stroke. The return of movement in his arm and leg was probably the result of reduced pressure on the brain.

So now it becomes clear that the part of the body damaged by stroke is directly related to where the brain is damaged. Since vision, for example, is regulated in the back of the brain, loss of vision following a stroke probably means the brain was damaged in this back part. And since Frank lost movement of his right arm and his ability to speak, the damage must have occurred on the left side of his brain.

Communication

Problems with speech and language, called aphasia, are acquired language impairments caused by some form of brain damage. Aphasia is characterized by a reduction of one or all avenues of communication—speech, hearing, touch, gesture, and the like. For most of us, it is hard to imagine not being able to talk for even one day. In this case our ability to communicate would depend on our desire and ingenuity. Nonverbal communication such as eye contact and sign language would be one way of communicating. There are other ways as well. Many people who are aphasics are considered more mentally and physically disabled than they really are because they cannot speak. But speech, the noises we make with our mouths, is only a part of language. Motions, noises, gestures, and expressions are also used in communication. A person with aphasia can still communicate and may even relearn to speak. While this relearning process may require the skills of a speech pathologist or speech therapist, family members can also help. There are things to do and ways to assist your relative who has become aphasic.

If your physician recommends that your family member see a speech therapist or speech pathologist, an evaluation will be performed by either of these professionals. During this evaluation, the following capacities will be assessed:

- What communication avenues are still open to this person?
- The speech therapist will evaluate not only if your family member can talk, but if she can understand requests and abstract ideas.
- The person's hearing will be tested not only to learn how she reacts to stimuli but also to see whether she can integrate sound and speech, both simple and abstract.
- Tactile communication will be evaluated—the person's ability to distinguish textures, sizes, and volume visually and to sense when she has been touched.

After a complete assessment, the speech therapist or speech pathologist will work to achieve recovery or adaptation. The loss of speech may be the most difficult adjustment for anyone to make, and here the love and encouragement of family members are vital to recovery. Suggestions provided later in this chapter will show you how to assist a family member who is recovering from a loss of speech due to stroke.

The First Stages of Coping

Emma did the right thing in having Frank transported immediately to a hospital. A person who is thought to be suffering from stroke should not be moved until professional help arrives to prevent further injury. Meanwhile the person can be made comfortable with the head elevated and assured by words and gestures. Stay calm; wait for the physician's assessment. Not all of the stroke's initial results will be permanent. A number of functions, damaged in the acute stage, may be partly or wholly restored with time and treatment. And, as we have seen, certain lost functions may be taken over and restored by nearby cell groups. Retraining for the damaged body functions should begin as soon as possible. Encourage the person to be independent. You will need assistance from the rest of the family, the physician, and the hospital's physical therapist and other health professionals. Chapters 12 to 15 can provide you with more information on helping your relative at home.

Immediately following the occurrence of stroke, it can be expected that the individual will become despondent. This is natural. It's a severe shock for anyone to see herself helpless and disabled. But not only do the majority of stroke patients survive—many return to an independent life. There are other cases, however, when a stroke, or a series of strokes, leaves the individual severely disabled and confused and in need of round-the-clock medical care. In either case, the support of the family is a major force in treatment of a stroke patient.

The American Heart Association and affiliates have had encouraging results with "stroke clubs"—periodic gatherings of stroke patients and their families where the various problems affecting stroke patients are discussed. Opportunities like these to vent frustration have helped many stroke patients and their families learn to cope with a trying situation. Just knowing they are not alone has helped many families overcome the handicaps associated with the aftermath of a stroke.

A friend of ours recently attended a stroke club meeting. At several points during the discussion a man seemed to want to speak, but each time he hesitated. Finally he stood up and began to talk. "I understand why my wife has trouble with the left side of her body," he said, "but I don't understand why she cries all the time. I don't mean to sound cruel, but my wife has always been strong and independent. She's battled problems before and this type of behavior is really unlike her. I've tried everything and, frankly, I feel like giving up too. Is this to be expected after a stroke?"

A stroke patient has many reasons for being depressed. Depression is, after all, a natural response to any great loss, and a stroke patient must adjust to many losses. The family's love and emotional support, combined with medical care and treatments, will assist in alleviating the depression. Sometimes the regaining of lost abilities signals the end of the depression.

There are times, however, when excessive crying is more than a result of depression from stroke. The crying may in fact be due to actual brain damage caused by the stroke. In the example just cited, the coordinators of the stroke club recommended the following guidelines. First, they suggested that the man determine whether his wife was crying because she was sad or whether there had been brain damage. This can be done in several ways. If his wife's outburst of emotion is not related to her surroundings or life, there is good reason to suspect brain damage. They then suggested that the next time she begins to cry, he should change the subject and snap his fingers to stop her crying. Abruptly changing the subject or snapping the fingers may break the crying spell and, in the end, help his wife by conserving her energy. They also suggested that he *ask* his wife if she is crying because she's sad. She might be able to tell him. Again, crying may be a result of depression from a stroke or it may be caused by brain damage.

Treatment and Recovery

Recovery from stroke depends on many factors—the extent and area of injury, the victim's age and previous physical condition, proper medical intervention, and above all time. When a large area of the brain responsible for a wide range of functions is affected, a great number of cells are needed to take over the lost functions. A large clot affecting a major artery, for example, can result in a fatal stroke or one that leaves an individual in a coma. Trunk or body control may proceed at a slow rate of recovery even with proper treatment. Attempting to teach the person to walk while lacking support of the trunk or torso is difficult at best and decidedly dangerous.

The part of the brain responsible for processing sensory information can also be damaged, causing the individual to lose all or part of her sensations from the involved side. She may lose her awareness of where parts of her body are in space or totally lack any feeling, as Michael did initially. In certain circumstances, a vague pain is constantly felt as the pain-sensing areas of the brain become "short-circuited." The loss of sensation, especially in the legs, is also a great limiting factor in rehabilitation as the brain requires adequate feedback in order to learn. The retraining of sensation is a matter for occupational therapists dealing with stroke rehabilitation. In many cases, it may involve using some of the remaining senses to substitute for the lost ones.

The return of movement after a severe stroke usually follows a pattern. One author described the return of movement in several stages which are condensed here for our discussion.[6] A person may move quickly through any stage or stop anywhere along the sequence. Rarely is there a complete return of movement following a stroke.

The first stage is a phase of no movement or muscle tone. As muscle tone increases after a period of time, movement begins. The extent of movement depends on the individual, but it is generally believed that certain stronger muscles return before others. Thus an affected leg or arm may produce only certain movements—the elbow bending and the wrist curling in the arm, for example, and straightening at the hip, knee, and ankle in the leg. Both movement patterns were seen in Michael's case. The patterns should slowly recede as the person gains control of the muscles that govern other movements.

Ideally, the control of movement should occur from the neck down through the torso and from the torso out through the extremities. This is roughly the sequence of development of movement in an infant. A person with adequate neck control can at least sit up and start retraining her trunk control and balance. The reverse, however, is difficult. A fully functional hand would hardly be useful if the person lacked the shoulder or elbow control needed to bring the hand up to the task in question.

A stroke patient may be referred to a physical therapist for assistance regarding movement. Occupational therapists can also help by working with fine movement, coordination, and adaptive skills. Physical therapists, working with the physician, are specialists in movement. Since rehabilitation after strokes is a developing field, treatment, philosophy, and technique may vary from therapist to therapist. Strokes present themselves in a wide variety of ways, too, so therapists must use different treatment programs and techniques for different patients.

The ability of the patient to benefit from rehabilitative therapy is a deciding factor in the return of movement. A physical therapist must be able to evaluate the extent of involvement and the level of recovery, weigh a person's rehabilitation potential based on social and other health factors, and from this appraisal establish appropriate goals. The active involvement of the stroke patient and her family is crucial to recovery as well. Any exercise program for a person who suffered a stroke should be approved by her doctor. Since certain movements and resting positions may actually hinder recovery, it is always best to get medical advice. A physical therapist will evaluate the person's capabilities and limitations and then recommend activities that are therapeutic. In evaluating a stroke patient, a physical therapist examines the amount of movement available in all joints passively. This is the range that a joint can go through even if a person cannot move voluntarily. If there are limitations, it would be pointless to expect the person to move *actively* without help through that range.

Various tests are made of the person's different sensory systems to evaluate any losses. Reasonable expectations can then be based on these findings. The manner of instruction and training will need to be adjusted accordingly. A person's reasoning abilities are often affected, too, and must be taken into consideration. Those with paralysis on the left side, for example, are sometimes impulsive and try activities beyond their capabilities.

It is difficult to prescribe the general exercises here that would be suitable for *every* family member who has had a stroke. Because of the differences in the way strokes present themselves, a program for one may be detrimental for another. Rather, seek the advice of the physician and physical therapist in all aspects of stroke care and treatment.

The information offered here on the causes and treatment of stroke will, we hope, give you the confidence to care for your elder at home or assist her during a hospitalization. Strokes affect people in different ways. We urge you to use love and imagination in supporting your relative recovering from a stroke. Your relative *can* improve, and your support may speed up those improvements.

Suggestions to Families

The following guidelines may be useful for families caring for a relative recovering from a stroke. If your family member has *right-brain damage* (left-sided weakness):

- Keep the house free of clutter—left hemiplegics are often prone to falls.
- Bear in mind that your relative may be careless and impulsive.
- Encourage step-by-step procedures for activities. In teaching your relative to get from a chair to a standing position, for example, remind her to clear all obstacles, properly position her weak leg, lean forward, and stand.
- Repeat your instructions again and again.
- Don't assume your relative can do more for herself than she is able.
- Don't forget to talk—the person with right-side brain damage still has her speech.

If your family member has *left-brain damage* (right-sided weakness):

- Remember that she may have perceptual problems.
- Keep your instructions short and precise—lengthy and complicated explanations tend to distract and confuse.
- Give constant reassurance to make up for deficits in perception.

- Encourage her consistently—she may tend to be slow and cautious.
- Remember that the inability to talk does not mean she cannot learn.
- Try to divide tasks into simple steps for easier comprehension.

If your family member is *aphasic:*

- Treat her as an individual with a communication problem, not as someone who is stupid, senile, or deaf. She is an adult. Although her behavior at the present time may be childlike, this does not warrant childlike treatment. If there is no hearing loss, don't shout or slow down your speech. It will not improve communication and may only cause further confusion.
- Keep explanations short and simple. If she doesn't understand, repeat and then rephrase the same concept and wait for a response. Even gestures should be kept to a minimum in order to avoid confusion and frustration due to fatigue and failure to understand.
- Encourage her in all her communication efforts, but don't *force* her to communicate.
- Let her make mistakes and correct them only if absolutely necessary. If you don't understand what she is trying to communicate, ask her to repeat it in words *and* gestures. Don't try to read into whatever she's said. She will learn through repeated mistakes; this is a normal learning process. Try not to speak *for* her unless absolutely necessary.
- Be honest. Don't pretend that you do understand when you don't. Don't read inferences into what you don't understand.
- Empathize. Imagine what it would be like to be in her place. Treat her as you yourself would want to be treated in the same situation. Never tease her or mimic her efforts to communicate.
- If she is paralyzed, talk to her from her good side.
- If she is bilingual, talk to her in her original language if you can. Many stroke patients revert back to the first language spoken as a child.
- If speech is absent, use gestures and visual clues to communicate. Be innovative.

- Pay strict attention when she's trying to communicate with you.
- Give her all the time she needs to respond. Don't show impatience or fear or irritability, as this may stop her from trying.

If your family member is *labile* (has unexpected emotional outbursts of crying, laughing, and swearing):

- Hold and reassure her. Sit with her and hold her hand. Be there. Your caring will be comforting and may stop the crying.
- Try to calm her down—perhaps by changing the subject quickly or snapping your fingers.
- Tell her to stop, but never shout.
- Don't be afraid to tell her you don't understand her.

If your family member has trouble *eating:*

- Be patient.
- Be prepared to help her if she starts choking. Talk to your physician or public health nursing service about procedures to follow if choking occurs.
- Make sure that someone is with your relative whenever she's eating.

We encourage you to stay involved in the care of your elder who has suffered a stroke. You can make a difference!

Notes

1. Dan Kaercher, "Do You Know the Warning Signs? Stroke," *Better Homes and Gardens* (July 1981): 11–13.

2. James F. Toole, *Diagnosis and Management of Stroke* (Dallas: American Heart Association, 1979), pp. 4–5.

3. W. M. Garraway, and others, "The Declining Incidence of Stroke," *New England Journal of Medicine* 300 (1979): 449.

4. Roy S. Fowler and W. E. Fordyce, *Stroke: Why Do They Behave That Way?* (Dallas: American Heart Association, 1974), p. 10.

5. Ibid., p. 4.

6. S. Brunnstrom, *Movement Therapy in Hemiplegia: A Neurophysiological Approach* (New York: Harper & Row, 1970).

11

Coping with Incontinence

AILEEN SAKADO
ALICE TALBOTT

Jane is worried. For the past month, her 79-year-old mother who lives with Jane and her family has wet her bed at least six times and has had an accident or two on the new living room couch. At first, Jane's mother seemed embarrassed and even apologized; but lately she seems completely unaware of the continuing problem. Jane's husband and children insist that something be done about her mother as well as the unpleasant smell of urine in the house. Jane doesn't know what to do without causing her mother embarrassment or creating even more tension in the household.

Bladder and bowel accidents can be the most frustrating problems to cope with for the older person and her family. The accident may cause the elderly person to feel anxious or distressed. Or, like Jane's mother, she may completely deny the existence of the problem or isolate herself from others. For families it is a trying time too. Some family members may begin to ask if it's time to think about institutional care. Others may keep trying to provide understanding and care at home. Remember that the inability to restrain a natural discharge (bladder or bowel incontinence) is not the inevitable result of aging. Rather, both are often symptoms that result from one or more environmental, psychological, and physiological factors. And some can be treated. In all cases, there are appropriate actions that can be taken to help a person with incontinence.

Dealing with Bladder Problems

Frustration and dismay are often the initial response to the elder's loss of control over her bladder. To cope with the situation and keep it from becoming more of a problem, you must objectively look for the cause. This is the basic step in solving the problem. There are several things to consider. The problem could stem from environmental, psychological, or physiological causes. Since it is easier to consider these possibilities one at a time, an environmental check is the first step.

Environmental Factors

Check your aging relative's residence in terms of the following aspects:

- Is the toilet close enough for the older person to reach it in time? The time between the urge to void and the actual release of urine tends to shorten as we get older. One easy way to avoid accidents is to make sure she is in closer proximity to the toilet.
- Is the bed up too high? If the bed is too high, a person is often afraid of falling when it's time to get up and go to the toilet. The bed should be low enough that when a person sits on the side of it, her feet are flat on the floor.
- Is there privacy? Some people hate to go to the bathroom when there are people milling about and kids running ahead to the toilet. It may seem easier to wait, but waiting could be too late.
- Are her walking aids adequate? Without proper walking aids—cane, walker, and so forth—getting to the bathroom could take longer than expected. Are the walking aids the right height and weight?
- Is the toilet cubicle large enough to accommodate a walker or wheelchair? A walker requires twenty square feet and a wheelchair thirty square feet. And it's helpful if the door to the toilet cubicle swings *outward*. It isn't essential but it helps if the toilet seat is elevated. Getting on and off the toilet is not as hard on sore, stiff joints when the seat is high. Grab bars or toilet seat arms also make getting on and off easier, too.
- If she's bedridden, is the urine-collecting equipment the problem? There are several types of bedpans. The *shovel* or *fracture* pan allows for minimal hip bending, so it's easier to get on than other types. But it doesn't hold as much urine as the others, and it can spill the contents easily when it's

removed. The *cutaway* pan is easy to grasp and, therefore, easier to handle. It has less capacity for urine than a concave pan, however, and feels less stable. The *concave* pan is very stable. It slides under easily and has a large capacity. It may be awkward to grasp, though, and it requires more bending of the hip than the fracture pan. In any case, check the bedpan for comfort. Is it too cold to get onto? Does it cut into the buttock? Does it slide too easily? If a male is using a urinal, be sure the handle is wide enough to accommodate arthritic hands comfortably. And check to see that the neck of the urinal or the bottle angle is placed for comfortable use.

If changing any of these things makes a difference, you have found the cause of incontinence. If the problem is not environmental, then psychological problems may be the cause.

Psychological Factors

Although deliberate incontinence is rare, psychological problems can cause incontinence. When Alan's wife died, he moved into his daughter's house at her insistence. Before long, however, he began to feel lonely and a little useless. It was at that time he began to have accidents at night. When his daughter, Susan, took him to the doctor, he was found to be in good physical condition. Susan, a social worker, suspected depression as the cause and encouraged her family to spend more time with Alan. In time, the number of his accidents decreased and eventually stopped altogether.

Incontinence can become a substitute for something—your task is to find what that something is. If in fact the problem is deliberate incontinence, you may need to seek professional help. Fear of falling is another cause. If the older person is unsteady on her feet, the fear of falling may prevent her from getting to the bathroom on time.

Physiological Factors

If the problem is neither environmental nor psychological, check for a physical cause. Consider:

- *Poor vision:* For most of us, sight is an important signal in bladder control. Find out if the person can *see* where the toilet is. If she can't, it could be very discouraging to think that there is no toilet around.

- *Hip stiffness:* It may hurt to get on and off a toilet or bedpan. Or maybe it simply hurts too much to walk over to the toilet.
- *Stressful situations:* Have you ever found yourself laughing so hard that you were in danger of letting go? If you haven't, you are unusual. If you have, then you can get some idea of the predicament of people who are very sensitive to stress incontinence. Lots of things could cause this internal stress—coughing, vomiting, sneezing, moving the bowels.
- *Constipation:* Not moving the bowels can cause bladder incontinence. Why is this so? Because of the pressure that an enlarged intestine can put on the bladder.
- *Dehydration:* It may seem unlikely that one could be dehydrated *and* incontinent at the same time, but this does occur. There are several kinds of signals that are sent from one part of the body to another, causing the bladder to release urine. One is a chemical signal. If the urine in the bladder is *concentrated*, as when a person is dehydrated, a signal is sent that causes the muscles to release the urine in the bladder.
- *Weak muscles:* Incontinence of the bladder could be due to weakening of the muscles—for example, through tissue injury (as from multiple childbirths) or from a recent bladder catheterization. When a bladder is catheterized, the muscles that hold and release urine become weak from lack of use. If this is the case, a physician can suggest exercises to strengthen these muscles.
- *Medication:* Diuretics (medicines that increase the flow of urine) can cause an urgency to urinate. Some people can't get to the toilet fast enough when they take them. Moreover, sedatives and tranquilizers can cause a person to miss the signals that precede urination. A person could sleep or relax right through the signal.
- *Infection:* Any kidney, bladder, or related infection can cause bladder incontinence. If you suspect this cause, consult a physician.
- *Disease:* Diabetes, rheumatoid arthritis, Parkinsonism, and other diseases can all cause bladder incontinence. If this is the problem, see a physician.
- *Mental impairment:* If your relative is confused and disoriented due to a stroke or for any other reason, consult your doctor for advice.

After you have evaluated the potential causes of incontinence, the next step is to determine the current urination pattern. Jack, for example, is a 69-year-old man who is mentally quite confused. He usually spends most of the day sitting with his eyes closed. Although he is able to speak, he often chooses not to say a single word. After a month of toilet accidents, his daughter sought the advice of the family physician. The doctor's first suggestion was that the daughter observe her father's toilet pattern. After two weeks of close observation, the daughter discovered that Jack would usually go to the bathroom around 7:30 A.M., 10:30 A.M., 1:00 P.M., 4:00 P.M., and so on. She also found that he would wander aimlessly without saying a word if he needed to go to the bathroom. The doctor suggested that a toilet schedule be developed which closely followed Jack's natural toilet pattern. The schedule would provide a definite routine for Jack and his family and, hopefully, would prevent the distress of toilet accidents. The doctor also reminded the daughter to watch for Jack's nonverbal cue, the aimless wandering, when he needed to go to the toilet.

Once you have discovered the urination pattern—when and how often the person urinates—you can combine this information with the cause of the incontinence and form a plan of action. You may then be able to prevent the frustration and embarrassment of toilet accidents.

Dealing with Bowel Problems

Bowel incontinence is the inability to control evacuation of rectal contents. Rather than being a natural consequence of aging, bowel incontinence is often a symptom of a variety of causes—physiological, psychological, and environmental. All too often, due to ignorance of its cause, it is a problem which is contended with rather than dealt with. Again it is a good idea to make a checklist, beginning with the environmental factors.

Environmental Factors

Many of the environmental factors which contribute to bladder incontinence may also contribute to bowel incontinence. For example, bowel accidents may occur when the person is immobile or confined to a bed and is therefore unable to go to the bathroom. They may also occur when the elderly individual is at a great distance from the toilet and unable to reach it in time. If these environmental factors are contributing to bowel incontinence, make the necessary changes in the environment.

Psychological Factors

Although psychological factors seldom cause bowel incontinence, two of them may contribute to the problem: prolonged isolation and depression. Prolonged isolation can lead to depression which in turn may contribute to constipation, bowel impaction, and bowel incontinence. When a person is depressed, mental as well as physiological functions are retarded. There is a reduction in activity, fluid and food consumption, appetite, and intestinal movement. One or all of these changes can contribute to constipation. The approaches recommended for bladder incontinence can also be used to relieve bowel incontinence due to psychological factors.

Physiological Factors

Constipation and bowel impaction are the most common physiological causes of bowel incontinence in the elderly. Numerous elements can lead to constipation. For one thing, changes in exercise pattern can precipitate constipation. When there is a decrease in activity—as when one is confined to a wheelchair or bed—there is less intestinal movement and the result is constipation. Diet and fluid intake probably have the greatest influence on intestinal elimination. Sufficient fluids—and foods high in roughage, bulk, and fiber—are necessary for regular evacuation. Therefore, a diet containing little roughage and a lack of fluids can lead to constipation. A third factor can lead to constipation when the older person ignores the urge to defecate. Failing to respond to the normal urge for defecation may result from environmental factors—see the section on bladder incontinence. But age-related physiological changes can also make the elderly more prone to constipation. Aging may reduce intestinal movement, decrease one's awareness of the urge to defecate, and weaken abdominal muscles which are necessary for normal bowel evacuation.

The second physiological cause of bowel incontinence is bowel impaction—the prolonged accumulation of bowel material which forms a hardened mass in the rectum. Bowel impaction is frequently due to constipation. It occurs when there has been no bowel movement for a long period of time. Any stool remaining in the large intestine for a long time will become hard, dry, and difficult to pass. Bowel impaction is a serious health matter since it prevents elimination of stool from the body. There are several signs of bowel impaction: no bowel movement for more than three days; abdominal and rectal discomfort; an enlarged abdomen; and diarrhea.

What can be done to prevent constipation and bowel impaction? Regularity of bowel evacuation is important. See if there is a time of day when incontinence is more likely to occur, as after a large meal. If so, the older person should be reminded or helped to go to the toilet. For the bedridden elder, a bedpan should be placed at such times. If there is no pattern to incontinence, assist the person to the toilet at frequent intervals— every two or three hours, for example.

Maintain bowel regularity by providing food high in bulk, roughage, and fiber—whole wheat flours, bran, rye, raw vegetables, raw fruits with skin. For the older adult who has difficulty with foods high in roughage due to poor dentures, see that the dentures are refitted or grind the food for easy consumption. Food with laxative action—prunes and prune juice, for example—is also recommended. Here are few more suggestions:

- Maintain adequate fluid intake by providing one and one-half to two quarts of fluid a day.
- Encourage regular activity. Exercises such as gardening, walking, and swimming improve abdominal muscle tone and intestinal movement—both of which are important for normal bowel evacuation.
- Suggest that the elder try a semi-squatting position when defecating. This position contracts the abdominal muscle to promote bowel evacuation.

If regular bowel habits are not achieved with diet, exercise, and positioning, it may be advisable for the older adult to consult a physician. A mild laxative or suppository may be ordered to stimulate evacuation. Suppositories should be inserted into the rectum about one-half to three hours before the usual time for defecation. If bowel impaction does develop, professional assistance should be sought. Usually the physician will order an enema prior to manual removal of the impacted stool. The stool is removed with gloved hands and with extreme care since the procedure may cause considerable pain.

Another physical and physiological cause of bowel incontinence in the elderly is the effect of drug therapy. A broad spectrum of medications such as sedatives and antibiotics may cause constipation or diarrhea. In either case, the result may be bowel incontinence. If bowel incontinence is a result of drug therapy, it is usually a temporary symptom lasting only while the drug is being taken. Again, consult your physician for advice.

Mental confusion or dementia is often cited as a cause of bowel incontinence. In this case the problem is due to the person's lack of awareness of the need to defecate. Find out whether your relative is aware of the need to defecate or is unable to control the urge. What can you do, then, as a concerned family member? You can start by reminding the older adult to go to the bathroom. You can also remind her where the toilet is and, if possible, have the toilet within sight. You can also seek professional help to resolve the confusion or at least maintain your parent's present capabilities.

Apart from the normal changes associated with aging, pathological changes may lead to bowel incontinence. Among the symptoms of these abnormal conditions are stomach and intestinal infections, diverticulitis, cancer of the colon or rectum, and irritable bowel syndrome. With all these conditions, you would observe a change in your relative's bowel habits. Be aware of these changes, and seek the advice of a physician.

Care of the Incontinent Adult

When someone you love becomes incontinent, it's natural to deny that the problem is more than a passing incident. It's natural, too, to become protective. When it is clear that some type of intervention is needed, however, it is wise to distinguish between your feelings of love and your ability to give the necessary care. Taking care of an incontinent adult is not a job for just anyone. If your spouse is incontinent, you must consider whether you are physically strong enough to look after her. If your parent is incontinent, her embarrassment (and yours) must be considered. It takes a certain objectivity toward excretions and genitalia to give the care that is needed. If you are not physically strong enough to provide this care or cannot overcome these embarrassments, that is understandable. You can show your love and respect by arranging for someone other than yourself to give that kind of care. The following information may help you to reach the right decision for you and your family member.

If a person is diagnosed as having irreversible bowel or bladder incontinence, or both, the next step is learning how to live with it. Above all you must learn to appreciate the emotional upset of the incontinent person. It is demoralizing, of course, to soil yourself; it is even worse when someone else has to clean you. And when the person who must clean you is an intimate relation, the situation can be even more uncomfortable. Under these circumstances, it is not uncommon for a person to withdraw emotionally and feel depressed. Laughter gives way to feelings of shame and embarrassment.

While the situation may be trying, there is no need for a lifetime of struggle and despair. Approaching the problem with objectivity and understanding, as well as following a set routine, may assist you in coping with—rather than being overwhelmed by—the problem of incontinence.

Probably the most important point in caring for an incontinent older person is the prevention of skin breakdown—a person with skin breakdown runs the risk of developing an overwhelming infection. A life-threatening situation may evolve from even a small opening in the skin or a mild urinary tract infection. To prevent this, you must remove the urine or stool from the skin as soon as possible. A simple procedure to follow is:

1. Clean the skin with a mild soap and water.
2. Rinse the skin well.
3. Dry the skin.
4. Use a mild lotion (such as Alpha Keri lotion or one that your physician recommends).

Repeat this procedure every time the person has been incontinent.

The next real problem is what to do with the soiled clothes, bed, linen, and floors. We suggest that you obtain a container with a tight-fitting lid that can be used for soiled clothes and linen only. Clean the linen and the container daily to prevent odor. Proper ventilation and light help remove unpleasant odors from the room and give a lift to sagging spirits. Use flowers and deodorizers liberally.

Mattresses and chairs will need protection from contamination with urine and feces. It may be a good idea to cover them with a protective sheet. The same protective covers are fine for the bed or other furniture, but they hold moisture close to the skin and heighten the risk of skin breakdown. It's better to protect both the bed *and* the skin. One way to do this is to get a sheet or pad that is water-repellent on one side and water-absorbent on the other. There are many pads available on the market. One kind, the Kylie pad, is composed of two layers. The surface next to the skin is water-repellent brushed nylon which passes urine into an inner layer of absorbent rayon that is interwoven to disperse urine. This pad is designed to pull urine away from the surface into a holding layer. When used with a protective sheet, the Kylie pad is said to keep both the skin and the bed dry. Such pads can be washed more than a hundred times without losing their absorbency.

Disposable protective pads are also available; we recommend the large size for adults. As a note of caution, however, you should be aware that the use of pads is so convenient it may *encourage* incontinence. Since it can take less time to diaper someone than it does to walk them to the bathroom, urge the incontinent person to let you know when she has to go to the toilet.

Protective garments get more approval from people than diapers and are sometimes advertised as adult briefs. Sizes are by hip and waist measurements. The superabsorbent polymers have a "gelling property" and hold much more liquid than others. If any of these briefs leak, it is usually due to a loose fit or a saturated pad. Be sure the leg closure is snug and comfortable. Be aware, as well, of the person's urinating schedule. Fiber-filled pads tend *not* to hold more than a cup and a half of liquid and thus can leak if not changed for a period of time.

For some older men an external catheter may be a useful solution to bladder incontinence. This device encloses the penis and catches the urine which is then passed into a bag worn on the man's leg. The bag is emptied and cleaned regularly to keep it sanitary. Although this appliance allows the incontinent older man to be mobile, many men finds its use uncomfortable and will not tolerate it. For women a variety of portable urinals have been developed.

People often mistakenly think that bladder catheterization is the best solution to bladder incontinence. Most physicians, however, only use it as a last resort. When a person has an indwelling catheter, bacteria can travel up the tube and cause bladder infection and urinary tract infection. If a person must have an indwelling catheter in their bladder, proper care of the catheter is essential to help prevent infection. High fluid intake (unless the doctor says otherwise) may also check bacterial growth and obstruction in the catheter. Since an indwelling catheter requires special care, consult a doctor if there are problems.

Be sure to use the proper body mechanics in caring for a person who is incontinent. You may suffer from unnecessary pain or a strained back if you use improper techniques in assisting or lifting your family member. Ask a physician or physical therapist or take a class to learn the most appropriate procedures. Many hospitals and community associations such as the Red Cross offer such classes. If your relative is bed-bound and requires the use of a bedpan, she may be able to lift herself onto it without your assistance. If she cannot, then you must learn a way to help her without hurting yourself. It helps to have a bed at least as high as your hip. Anything higher or lower can strain your back.

In assisting your relative onto a bedpan, it works best to have the bed flat. Have your relative roll over to the side away from you, and place the pan next to her buttocks. Then have her roll back onto the pan. If you're able, raise the head of bed or place pillows at her back to support her in a sitting position. (She'll be more comfortable if her knees are bent.) Then give her privacy and sufficient time.

To remove the bedpan, lower the head of the bed or remove the pillows so that your relative is lying flat. Then have her roll away from you onto her side. (Hold the pan as she rolls so that it does not roll with her and spill.) From that position, you can easily remove the pan and clean her.

This method can also be used when changing the bed linen while the person remains in bed. Your relative should be lying flat on the bed. Have her turn away from you and as far on her side as possible without falling off the bed. Roll the dirty linen tight against her body. (The linen will look like a roll the length of the body.) Then lay half the clean linen in place lengthwise on the bed and roll the other half tightly against the dirty linen. Next have her roll back toward you over the dirty and clean linen onto the clean linen half which is in place. Finally, go around to the other side of the bed and remove the roll of soiled linen and pull the roll of clean linen into place.

The care of an incontinent older person may at times be frustrating and seem never ending. Remember, however, that toilet accidents are not the inevitable result of aging but may be a symptom of environmental, psychological, and physiological causes. You'll have to remain objective in order to identify the cause of the problem and determine the most appropriate care. Try discussing the problem with your older family member. It may relieve the strain of a situation that can be embarrassing to both family and older adult alike.

PART THREE

AS DEPENDENCY GROWS

12

Keeping Your Relative
Mobile and Independent

MARY BRENEMAN
COLETTE BROWNE

Jacob, a 66-year-old retired accountant, suffered a serious stroke that affected the right side of his body and his ability to speak. After months of physical therapy treatments, he is now able to ambulate, or walk, with a four-point cane and a little assistance from one person, primarily to help him keep his balance. He has regained strength on his right side but still requires daily exercises for further recovery. Jacob is being discharged from the hospital where he has been for the past two months. His wife, Virginia, has been attending his physical therapy sessions to learn how she can help him at home. Because Jacob's discharge has been thoroughly discussed by Jacob, Virginia, and the hospital staff, his family is looking forward to his return home with great enthusiasm rather than trepidation.

Many families, however, do not share this family's confidence in taking care of a disabled person at home. Their reluctance is often based on a lack of knowledge. Many families believe that only the very skilled can assist in therapy and exercise. This is not true. We now know that family members can learn many of these techniques when instructed by a trained professional and can use them successfully with their disabled relative at home.

The Crucial Questions

When someone is to be discharged from a hospital or other facility, there are many aspects of care that the family must consider. What types of treatment should the person be given? Who should provide it? What about medications? Is the new residence safe? Who can the family call if a problem arises? Consider the case of Gloria, a 78-year-old retired teacher. She never dreamed she would end up in a hospital until she slipped in her bathroom one evening and fractured her hip. She was brought to the hospital by a neighbor and underwent surgery to stabilize her hip. Gloria was hospitalized for three weeks. During this time, she received physical therapy and was taught to walk with a walker. When it was time for discharge from the hospital, the social worker from the hospital assisted Gloria and her family with the arrangements back to her son and daughter-in-law's home, where she had been living for the past year. What knowledge and skills were needed to keep Gloria at home safely? How could her family promote her independence and prevent any loss in functioning and strength? To address these concerns, Gloria and her family needed to ask certain questions of the hospital staff prior to discharge:

- Can Gloria walk safely by herself or does she require some help?
- Is she able to get to the bathroom alone or does she need assistance?
- Can she get out of bed alone? How can she be moved to her wheelchair from her bed?
- If she requires some assistance, what is the safest way for her family to help her without injuring her or themselves?

Now let's look at some answers to these crucial questions.

Can Gloria walk safely alone or does she need assistance? The doctor and physical therapist are the ones to answer this question after a careful assessment. Many older adults use a walker or cane to give them stability or to take pressure off a sore extremity (leg or arm). There are a variety of assistive devices to consider before deciding which one is appropriate. The function of a walker is for support when walking. A pickup walker is a U-shaped appliance with a base of four legs and two side bars. (See Figure 3.) A rolling walker has wheels on the two front legs to allow ease of movement. A single-point cane is used primarily for those who have a slight balance problem. A quad cane has a base of four legs which can be used for bearing

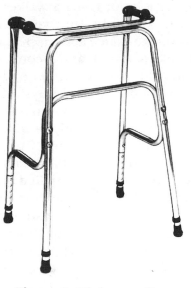

Figure 3. Pickup walker
Photo courtesy of Lumex

weight; this cane is used when the arms are not of equal strength or one arm is in a cast.

Many are able to get around safely by having the additional support of a cane or walker. But some people need another person to help them with walking. Perhaps they are too unsteady to depend solely on an assistive device. Or perhaps their legs are weak and they need someone to stand by in case their legs buckle. If Gloria requires assistance while walking, it may help to place a belt around her waist. This precaution is highly recommended for safety reasons. When Gloria does walk, her family can stand to one side and keep one hand on her belt. In this way, assistance can be provided quickly by simply grabbing onto the belt if Gloria starts to lose her balance. Gloria should never be grabbed by her arms (or under them) to prevent her from falling as this action could dislocate her arm or break it.

If Gloria is mildly unsteady on her feet and has a tendency to lean her body to one side, stand on her opposite side as she walks. This precaution helps her to establish balance. Don't stand on the side she is leaning on—this will only encourage her to lean *more* on whatever support is available. If, on the other hand, Gloria is quite weak, it may be a good idea to have a chair nearby. Then if she tires, or if her knees buckle, she can quickly sit down. If she's not using a walker or cane, it would be a good idea to let her hold onto your hand. She may feel more secure with your guidance and support and may therefore be more willing to take that first, and second, step.

Is Gloria able to get to the bathroom by herself or does she need help? Again, your doctor and physical therapist are the people to ask. If Gloria is ambulatory—in other words, is able to walk by herself—she would probably be able to get in and out of the bathroom without much trouble. The most difficult part may be getting on and off the toilet seat and in and out of the bathtub. Grab bars may have to be installed on either side of the toilet seat and bath if she needs support in sitting down or standing. Otherwise, a sink or vanity can be used for the same purpose if it's sturdy and nearby. Raised toilet seats are available at most orthopedic and medical supply stores. But before you purchase or rent such equipment, seek the advice of a trained professional.

Can Gloria get out of bed alone? Or is assistance required? Again, Gloria's doctor and physical therapist should be asked for their opinions. As Gloria's needs change, her family should inquire whether she will be able to accomplish this task alone one day. How can Gloria be moved if she is able to walk but needs help getting in and out of bed? First, ask Gloria to sit on the edge of the bed, and position yourself directly in front of her. Make sure her feet are firmly on the ground, at least six inches apart. Place a belt around Gloria's waist so you can use it during the transfer. Have her push up from the bed with both hands while you help to pull her up by holding onto the safety belt. Now, with Gloria's cooperation, gently come to a standing position. Never rush her once she is on her feet. Take your time. Remember to explain what you are doing—she may be able to help you.

What about transferring her from a bed to a wheelchair? Let's consider the procedures to follow if a bed-bound relative asks to be put in a wheelchair. First, explain to her the steps you are about to take. Again, she may be able to help you. Next, help her sit on the bed with her legs hanging over the side. Make sure the wheelchair is close to that side of the bed. The wheelchair should be in a locked position. Stand directly in front of her. As she pushes herself up from the bed, grasp onto the safety belt and gently help pull her up to a standing position. Now, with her back to the wheelchair, gently lower her into it. Sometimes a nightstand placed by the bed makes it easier to get out of bed as it can be used to support a person. Unlock the wheelchair if you're moving her to another room. At any time during this procedure, if your relative complains of pain and looks dizzy, return her to bed for rest. (To return her to bed, simply reverse the procedures.) During these steps, try to watch your relative's feet so they don't get caught in an uncomfortable or dangerous position. Wheelchairs can sometimes tip over when too much weight is put in the front. To prevent this from occurring, be careful of weight distribution.

What is the safest way to move Gloria without her family hurting themselves? When faced with the task of moving and lifting another adult, relatives often become concerned for their own health. This is natural. Family members need to be careful when lifting another adult or assisting with walking to prevent injuries to themselves. Sometimes the safest way to transfer a person may be through the use of a mechanical Hoyer lift. The Hoyer lift may be used under three circumstances: if the person is unable to offer any assistance at all during the transfer; if the caregiver is physically incapable of giving the necessary assistance; or if the caregiver who transfers the person several times a day becomes fatigued. The person is placed on a canvas lift which is then attached to a mobile hydraulic lift. She can then be transferred from bed to chair and back again with a minimum of physical exertion. Hoyer lifts are most often used in hospitals but may be purchased or rented from a medical supply store for home use.

Remember—an injured caregiver is not very helpful to a disabled and dependent older relative. Proper body mechanics are essential in protecting your back and other body parts from injury.

Body Mechanics

"Body mechanics" means making the best use of the body to accomplish a task while avoiding strain. Every day we all put our bodies through a rigorous test of bending, stretching, running, lifting, kneeling, and so on. Usually, our bodies are receptive to the demands we place on them. But sometimes we push them beyond their endurance. A sore muscle or a strained back may be the signs that tell us we should not have shoveled that snow or lifted that heavy package by ourselves. Body mechanics—the proper use of our bodies when doing such tasks—could have prevented these aches and pains that can become serious if ignored.

Moving your relative is not, we realize, the same thing as shoveling snow. Even so, the same precautionary steps can be taken to ensure that you don't injure yourself trying to help a relative. Consider the following questions for your safety.

How much does your relative weigh? Can she support some of her own weight? If you weigh only a hundred pounds, you should not expect to be able to support a relative twice your weight. How is her weight distributed? Is she very tall? Since most people's weight is centered at their middle, the waist is a good body part to support with most of your own strength.

How are you going to move your relative? Think ahead. Obviously, you don't want to drag anyone on the floor. Instead you can lift, roll, or guide her with your own physical and emotional support. Here are additional guidelines (see Figure 4) that may help you to move your relative safely while protecting your own health:

- Never use your lower back to lift, and never bend over to help your relative move. Bend your knees slightly and use the strong muscles of the arm, thigh, and buttocks to lift.
- Always place yourself close to the person you'll be moving. Avoid stretching.
- When lifting someone, keep your body like a triangle—with your feet spread apart a good six inches for strength and balance.
- If your relative's bed is not a hospital bed (does not raise up) protect your back! If you must stand while working with your relative, place a stool or footstand by your feet. Placing one foot on the stool will help relieve the pressure on your back if you must bend over.
- Transfer your relative to her strong side. She may be able to assist you more this way. Again, a belt can be very helpful to grab onto if a fall is imminent.
- If someone is helping you or you want your relative to help you, count out loud to involve everyone: "On three, let's lift . . . one, two, three!"

(a) Minimal assistance

Stand at person's weak side. Support weak arm with your hand as pictured and grasp belt at person's back. Have person *slide forward to edge of bed* before attempting to stand.

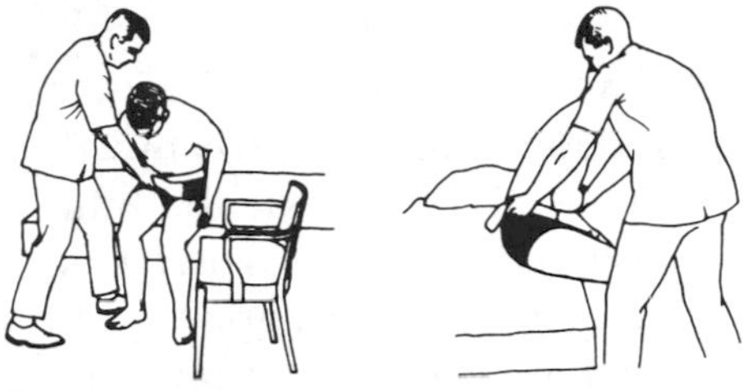

(b) Full assistance

Step 1:
Place belt around person's waist. Stand facing person. Grip belt with both hands at person's sides. Slide person forward until both feet can be placed flat on floor.

Step 2:
Block person's weak knee with your knee. Tell him that you are going to help him stand on the count of 3. Rock him forward on the count of 1, rock again on 2, and then on the count of 3 pull him forward and up. Be careful to bend *your* knees and keep *your* back straight to prevent injury to yourself. You may find that the person will feel more secure if you allow him to place his arm around your shoulder.

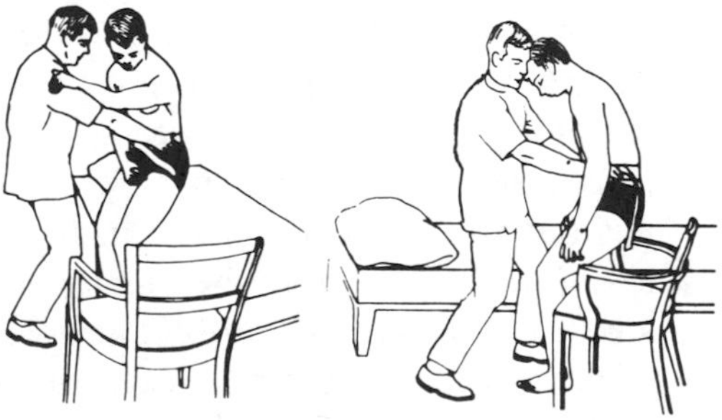

Figure 4. Moving your disabled elder

Adapted from *The Patient at Home* by M. R. Barnes and C. Crutchfield. Thorofare, N.J., SLACK Inc., 1973. © Reprinted with permission.

- Think ahead! If you're lifting your relative from the bed to a chair, have the chair nearby to avoid unnecessary movements or delay.
- Love is therapeutic. Encourage your relative to do as much independently as possible. Praise a good effort.
- Stress abilities, not disabilities! You can prevent much discouragement and frustration when you focus on what your relative *can* do as opposed to what she cannot.
- Activity promotes more activity. Exercises can increase circulation to the body part being exercised.

Using a Wheelchair

For some older people, a wheelchair represents their only source of mobility. Weakened muscles, arthritic and painful joints, or impaired peripheral vascular health do not necessarily mean the person can no longer be independent. A properly fitted wheelchair should be chosen after you've taken into account the older person's needs along with architectural barriers within the home that may make the wheelchair useless. If you observe your relative struggling in and out of a wheelchair, unable to maneuver it, or refusing to use it, ask for professional advice. Since there could be many reasons for these problems, it's best to ask a health professional for an evaluation of your relative *and* the wheelchair. They may not be compatible.

Safety is obviously the highest priority in selecting a wheelchair. Comfort, however, should not be ignored. Most older people will do well in a fixed-back chair, but do seek the counsel of a professional in your selection. Forward mounts can be purchased to prevent tipping forward when a person tries to get out of the wheelchair. If an older family member is paralyzed, think about a wheelchair belt. This restraint is much like a seat belt in an automobile and can prevent injuries from accidents in much the same way. For those who spend a great deal of time in a wheelchair, the upholstery in the seat and back should be durable and comfortable. Make sure there's adequate circulation of air in the wheelchair seat to prevent pressure sores from developing. Be sure to watch for the development of bedsores on the tailbone, too.

There are several important points to remember that will make pushing a wheelchair with a rider both easy and safe. The main parts of a wheelchair are the brakes, footrests, handle-bars, and tilting rods (see Figure 5).

The *brakes* are located on both sides of the large tires. Remember to lock them whenever you park the chair or let go of the handlebars. The *footrests* are located on the bottom front of the chair for the elder's feet. Before the elder gets in or out of the chair, lift both footrests up to allow easy and safe entry or exit from the wheelchair. The *handlebars* are located on the top of the chair back. Grip firmly and bend your arms at the elbows to lessen stress while pushing. Remember to push with your arms, not your back. The *tilting rods* are two pipes close to the ground in the rear of the chair. These rods are used to make moving over bumps easier. First grasp the handle firmly; then put one foot on one of the rods and press down gently. (This action requires more caution than energy.) The front wheels of the chair will then lift up over the bump.

To move a wheelchair up and down a step or curb, tip it slightly backward by stepping on the tilting rods. Then push the chair up the curb. The wheelchair should descend the steps backwards. Be sure to *back down* any decline so the elder does not fall out.

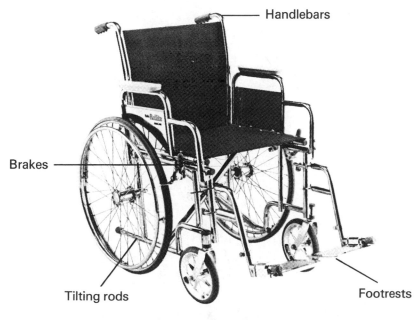

Figure 5. Main parts of the wheelchair
Photo courtesy of Invacare Corporation

Remember that your relative still has the same basic needs and drives she had prior to her disability. We all want to be independent and to do as much for ourselves as we can. Too much help, therefore, can lead to helplessness. Again, *observe* your relative. See what she is capable of doing and let her do it! By promoting self-care, you are also encouraging self-respect.

13

Encouraging Self-Care

CATHY COLLADO
JANE ROGERS

Among the basic needs that must be satisfied in order for us to feel good about ourselves are the need for love, a sense of belonging and achievement, independence, and self-esteem. With aging, however, come many physical and mental changes that can discourage or prevent us from fulfilling these needs. Of crucial importance to feelings of independence, achievement, and a healthy self-image is our ability to look after ourselves— our capacity for self-care. Self-care refers to eating, dressing, bathing, and caring for our own bathroom needs independently. As adults we tend to take these accomplishments for granted until a disability develops that prevents self-care. The self-care skills of those who have become frail due to the combinations of age and illness are often ignored by well-meaning family members who do things *for* them, not with them. Often, older adults are robbed of their privacy, rushed because they are slow, or criticized because they forgot instructions. Consequently, families may think it is actually easier to feed, dress, and bathe them—all of which fosters a gradual growth of dependency, not independence. If we could put ourselves in this older adult's situation, we would lose our self-respect from having our ability to make decisions, even small ones, denied and all our personal tasks done for us. Too much care does not always equate with caring. Rather, it is the adult's abilities, not disabilities, that need to be stressed in order to promote independence in self-care skills. This encouragement may well improve her self-esteem and can ease certain responsibilities of the family as well.

Changes Affecting Self-Care

The most common changes that affect one's ability for self-care are a loss of energy, motivation, and mobility; weakness in the arms and legs; pain, poor vision, recurrent illness, and confusion. These conditions need not prevent a person from actively looking after herself, however. Here are some general suggestions for your guidance:

- *Loss of energy:* If your family member doesn't seem to have the energy she once had, you can conserve what energy she has left by rearranging the bathroom, shower, bedroom, and kitchen so that essential items are placed within arm's reach while she's sitting or standing in one place. One friend, for example, whose mother is bedridden, has the telephone and television by her mother's nightstand for easy access. She also keeps a tray of beverages, snacks, and hobby and reading material nearby to allow her mother some independence as well as to prevent boredom. You can also plan to carry out all necessary tasks in one room before moving on to the next and thus avoid having to go back and forth to the same room.
- *Lack of motivation:* If your family member doesn't seem to want to do anything, you can show your appreciation after she has completed certain tasks. A sincere "that's great," or "I love you," is often a very effective reward. Some families use favorite foods and special outings as incentives to spark interest and desire for self-care. Sometimes making a deal will encourage initiation of a task. If your family member is not cooperating with buttoning, for example, ask her to button the first two while you button the last two.
- *Decreased mobility/weakness in arms and legs:* Loss of leg and arm strength is often a problem. The older adult should be encouraged to use the stronger limbs to compensate for the weaker ones. Don't ignore the weakened extremities, however, as they will only lose more strength.
- *Poor vision:* Since poor vision is common in older adults, be sure to provide adequate lighting in all rooms to prevent accidents. Touch can also be used to encourage self-care skills by letting the person with poor vision know you are there for support.
- *Recurrent illnesses:* Changes in your relative's behavioral,

mental, and physical condition should be reported to your physician. What may look like a minor ailment or just "old age" may actually be a symptom of a serious disease. Pneumonia, for example, is afebrile (no fever) in the aged—confusion is the symptom instead. As a health measure, take your family member to a physician at least yearly and more often if problems arise.

- *Confusion:* A confused older person needs more direction and encouragement to complete self-care tasks. Allow her to do as much for herself as possible. Refer to Chapter 8 for helpful suggestions.

As we continue to proceed with specific self-care tasks, an open mind is recommended. This may help you attempt some of the suggestions provided before jumping to any conclusions that "Grandma just won't do that." Give yourself a chance. Give your elderly family member a chance, too.

Independence in Self-Care

Self-care encompasses activities of daily living such as dressing, grooming, bathing, and eating. Recommendations on these activities are addressed separately in the following sections, but all are geared toward encouraging independence. Remember: You can make a significant contribution to your older family member's health and self-esteem when you encourage independence and good hygiene.

Dressing

Even if your family member rarely leaves the house, it's still a good idea to encourage dressing. You can assist her by making sure her clothes are clean and comfortable. There are three ways that encourage self-dressing: the pullover method, the hemi method, and a combination of the two. We'll begin with the three dressing methods for shirts and dresses:

- *The pullover method* is appropriate for those able to bring at least one hand over the top of the head and back behind the neck. Here are the instructions for putting on a garment:

Place the garment on the lap with the front facing up and the collar nearest to the body. Place the left hand in the left sleeve and the right hand in the right sleeve. Raise both arms and allow the garment to fall down the arms and over the head. (See Figure 6.) To remove the garment, grab the neckline or collar from behind the neck with one or both hands; then pull the garment over the head and pull the arms out of the sleeves.

- *The hemi method* is ideal for those who have suffered from a stroke or are weak on one side of their body. This method also applies to anyone who has pain in their arms such as those suffering from arthritis. Here are the instructions for putting on a garment: Place the weak arm through the sleeve first and then pull the sleeve up over the elbow. Grab hold of the garment's neckline and position the garment on the shoulder of the weaker arm. Reach behind the neck and grab the rest of the garment to insert the stronger arm into the sleeve. (See Figure 7.) To remove the garment, reverse the method of putting it on. Remove the strong arm from the garment and pull the garment off the weak arm.

- *The combination method* sometimes makes dressing easier than either one of the methods alone. She may put on a garment by using the hemi method, for example, but use the overhead method to take it off (or vice versa).

The dressing methods for trousers and pants can be done lying in bed, in a sitting position, or while sitting in bed. We'll begin with the method for putting on trousers while in bed. (This method may be useful if one leg is weaker than the other.) To put on the trousers, sit up in bed. Pull the knee of the weak leg up so the thigh is almost up against the chest. Place the weak foot in the trouser leg. Push the knee back down to straighten the leg as it enters the trouser leg. Then place the strong leg through the trouser. Be sure that the foot of the strong leg is entirely through the trouser. Push the strong leg to lift the buttocks off the bed while pulling the trousers up to the waist. If the person has trouble lifting the buttocks, have her rock from side to side and pull the trousers up gradually. To remove trousers, lift the buttocks or rock from side to side to push the trousers down while in a lying position. Remove the strong leg from the trousers first. Then get into a sitting position, pull the knee of the weak leg up, and remove the trousers from the weak leg.

To put on trousers while in a sitting position, hold the waist of the trousers low enough to insert both legs one at a time. (Feet should be showing from the other end.) Hold the waist of the trousers with one hand and use the other to help you stand. Upon standing, bring the trousers up and fasten them at the waist. To remove the trousers, unfasten them in a standing position and let them drop to the floor. Then sit down and kick the trousers off the legs. A stick can be used to pick trousers off the floor instead of stooping or squatting.

As before, it may be easier to combine methods. It may be convenient to put trousers on in bed, for example, and to remove them while sitting.

We turn now to the dressing method for putting on socks while in a sitting position. Use the strong hand to cross the weak leg over the strong one. Using the strong hand, work one sock onto the foot and then place the weak foot on the floor. Use the same method with the strong leg. If this is a precarious sitting balance, use a chair with a back or arm supports for safety—except for those who have had hip fractures on either side. It is not unusual for the elderly to require assistance here due to their body's loss of flexibility. And are socks really necessary?

To put on shoes while in a sitting position, use the strong hand to cross the weak leg over the strong one. (Those who have had hip fractures, however, should not cross the legs—keep the shoes on the ground and *lift* the leg into the shoe.) Slip a shoe on the foot as far as possible. If the shoe does not slip on completely, place a long-handled shoehorn at the heel and then reposition the weak leg on the floor. Push down, easing the foot into the shoe. Sometimes it is helpful to push down on the knee to help ease the foot into the shoe. Once there's a shoe on the weak leg, position the other shoe on the floor and slip the strong foot into the shoe using a shoehorn.

Now here are a few suggestions regarding shoes and socks

- Socks should not be so tight that they limit circulation of the legs and feet.

1. Put shirt on lap, label facing up, with collar next to abdomen and shirttail draped over knees.

2. Open sleeve for weak arm. Pick up weak hand and put into sleeve.

3. Pull sleeve up over elbow.

4. Put good hand into armhole. Raise arm out and up to push through sleeve.

Figure 6. The pullover method of putting on a shirt

5. Gather back of shirt from tail to collar.

6. Hold gathered shirt up. Lean forward. Duck head and put shirt over head.

7. To straighten shirt, lean forward, work shirt down over shoulders, reach back, and pull tail down.

1. Put shirt on lap, label facing up, with collar next to abdomen and shirttail draped over knees.

2. Open sleeve for affected arm. Pick up affected hand and put into sleeve.

3. Pull sleeve up over elbow.

4. Grasp collar at the point closest to good side.

Figure 7. The hemi method of putting on a shirt.

5. Hold tight to collar. Lean forward. Bring shirt up, around, and behind to good side.

6. Put good hand into arm-hole. Raise arm out and up to push through sleeve.

7. To straighten shirt, lean forward, work shirt down over shoulders, reach back, and pull tail down.

- Slip-on shoes are easier to manage than laced shoes.
- Shoes with Velcro fasteners are also available.
- A long-handled shoehorn may be used instead of bending over and possibly losing balance.

The following hints for independent dressing have proved useful for others:

- Keep clothes clean, attractive, and in good condition.
- Clothes that are one-half to a full size larger are easier to remove and put on.
- Open-front garments are recommended along with large buttons or zippers down to the waistline or lower.
- Back-opening garments, pullover shirts, snaps, hooks, small buttons, and snug clothing are not recommended.
- Stretch fabrics can ease the dressing process.
- If buttons or zippers are too difficult to manipulate, use Velcro instead.
- Be *consistent* in the dressing method you choose.
- Allow plenty of time to dress and undress.
- Let her know how she's doing through praise and a mirror.
- Conserve energy by *planning* the dressing methods.
- Encourage independence in dressing—removing clothes is usually easier than putting them on.
- If self-dressing is not possible, encourage the older adult to have a say in choosing what to wear.

Grooming

Grooming refers to hair care, washing and wiping face and hands, dental care, makeup, and shaving. If your family member is able to walk, encourage grooming to be done in the bathroom. All grooming items—shaver, soap, toothbrush, toothpaste, towels, and the like—should be within arm's reach. Place all grooming items in one drawer to avoid confusion. A stool or chair may be placed near the sink in case the person tires easily while standing. Remember that grooming can also be done in the shower.

If your older family member is restricted to a wheelchair, encourage grooming to be done in the bathroom. If the wheelchair cannot be positioned facing the sink, position it sideways. It may be helpful to place a plastic container containing all necessary grooming items on her lap while the wheelchair is positioned sideways. It may be easier to groom in the shower.

If the older person is restricted to the bed, encourage grooming while sitting up in bed. Grooming items may be placed on a nightstand or bedside table. It's often a good idea to place a plastic container holding all the essential grooming items on her lap.

Here are a few one-handed techniques (primarily for those who have one-sided weakness due to a stroke). Place the toothbrush handle in the mouth with bristles facing up; squeeze toothpaste onto the brush; then use the strong arm to brush teeth. Brush dentures while in the mouth and remove them to rinse. Use a small, lightweight thin towel to wash and wipe the face. Match the size of the towel to the hand size. Use the strong arm to wipe the weak arm.

Bathing

Since most of us consider bathing a matter of privacy, encourage independence in the bathroom. But bathing must also be safe. You can promote safety *and* independence while bathing by observing a few guidelines:

- Bathroom equipment must be both comfortable and safe (see Chapter 14).
- Washcloths should be small, lightweight, and thin. A thin nylon towel is recommended due to its light weight and ability to hold suds. A long-handled back brush may also be of assistance.
- Flexible shower hoses allow control of water and rinsing. (Bathing equipment may be purchased from various vendors listed in the Yellow Pages under "Hospital Equipment and Supplies.")
- If the older person is able to wash her face and other body parts while in the bathtub or shower, encourage her to do so. Assist only when absolutely necessary.
- All necessary items should be placed within arm's reach while sitting on the bench in the shower or tub.

- To wash the back, use the back brush or a long towel.
- A sponge bath can be given in bed or on the toilet.
- Remove all scatter rugs to prevent slips and falls.
- Be sure that both the feet and the floor are dry before stepping out of a shower or tub.
- Soap on a string keeps the soap always in reach. A pouch made of net fabric attached to a string serves the same purpose.
- If the older person's grasp is weak, terrycloth mittens may serve as a hand towel.
- Don't sit on the tub or shower floor—it's too difficult to get up.
- Don't use towel racks as grab bars—they aren't sturdy enough.
- Enter and exit the shower or tub sideways, not facing forward or backward. If, for example, the older person enters the bathtub sideways with left leg first and right leg second, she'll find it impossible to sit in the tub. If she enters the tub facing forward, she must pivot and then sit. Remember: The greater the number of steps to a task, the harder it is to do, the longer it takes, and the more energy it requires.

For those who have limited use (or no use at all) of one arm or leg, here are some hints for bathing in a sitting position:

- When washing under the strong arm, fling the washcloth under the arm. Flush the strong arm against the body and pull the washcloth out simultaneously.
- When washing the remainder of the strong arm, place the washcloth over the thigh of one leg and rub the strong arm over the washcloth.
- When washing the feet, throw the washcloth down on the feet and rub it over the weak leg.
- Wash the strong leg by crossing it over the weak leg and then using the strong arm to wash. Do not, however, use this method if the older person has fractured either hip.
- Wipe the body while sitting on the tub bench.
- Dress immediately after exiting the shower or tub so the grab bar can be used for support. (If the toilet is near the shower or tub, the elderly person may choose to sit there to dress.)

Feeding

Feeding is entirely different from eating. *Feeding* is the coordination of brain and arms to bring food to the mouth for *eating*. Here are some recommendations to encourage independent feeding:

- Using the "clock system" described in Chapter 5 may be helpful for those with poor vision. It will eventually help your family member to find her own drink, napkin, plate, and fork.
- If her grasp is weak, build up the handle of the utensil by wrapping a hand towel around it.
- If the plate is sliding around the table while she's trying to scoop food, use a heavier plate with a damp towel beneath it.
- Dishes with ledges, found at medical supply stores, can reduce the amount of food that falls off the plate. Dishes with separate compartments are also useful.
- Straws are useful if she's unable to hold the cup or drink from it.
- Sometimes lightweight plastic bowls are easier to eat from than plates. Bowls may be lifted right up to the mouth to minimize spillage.
- If metal utensils are too heavy, use plastic.
- If she can't distinguish her food from the plate, use a plate with a solid color. White brings out the color of most foods. Don't use green or brown, though, since they're the same color as vegetables and meat.
- If only half of the food is being eaten (right half or left half), your relative may have homonymous hemianopsia. This condition, primarily found in stroke victims, results in an impairment of one-half of the eyes' visual field. If you suspect she has homonymous hemianopsia, encourage her to turn her head to the left side and use the vision on the right (or vice versa). This process, called scanning, will broaden her visual awareness on the left side. Sitting on her left side and asking that she look at you when talking will also encourage her to look at the left side. Reverse the method if her right visual field is impaired.
- Adjust the chair or table height for comfort.
- If she's independent in eating, but messy, you can provide an

apron or bib. You can also spread newspapers under the table
to avoid staining the floor or rug.

• If utensils are too difficult to handle, try using more finger
  foods. Sandwiches and other foods can be cut into small
  digestible parts that can be eaten with the fingers.

If the older person appears to be having problems swallowing
or is choking frequently, inform your physician. These are *not*
feeding problems and may be serious.

How to Grade Tasks

We have discussed activities of daily living and suggested ways
in which families can encourage their older relative's independence. However, different degrees of assistance are called for in
different cases. What if our recommendations do not seem to
suit the older person in your care? How much help is too much
and how much is too little? There is a process called *grading*
that can help you to determine the right amount of assistance.
Grading defines the steps of a procedure and then modifies
them to accommodate the older person. Here are some examples of grading a task to accommodate the individual's needs
and encourage her independence. If the task is to feed herself,
you must first determine the steps involved in the task. While
feeding seems natural enough, it actually involves five basic
steps:

1. Find the food.
2. Pick up the spoon or fork.
3. Bring the utensil to the food and pick it up.
4. Bring the utensil from the plate to the mouth.
5. Return the utensil from the mouth back to the plate.

These steps must be modified for a person who has suffered a
stroke and, say, has only one functional arm. In this case, the
person must:

1. Find the food.
2. Pick up the utensil. (If it's too hard to find, place it on the
   plate. If it's too heavy, use plastic.)

3. Bring the utensil to the food to pick up the food.
4. Bring the utensil from the plate to the mouth.
5. Return the utensil from the mouth to the plate.

Another task that can be graded is dressing. If the task is to fasten the front of a shirt, small buttons are the most difficult. Large buttons are somewhat easier, then a zipper, a zipper with a large ring, and finally Velcro for easiest handling.

By observing how much your family member is able to do with each separate step, you will begin to understand your own role in independent care. Attempt various methods and grade the task if necessary. Be patient in teching a new method.

Teaching the Older Person

As a caring family member or friend, you may often feel overwhelmed by what lies in front of you. Teaching independence can itself be a challenging task. Even so, there are rewards. Be encouraging, yet firm, and offer sincere praise when each step of a task is accomplished. If the person is trying a new method, praise her just for the attempts alone. Offer step-by-step instruction and demonstrate the steps if necessary. Correct her errors immediately. Keep your instructions short and simple. If you find yourself becoming frustrated, leave the room for a few minutes, take a few deep breaths, and return when you are feeling calm. If you're not quite sure the person can do the task, you may want to observe her unobtrusively to avoid accidents such as eating the soap or drinking the hair tonic. You can also leave her for a while and then return to see how she's handled the task. Be consistent and kind in your instructions. You want her to taste success, not failure. Never demand performance; frustration may be the unhappy result. We suggest you attempt a method for at least a week before deciding to switch to another. It's difficult for *anyone* to learn a new method for grooming and the like, especially when the method keeps changing. Be realistic in setting your goals. If the methods you've attempted don't work, maybe your expectations need to be lowered. This is often difficult to do, for family members may not be able to accept their relative's disability as permanent. They should discuss these fears with their physician. If, however, the older person is capable of raising her arms up and down, touching the back of her head, placing her hands on her hips, making a fist, and opening her hands, she should be able to handle most self-care skills independently. Support her attempts to do so.

Preventing Dependence

In the preceding pages we have provided hints to increase your relative's independent performance in the activities of daily living. Equally important are the following suggestions for *maintaining* her present level of independence:

- *Encourage participation in household chores.* Everyone wants to feel needed. Perhaps, for example, you notice your mother is able to button shirts when she folds clothes but she's unable to button her dress. Since you know she should be able to button her clothes because she did so when folding, bring that to her attention. Encourage your father to continue the yard work as his job around the house. Praise can boost a sense of accomplishment. Use it generously!
- *Stimulate orientation.* Orientation is the ability to identify the date, time, place, and people. Put up calendars with large print and mark the days as they go by. Place clocks in every room. Encourage conversation relating to current events. Routines are especially helpful—for example, always eat meals at certain times and begin specific chores at certain times. It's extremely easy to forget what day it is if there's no reason to remember. Haven't you ever experienced this feeling on vacation?
- *Encourage independence by reducing unnecessary assistance.* If you're not providing assistance, check on her self-care performance from time to time.
- *Encourage activity.* Provide rest periods and nutritious meals. As long as muscles are being used, strength and circulation will be maintained. Daily physical exercise is necessary for preventing stiffness and weakness.
- *Participate in your family member's care.* Every member of the family should pitch in to avoid heaping all of the tasks on one family member.

Two final points are worth restating. First, not all older people require this type of assistance and instruction. Most don't. If you believe your family member does require your intervention, discuss the matter with your doctor and an occupational therapist. Second, remember to assess your elder's capabilities prior to helping. Doing too much, in the end, can rob her of her independence. Those physically and mentally able to look after themselves should be encouraged to do so if for no other reason than their self-esteem. An occupational therapist is a trained professional who may provide further suggestions for your elder's self-care. You may reach an occupational therapist at most hospitals and home care agencies.

14

Providing a Safe Home Environment

MILDRED RAMSEY

When Susan brought her mother home from the hospital after a slight stroke, she wasn't prepared for what happened. First her mother nearly fell as they started up the four steps to the entrance of the house—Susan grabbed her around the waist just in time to prevent a fall. Then she had to lift her mother bodily from one step to the next because her legs were so weak. By the time they reached the front door, Susan was trembling all over from fright and physical exertion. As they passed through the door, Susan's mother grabbed at the door frame, an act which only hindered her from getting inside more quickly. Then she caught her toe under the edge of a small throw rug and nearly fell again. Despite the pain from her strained back muscles, Susan managed to maneuver her mother around an end table to the nearest seat, a low sofa. "Mother!" Susan exclaimed. "You were walking just fine at the hospital. What happened?" Her mother burst into tears. "I don't know," she cried. "On the steps, my legs just wouldn't go—and now I have to go to the bathroom!"

Susan was in for another shock when she discovered her mother was unable to get up from the low sofa. Once again she strained her back lifting her mother to a standing position. "What is going to happen next?" she asked herself as she helped her mother down the hallway. "And how will I ever be able to return to work?"

Susan discovered some of the basic facts about safety in the home the hard way—the way people often do. It is unfortunate that some elderly people have to experience falls and other mishaps because a few simple safety factors have not been put into effect in their living environments. It is also unfortunate that caregivers injure themselves because the home is not properly safeguarded.

Most homes have not been built with elderly persons in mind. Young people who are planning new houses don't stop to think that they will be old one day and the flights of stairs which are so easy to climb now may make access to their dwelling impossible in later years. Bathroom doors and interiors are often too narrow to be used when a wheelchair becomes necessary. Even apartments in housing projects built especially for the elderly have many barriers, undoubtedly the result of designs of planners who do not understand the special needs of the aging.

Although some dwellings—especially those with many stairs —can never be made safe for independent living for the elderly, most can be altered inexpensively to reduce the possibility of accidents. It is just as important that family members take special precautions on their own behalf against strained muscles, lack of sleep, and overtaxed physical and mental resources by providing appropriate equipment to aid in the care of their elderly.

Susan's mother moved about with ease in her hospital room, but the extra muscle strength required for climbing stairs just wasn't there. Had Susan followed a few general rules for safety before bringing her mother home, her bad experience could have been avoided altogether.

Safety Rules

The following general rules apply to any dwelling for an elderly person:

- *Steps and stairs should always have handrails.* In the elderly, muscle bulk and strength decreases along with coordination. Moreover, visual problems can impair judgment about the height and position of steps. A handrail, therefore, gives a great sense of security. Strength in the arms provides the additional boost the legs often need.
- *Throw rugs should be eliminated.* Visual problems, muscle

weakness, and poor coordination reduce an older person's ability to negotiate throw rugs.

- *All walkways should be kept clear.* All electrical cords, toys, wastebaskets, and carelessly placed chairs and end tables should be eliminated wherever an elderly person walks. Get rid of excess furniture, too.
- *Chairs should have high, firm seats.* Weak leg muscles make it difficult to rise from a low surface. A favorite chair that is too low can be raised on wooden blocks to a height that will enable the elderly person to rise with little or no assistance and thereby reduce the chances of falling.

How do you go about determining solutions to *specific* problems in a house or apartment? Each room has its potential dangers which are closely linked to the dependency level of the elderly individual. With a few changes, however, the bedroom, bathroom, and kitchen can be made safe for an elderly person whether she can walk unassisted, must use an appliance, or is in a wheelchair.

The Bedroom

The bedroom often has a crowded collection of furniture that has built up over the years. The first thing to do is eliminate all the furnishings that are not necessary. A bed, a chest of drawers, a bedside table, a chair or commode chair—these are the only pieces of furniture necessary in an elderly person's room.

If your relative is bedridden, the following safety precautions should be taken:

- *Use a hospital bed.* One of the most important features of a hospital bed is that its height can be varied. For the caregiver, this feature is indispensable in reducing back strain. Raising the bed to hip level prevents unnecessary stooping and bending.
- *Make sure that side rails are up except when care is being given.* Side rails prevent accidental falls out of bed. They also aid a bedridden person in turning from one side to the other. If a hospital bed is not being used, portable side rails can be obtained.

- *Position the bed for easy access from either side.* Care given within easy reach of the elderly person eliminates reaching across the bed, which causes back strain.
- *Use a draw sheet to help change the bedridden person's position without straining your back.* A twin sheet folded in half crosswise and placed over the bottom sheet can be grasped and pulled firmly in the desired direction without undue back strain for the caregiver or body strain for the elderly person.

If she is confined to a wheelchair, the following safety precautions should be taken in the bedroom:

- *Use a very firm mattress.* A soft mattress makes transfers and maneuvering difficult. If the bed is used for sleeping only, a hospital bed is not necessary.
- *The bed should be the same height as the seat of the wheelchair—with cushion.* Transfers are easier to make if surfaces are at the same level. Standard beds can be raised on blocks if necessary.
- *Before transferring, always be sure that the brakes of the wheelchair are on and the footrests have been flipped upward out of the way.* If the arms are removable, remove the one next to the bed.
- *Transfer the person from her strong side.* If the person has left-sided paralysis from a stroke, be sure the wheelchair is placed so that her right side is next to the chair. If the bed is pushed against a wall so that only one side can be used, sit her up and move the chair alongside the bed toward her right side. Return the chair pointing in the opposite direction so the transfer back to the bed will also be made from the right side.

If your aging relative is ambulatory, she may become disoriented during the night. To avoid accidents, the following precautions should be taken:

- *Keep a night light on in the bedroom and bathroom.* These dim, inexpensive bulbs plug right into the wall socket.
- *Make sure slippers and other clutter are out of the way.*
- *Place a commode chair beside the bed if getting to the bathroom alone safely is a problem.* In this way she can slip right

from the bed onto the chair and back again without taking any steps. With the seat down, the chair can be used as a regular chair.

Sleep patterns in the elderly can be severely affected by acute illness, various debilitating diseases, and dementia. The elderly person becomes restless and active during the nighttime hours. Perhaps nothing affects a caregiver more adversely than being aroused from sleep night after night because of an aging relative's restlessness. Moreover, some of these older relatives are in great danger of falling and sustaining hip fractures or other serious injuries while up and around. A good solution to this problem is judicious use of restraints.

When restraints are suggested as a method of dealing with the problem of night wandering, the caregiver's reaction is often one of horror. "Oh, no!" a daughter will say. "I couldn't tie *my* mother down!" Actually, most restraints on the market are well designed for comfort and mobility. They are capable of making an individual safe without feeling tied down. Bed restraints allow a person to sit upright in bed and to roll to either side, but they prevent getting out of bed. For the caregiver, a restraint can make the difference between a good night's sleep and a night full of interruptions. Often such a restraint will encourage an elderly person to go back to sleep when she finds she can't get out of bed. Restraints are also useful for wheelchair-bound and bedridden patients to help keep them correctly positioned and safe.

The Bathroom

For the elderly, the bathroom is probably the most dangerous room in the house. In the first place, other family members may leave the floors wet and slippery. Bathroom fixtures are exceedingly hard and can cause serious injury if an elderly person falls and strikes one of them. Furthermore, bathrooms are often narrow and small, making them difficult for a person in a wheelchair to use. In spite of these problems, most bathrooms can be made safe and functional for elderly individuals. The cost of much of the equipment recommended here is covered by Medicare.

In general, it is always best to remove glass doors on showers and tubs and replace them with curtains. Such doors impede transfers and can easily shatter if fallen against. Place friction strips on shower floors or tub bottoms to prevent slipping. Keep bathrooms as warm and free of drafts as possible because the elderly chill more easily than younger persons do. Finally, a temperature control mechanism can be installed by a plumber to prevent scalding.

Using the Toilet

The following items can aid in making it safe and easy to use the toilet:

- *Raised toilet seats:* Often toilet seats are too low for the elderly to sit and stand with ease because their leg muscles are weak. Raised toilet seats are inexpensive and can be installed or removed in a few seconds. The added inches in height can mean the difference between dependence and independence in the bathroom.
- *Grab bars:* Grab bars placed at shoulder height on the walls near the toilet greatly assist the elderly person to sit and stand.
- *Safety frame:* Tubular arms which attach at the back of the toilet give security while she's seated and aid in standing and sitting. They can be used in conjunction with raised toilet seats and in place of grab bars.
- *Wheeled commode seat and safety frame:* On casters, it can be used as a commode chair in the bedroom or wheeled into place over the toilet. It can also double as a shower chair.

Using the Shower

The most sensible method of bathing for most elderly people, whether handicapped or not, is to use a shower stall with no entrance barrier. (That is, the shower floor begins flush with the bathroom floor and has no ledge.) Inside there should be a shower bench that is high enough to make sitting and standing easy. A grab bar should be installed facing the seated person so that either arm may be used to facilitate sitting and standing. The shower head should be movable (attached to a long hose or metal coil) and capable of being directed to all parts of the body while held in the hand or attached in the usual fashion. If the elderly person is too debilitated to be transferred to a shower bench, she can be wheeled into the shower on a shower chair. Shower chairs have small caster wheels and require much less space than wheelchairs—meaning that they can pass through narrow bathroom doors and fit into small shower stalls.

Few bathrooms, however, are equipped in such ideal fashion. More often, shower stalls are built with at least a six-inch-high ledge. Others have walls as high as twenty inches to step over. How can you safely transfer to a shower a stroke victim or an elderly parent with weak legs or severe arthritis? Two possible methods are suggested here: the *chair-bench method* and the *wheelchair-bench* method.

First we'll consider the chair-bench method. Outside the shower, place a straight wooden chair with its side beside the ledge of the shower. Inside the shower, place a shower bench. The elderly person should sit down on the straight chair, swing both legs over the ledge into the shower, and slide over onto the shower bench, using the grab bar or the help of a caregiver to pivot onto the shower bench. The caregiver can often best assist in the transfer by standing inside the shower if there is room. After bathing, the transfer is reversed—the legs are now swung over the ledge onto the bathroom floor before the elderly person is slid onto the chair.

Now let's look at the wheelchair-bench method. If there's sufficient room in front of the shower stall, the chair can be wheeled to face the shower ledge and the elderly person's legs can be placed inside the shower with her hips near the edge of the wheelchair seat. With a little assistance, the person can be slid across to the shower bench. If she has good use of her arms, she can help by using the arms of her chair and the edge of the shower bench for lift. A wheelchair can also be angled in sideways next to the shower ledge once the chair arm next to the shower has been removed.

Using the Tub

In some homes and many apartments (even those constructed specifically for older adults), a bathtub is the only means available for bathing. Some are tub-shower combinations, which make adjustments much easier. Bathtubs are extremely hard—if not impossible—for elderly people to get into. They are even harder to get out of. Muscle weakness combined with arthritic limbs can render a tub useless in an older person's bathroom unless you install appropriate equipment to make bathing easier. The following guidelines should be followed for ease and safety in tub bathing:

- *Select an appropriate tub bench.* The safest and easiest tub bench to use has legs both inside and outside the tub. A person can be seated on a portion of the bench which extends outside the edge of the bathrub. Her legs can then be swung inside the tub and she can be slid across the bench to the proper position for bathing. A small back on the bench gives extra support.
- *Use a movable shower head.* A shower head which is attached to a hose from the faucet (if it is not a tub-shower combination) or installed in place of the fixed shower head will make bathing easier and more pleasant. It is especially helpful in cleansing and rinsing the crotch.
- *Have towels and dry clothing at hand.* Quick drying and dressing in a warm bathroom will prevent chilling when your relative enters cooler areas of the house.

The Kitchen

Volumes have been written about appropriate kitchen designs to help handicapped individuals function in that setting. Redesigning a kitchen is very expensive, however, and is rarely done for handicapped elderly persons. Instead, services such as Meals on Wheels are utilized if she is unable to prepare foods, or an aide is hired to shop and cook ahead.

Family members become greatly concerned when an aging relative is left alone and persists in turning on the kitchen stove without remembering to turn it off again. If the elderly person is hard of hearing, she may forget to turn the kitchen faucet off and may flood the floor. Here are some suggestions for handling dangerous problems in the kitchen:

- *Turn off the electricity for the stove at the master switch.* Leave foods for lunch in thermos containers on the counter.
- *Heat foods in a microwave oven.* Leave foods in appropriate

containers for microwave use. The oven will turn off automatically.

- *Install a signal light for the hard of hearing.* Special signal lights can be installed to warn her that water is running, the doorbell is ringing, or the stove has been left on.

Emergencies

"I worry so much about mother being home alone during the day that I just can't do justice to my job," Susan thought as she sat at her desk. She had made the home as safe as possible, and her mother had improved sufficiently to be left alone. Yet the nagging possibility of a fall or another stroke occurring during the day hung over Susan's head. She wouldn't call her mother because her mother tended to rush nervously to the phone. Yet Susan needed some way of reassuring herself that her mother was all right.

When a parent is left alone all day, there is no fail-safe way of preventing accidents. A family must often decide between taking some risks or placing a parent in an institution. The family may not be well enough off to afford day care or in-home care for the elderly person. Usually, some element of risk is worth taking to ensure the happiest setting for an elderly loved one. Ways can be worked out to check during the day on the welfare of a relative who has been left alone at home. Here are some examples:

- *Install a specially equipped telephone.* The telephone company can install a phone which will dial a single, specified number when the instrument is lifted from its cradle. Thus an elderly person can lift the instrument during an emergency or at predetermined times during the day and reach a family member.
- *Place a whistle around the elderly relative's neck.* Then she can blow the whistle to signal an emergency and summon help even if the telephone cannot be reached. Cooperating neighbors should be given a key to the house or apartment.
- *Make daily phone checks.* If an elderly person lives alone and has no family members in the same city, phone checks can be arranged seven days a week to make certain she is all right.

This telephone call should be made at the same time each day and should be expected by the elderly individual. If there is no answer, emergency help can be called in.

Your local social service agency may be helpful in arranging this service.

In conclusion, most homes can be made safe and comfortable for the elderly at various levels of dependency. The safest method of carrying out an activity is usually the most efficient one. By making appropriate changes in the home, caregivers are also helped to conserve their physical and mental resources.

15

Community Services: Help Does Exist!

HAZEL BEH
DIANE MURAYAMA
MILDRED RAMSEY

Steve gripped the steering wheel of his car as he drove away from his mother's apartment building. How was he going to tell Marian he would have to move his mother into their home? The two of them would never get along, he thought. Marian was such a perfectionist and his mother was so messy. Yet what was he to do? He knew his mother could no longer go up and down the two flights of stairs to her apartment. Her arthritis was so bad that her laundry had not been done, the apartment was dirty, and she couldn't get in or out of her bathtub any more. Worse, she wasn't able to shop for food and prepare meals and she was losing weight.

It is usually a shock for family members to be faced suddenly with the growing dependency of an aging relative. It isn't that one has not thought or worried about what will happen to Mom and Dad when they can no longer take care of themselves. Rather, it's a case of not knowing what can be done when dependency grows. Often only two options seem available: put Mother in a nursing home, or care for her in the home of a family member. In actuality, services do exist that can help aging relatives remain as independent as possible while giving families as much assistance as needed. But how do family members learn about these services? Who can they turn to for assistance?

Steve was fortunate. He spoke with his neighbor Louise, who was able to give him some valuable advice.

"What am I to do, Louise?" Steve asked his neighbor as they stood talking in front of her house. "You didn't seem to have any trouble when you brought your mother home to live with you."

"Oh, I would have if I hadn't gotten the right kind of help."

"What kind of help are you talking about? Marian doesn't like help in the home."

"If you had a legal problem, wouldn't you go to a lawyer?"

"Right."

"Well, following the same line of reasoning, you need to consult a professional about your mother. Someone who has specialized in the field of aging can talk with your mother as well as Marian and help find a satisfactory solution to the problem."

What's Available?

Most communities have agencies that specialize in working with aging clients. The staff who work for these agencies are usually able to do a complete assessment of an elderly person and the situation. These professionals are also aware of the community services that are available. After an assessment is made, family members and the elderly relative will be presented with options to suit their situation. The professional staff, usually social workers, will then continue to support the family in the arrangements they have chosen.

Although the assessment is the most thorough way of determining what services are needed, information and referral without an assessment is a service provided in some communities. City, county, and state listings usually have a telephone number that can be called for information on specific services for the elderly. Your city and county may also have outreach workers who will come to your home and make recommendations. You can ask these workers about other agencies that serve the elderly. Most are free of charge.

In learning about the array of services that are available it is well to keep in mind that the aging population is growing and that some programs are suffering financial and staff cutbacks. This means there may be a frustrating waiting list for the service you need most. Don't give up. Persistence eventually pays off in these cases, so by all means place your name on the waiting lists where necessary. In the meantime, explore other options for assistance.

Some communities may be more responsive than others to the needs of their older population. To help you find the programs that may be of assistance to your older family member, let's take a look at several types of services that may be useful, including transportation, housing, finances, and home care.

Transportation

When the needs of older people are being considered, transportation often takes a back seat, so to speak, in priorities. Yet suitable transportation is of great importance to older adults. In fact, many say it is their most serious problem. Transportation may determine whether or not an elderly person has access to life-supporting services and recreational activities. Certainly transportation must be available if she is to coordinate her housing, medical, financial, and recreational needs.

Take the case of Nora, for example. Nora is eighty years old. She has no immediate family members and most of her close friends have passed away. She is suffering from poor health and should be seeing her doctor almost every week, but she can't because transportation is a problem. She's unable to take the city bus because she has trouble boarding. If she had transportation that picked her up at the housing project where she lives, she'd be able to see the doctor regularly.

In this case transportation services can make the difference in whether or not Nora will receive the necessary medical care. In some communities, curb-to-curb or door-to-door transportation for the elderly is provided by government-subsidized or private companies. Many welfare departments may also allow certain clients to take the taxi to the doctor. Clearly, then, the availability of affordable transportation can have a significant impact on the older person's health.

Studies have shown that adequate transportation plays an important role in a person's view of life. Lack of transportation can narrow a person's life space and limit contact with others. Social contact with friends and family may be impossible if there's no way to reach them. Without suitable transportation, elderly persons may decide that it's much easier to remain at home until someone visits them. The decision to isolate themselves may lead to a crisis, however, if visitors are infrequent. More complex problems such as alienation, depression, and malnutrition may be the sad result for older people who cannot obtain transportation.

Ruth, now seventy-five years old, is a widow who lives alone in her own home. Since her husband's death two years ago, she has become more reclusive and rarely leaves her house except to check the mailbox. In response to a call from a concerned neighbor, a community outreach worker visited Ruth. The worker found that Ruth was in fact managing well in her daily affairs. The worker also discovered that Ruth had made arrangements with a local store to deliver her groceries. Since she was unable to drive, however, she had not gone shopping since her husband's death. Although clothes shopping was one of Ruth's favorite activities, she was unwilling to ask her friends or neighbors for a ride and was now embarrassed about her appearance and refused to socialize with people. In this case the outreach worker was able to arrange transportation and escort services for Ruth. The escort worker was able to win Ruth's friendship and provided personal assistance as well as encouragement and company during her first shopping outing in two years.

The need for transportation services depends on the older person's personal situation and physical abilities. Responding to this problem early, however, may often alleviate more difficult problems in the future. The availability of these services depend on the financial and community support for special transportation arrangements for the elderly.

Government agencies such as the state executive office on aging, the county area agencies on aging, and the information and referral offices in most communities should be able to provide information on transportation for older family members. Community social agencies may also be contacted when seeking transportation for the elderly. One final note: Remember to ask if there are eligibility requirements or a fee for the service. While some are free, others are not.

Housing

For most people, home is more than shelter—four walls and a roof over the head. It represents a place to return to, a place where we feel safe and comfortable among treasured and familiar possessions. It is a place where loved ones gather; a place to relax and be yourself. Yet home can also mean living in a dilapidated house or being miserable and lonely in a bare room at the top of the stairs with only a light bulb dangling from the ceiling. Home can even be just a park bench. For some, home may not be a happy place or offer any sense of freedom and security.

For many older persons, home may mean all that we have mentioned and significantly more. It is a part of their identity and a place that enables them to maintain their independence and control over their own lives. As they experience changes in their lives, familiar surroundings become essential to their sense of well-being. Perhaps these are some of the reasons why so many older people refuse to move or try to hang onto their homes no matter what the cost.

Whatever the concept of home, finding the right place to live is a significant concern. To older adults who are experiencing physical changes and perhaps chronic illness, living on fixed incomes and having less mobility, finding appropriate and affordable housing is of even greater concern. Only 5 percent of the population aged sixty-five and over resides in institutions. Where, then, do most older people live? The majority remain in the community, and so it is no wonder that housing is one of their greatest concerns.

In trying to find suitable housing for older people, one must not only understand their needs but know the agencies in the community that can help. Specific questions on housing may be answered by the local housing authority or the U.S. Department of Housing and Urban Development (HUD). Check your telephone directory under the governmental listings. Keep in mind that location (accessibility to services, proximity to family, friends, shopping areas), safety, and cost of shelter must be considered when you are deciding on housing. Be aware, too, that in some localities the demand for housing may exceed what is available.

Often the housing needs of the elderly are only part of the problem. It may be useful to seek the services of a professional to sort out the problems. In some instances, homemaker or housekeeper services may help your older family member to remain in her own home. In other situations, it may be best to have your elder move into the home of a relative or a group home or even hire a live-in companion to meet all of her needs.

Small group homes, in which three to five older adults share a house, offer an alternative to people who for various reasons can no longer live alone but do not need nursing care. These homes encourage the individual to maintain independent daily living activities, but they also offer support services.

Older persons who own their homes may want to consider sharing their living accommodations—especially when the house has become too large and expensive to maintain alone. Some communities have programs which match older people to younger persons for purposes of sharing a home. Each person participating in the program benefits: The home sharer has companionship, a place to live, and a sense of worth in sharing the household responsibilities; the home provider not only gains help in managing the house but receives companionship and a feeling of security from knowing there is someone else in the house.

Other community resources should also be considered: the local executive office on aging, regional agencies on aging, and office of information and referral. These agencies can refer you to other offices dealing with housing problems for older people.

Questions on qualifications for the different programs should be raised when looking for housing. Each program has its own eligibility requirements. Be sure to get information on the services available for housing projects, group homes, and rentals in order to find the best living arrangement for an older person.

Finances

Henry and his wife, Susan, thought they had planned their retirement carefully. In addition to his Social Security of $400, Henry had a monthly private pension of $400. Since their rent was $300, the remaining money seemed more than adequate for their simple needs. But when Henry developed a chronic lung ailment, they found that Medicare did not begin to cover the costs of his frequent visits to the doctor and his expensive prescriptions had to be paid for from their savings. After lung surgery and a subsequent heart attack, Henry required the services of a nursing home which cost $2,000 a month. After Medicare paid its share for the first one hundred days, Henry and Susan applied for state aid (Medicaid). Susan found she had to reduce her entire savings to a nominal sum in order to remain eligible for Medicaid—even the money she had saved for her future. She also found that her share of their income did not keep pace with her rent increases. And when Henry died, she was left without savings, without a partner to share the work of daily life, and without an adequate income.

This tragic story is repeated all too often. A large percentage of elderly people live well below the national poverty level. Some thought they could live on Social Security benefits alone. Many thought Medicare was adequate health insurance. Others planned for retirement but not for extraordinary inflation year after year.

When income is inadequate, Supplementary Security Income, a federal program for the aged, blind, or disabled with very low income, is the financial assistance to seek. Application should be made with the Social Security office in your community. In many areas the state government further subsidizes the poor to bring them up to the state's poverty level. The state welfare system also administers food stamps and Medicaid programs which further stretch an older person's income. Each state's welfare program has its own rules about property ownership, assets, and savings. Since these rules change often, the best advice is to go ahead and apply but be sure to disclose everything. If an elderly person seeks additional help from family members, government entitlements may be reduced. Supplementary Security Income, for example, has a maximum amount the elderly may receive as quarterly gifts before being penalized. Be cautious, therefore, in accepting help from others when government entitlements are involved. If the government discovers unreported income or failure to report overpayment, serious legal problems may arise.

Sometimes an older person's income is above the entitlement levels but still inadequate. While many family members feel they *ought* to assist their elders, others believe it is not their responsibility. Many older people refuse to accept help from their children—regarding it as the ultimate failure or finding the feeling of indebtedness intolerable. Family members might do better to offer a regular small amount that can be counted on but accepted without obligation.

Lillian received a monthly check for $50 from her son. At first she told him she didn't need it, but he insisted—it was small payment for her devotion, he said. He told her to treat herself to something special even though he knew it would more than likely be used to pay for medicine or the utility bill. This proud old woman and her son kept up a charade—that she would treat her friends to a fancy dinner—until the day she died.

Sometimes it makes economic sense to help an elderly parent. When children expect to inherit a family home or heirlooms, perhaps they should consider helping so that their parents are not forced to liquidate their assets. Occasionally, though, it is advisable for the elderly to sell their home. Consider the case of Elizabeth, an eighty-year-old widow. She had only a small income ($250 a month) and no savings but lived in a house currently valued at $200,000 (not uncommon in many large cities nowadays). If she sold her home and established a trust for herself, she could live comfortably on the income in an easy-to-care-for apartment. It would be wise for family members to discuss the options thoroughly and seek the advice of professionals when making such decisions.

When personal, family, and government resources prove inadequate, some older adults can turn to local charities, churches, or foundations. Some organizations disburse money for specific groups of people, certain ethnic groups, or people with specific problems. Often they can find a solution to financial problems when no one else can. Social service agencies or trust companies can help locate charity funds. Most communities have at least short-term or one-time help available.

Since each government program and each charitable trust has its own rules about assets, income, home ownership, personal deductions, and other eligibility requirements, seek out a social service agency to help with the application process. Be persistent. And be sure to apply for financial assistance, if it's needed, even when you're unsure of your relative's eligibility. Veterans (and spouses) of both world wars, Korea, or Vietnam should remember to check on their VA entitlements, especially benefits for medical treatment and for those with low incomes.

So many items are required when applying for assistance—insurance policies, receipts, bankbooks, canceled checks, and the like—that the process can seem intimidating to an elderly person. Family members who accompany their relative, interpret questions, and represent them can often make the difference between acquiring or being denied assistance.

For older adults who grow increasingly confused or incapacitated by illness, family members may need to increase their responsibilities. Their relative may give them power of attorney so they can transact business for her. If poor judgment or indecisiveness regarding finances is evident, try to find out the cause of the problem. If the dementia is irreversible, family members may seek guardianship of the estate to protect their relative's assets as one option. The final step, guardianship of the person, is required for older people who need others to make decisions regarding their physical care. To protect the older person's civil rights, guardianship involves a court procedure. Call your local legal aid program for information on taking these steps or for direct help if the elderly person falls into a low-income category.

Obviously the best time to plan for old age is long before retirement. All family members should be involved in planning for the future. If a son always expected the family home to be willed to him, he may need to help his parents safeguard it. If an older woman has always said she wants to remain in her home at all costs, family members should try to help her. Some parents even make clear how much help they are willing to accept, perhaps saying, "I never want to live in your home—I could never be happy knowing I was causing economic hardship for you." Others, believing that families are bound by ties and obligations, are devastated if their children don't help them.

The older adults who are poor today will probably die poor. Little can be done to change their plight. Their fate was determined in their young and middle years. Subsequent generations, therefore, should keep the following points in mind when planning for their own future:

- Social Security was never meant to be a total retirement income.
- Private pensions that don't keep pace with inflation will probably be inadequate.
- Study the surviving spouse benefits in pension plans and make plans accordingly.
- Family property, always a special concern, can sometimes be protected if planned for in advance. See an attorney specializing in public entitlements.
- Supplement Medicare with other health insurance unless you are in a low-income category and qualify for Medicaid.

- Keep family members apprised of your wishes and informed about all financial matters so they can help if you are ever incapacitated.

Home Care Services

When your older family member is homebound and unable to use the services out in the community, home care services may be beneficial. Home care is not a single service. It is a range of services, provided by paraprofessionals as well as professionals, that may include home health care, personal care, chore services, meal services, and companion services. A physician's order is not required to obtain all home care services. The cost varies and may be covered by insurance.[1] Be sure to choose the appropriate home care service to assist you in caring for a homebound family member. Contact the regional agency on aging or a social service office in your community to find out what resources are available to you.

Case management services can also assist you in this area. Trained professionals can identify, monitor, and obtain services to keep frail elders at home after a thorough assessment. Again, contact your regional office on aging for the name of a public or private agency that provides case management services.

When Albert was discharged from the hospital after suffering a severe stroke, home health care services were ordered by his physician. A registered nurse, speech therapist, and physical and occupational therapists provided regular treatments in his home for several weeks. A home health aide arrived three days a week to assist with bathing and giving an enema when necessary. Special equipment, such as a shower bench, raised toilet seat, grab bars (none of which are covered by Medicare), were ordered by a physical therapist to make the bathroom safer and more efficient for Albert's use. Because of the severity of his stroke, a wheelchair was deemed necessary for any outings. A doctor's order for the wheelchair was obtained so the cost could be reimbursed by Medicare. Albert and his wife soon learned, however, that only certain pieces of equipment are covered by Medicare. Within six weeks following his hospital discharge, Albert, with the help of his wife, was able to carry out the techniques he had learned from the therapists, but his condition had reached a plateau. Unfortunately, his home health care visits were then discontinued, as they would no longer be reimbursed under Medicare regulations and Albert himself could not pay for them.

In general, the rules for obtaining home health care that is fully covered by Medicare under both plans A and B, for an indefinite period, are as follows. (These rules are of course subject to change.)

- The person must be homebound.
- The care must not be considered maintenance unless it involves the changing of a catheter, a nasogastric tube, a dressing, or a similar service that requires skilled nursing.
- The treatment received from physical therapy, nursing, or a dietitian must be given with the assurance that the patient's condition will improve. Once a plateau has been reached, such visits must stop.
- Home health aides can be assigned to give baths and general care so long as a nurse, speech therapist, or physical therapist is assigned to the case. Under Medicare, this service is never available for maintenance only.

Many older persons and their families are not aware of what is available to them through their local home care agencies or what is fully reimbursable under Medicare. Unfortunately, this is often true of their physicians as well. Most physicians, however, will gladly order home care and equipment covered by Medicare when it is warranted—if they are requested to do so. If family members believe that their relative may qualify for this service, they should call the physician and discuss it (or have a social services agency do it for them).

Once professional home health care was discontinued, Albert's wife soon realized that without the visits of a home health aide, she would need to find additional help. Because their income was limited, she could not afford to pay much, however. A social worker from a case management agency in her town helped her to apply for a respite worker trained to provide general and personal care. The social worker also applied for a senior companion who could stay with Albert while his wife went shopping or on a much needed outing. The senior companion also enrolled Albert in a health maintenance class for handicapped elderly, where he could participate in exercises and other group activities. He used the special handicapped van service which accommodates those in wheelchairs to get to the sessions.

In most communities, the services of respite workers and senior companions are available. Because of the demand for these workers, there is often a long wait before one can be found. In the meantime, help is available, for a fee, from health care companies or from individuals in the community. Social services agencies may be of assistance in locating these services.

Margaret had different problems. At the age of eighty-two, she lives in a public housing project for the elderly. She suffers from arthritis and is largely homebound. She had formerly enjoyed having lunch at a nearby meal site for the elderly, but now her noon meals are being delivered to her. Twice weekly a chore service worker, acquired through her local public welfare agency, spends four hours cleaning her apartment, doing the laundry, shopping, and preparing food. Margaret is eligible for this service because of her low income. She also receives great reassurance from a daily phone call arranged for her through a volunteer program in her community. Once weekly, her friendly visitor, another community volunteer, spends an afternoon with her, talking, playing cards, and going for short outings. These services are enabling her to remain in an independent living situation. Similar services are available in most communities. Check with an information and referral or social services agency for eligibility requirements and application procedures.

Another service is hospice care. In the past few years, hospice programs for the terminally ill have been gaining acceptance in many communities. Hospice care is based on a team approach with the dying person, family members, and health professionals working together to make the end as comfortable as possible. Hospice assists the dying with two of their major concerns: dying in pain without dignity and burdening their survivors with financial debts for their medical care. Under Medicare, choosing this kind of care when nearing the time of death can be both an emotionally and a financially wise decision. Choosing hospice care with a Medicare-certified facility allows the dying person to remain at home in familiar surroundings with loved ones while receiving supportive care. It also allows the hospital facility to be used when the care becomes overwhelming for family members. The facility agrees to assume this care as long as the person is alive. Treatment is directed toward controlling pain and symptoms. Discuss hospice care with your older family member and physician.

There are many ways that family members can assist their dependent elderly relatives. Community programs may offer a variety of services to help supplement your care. A word of caution, however. Increasing numbers of elderly persons will be requiring assistance from others, so be prepared to seek other alternatives. Be patient. And be creative in working out your solutions.

Notes

1. Carol Kikkawa-Ward, "Home Care," *Report on the Ola Na Iwi Conference* (Honolulu: Executive Office on Aging, 1984).

16

From Care at Home to Nursing Home

BEVERLY KLOPF

Everything is farther away than it used to be—it's twice as far to the corner and they've added a hill, I notice. I've given up running for the bus—it leaves faster than it used to. It seems to me they're making stairs steeper than they used to in the olden days, and have you noticed the smaller print in the newspapers lately? There's no point in asking anyone to read aloud. Everyone speaks in such low tones I can hardly hear them. The material in dresses is skimpy now, too, especially around the hips and tummy. It's almost impossible to reach down to put on my shoes. Even people are changing. They're so much younger looking than they used to be when I was their age. On the other hand, people my own age are so much older looking than I am. I ran into an old classmate the other day, and she had aged so much she didn't even recognize me. I got to thinking about the poor thing while I was combing my hair and then glanced at my own reflection and, confound it, they don't even make good mirrors anymore.[1]

We may all chuckle at this story; and if we do, it may be because few of us wish to admit we are aging. Growing old is often regarded with alarm by people because they view aging as synonymous with inevitable physical and mental decline. Yet aging is a normal, gradual process which follows no single pattern. Each of us will grow old differently.

Most older adults, as many as 95 percent of those over the age of sixty-five, continue to live in the community in which they spent much of their lives, living either by themselves, with a spouse or friends, or with other family members. The remaining 5 percent have, for a variety of reasons, become overwhelmed by disease and the many changes that accompany the aging process and are institutionalized. It is this population, composed of the frail and vulnerable elderly, who need special care, the sort of care offered in institutions.

What do we mean by institutional care? When does a family member require additional care, if ever? And how do you go about choosing an institution?

What *Are* Nursing Homes?

Care away from the home is determined by a person's needs. Five levels of such care are available: acute care, skilled nursing care, intermediate care, care homes and boarding homes. Skilled nursing care and intermediate care facilities often are referred to as "nursing homes." Today's nursing homes, while predominantly serving the elderly, are actually for the young as well. They are for convalescents of all ages who need therapeutic care prior to returning home as well as for those who need long-term care.

Acute Care

Acute care is the round-the-clock care a person receives in a hospital after being admitted for illness or injury. Acute care is not nursing home care. The doctor usually makes daily visits to manage the necessary treatment as in the case of Frank and Betty. Frank, an 85-year-old man who was admitted to the hospital and diagnosed as having had a stroke, is nonresponsive and requires daily visits from his doctor. He needs acute care while he is being diagnosed with tests and X rays and while his medical condition is being carefully monitored. On the other hand, Betty, who is seventy-five years old, went in the hospital after she fell at home and fractured her hip. She had surgery to repair the fracture and now needs physical therapy to regain her ability to walk. She also requires acute care at this time. As for Frank and Betty's hospital costs, Medicare, Medicaid, and most private insurance companies will cover all or part of the expenses.

Skilled Nursing Care

As we continue to follow Frank and Betty, we will see changes in their physical condition. Frank begins to respond to his care but is unable to swallow, preventing him from eating. He now must be tube fed. He needs training so that he can regain his functional abilities, such as walking, which are impaired. As his medical condition stabilizes and shows improvement, he will be certified by the doctor to require skilled nursing care. Rehabilitation and tube feeding can be taken care of at that level. As for Betty, she has recovered from surgery and no longer requires daily visits from her doctor. She is continuing physical therapy for walking and is considered to require only skilled nursing care now.

The skilled nursing level, where we now find Frank and Betty, is less intensive than acute care. It is for persons who are in need of round-the-clock nursing services for convalescence and rehabilitation, but now the emphasis is on nursing and therapeutic care. The patient's condition, no longer acute, is stable enough that the doctor's visits can be limited.

Medicare pays for services in a skilled nursing facility after a patient has spent three days in an acute care hospital. Care and treatment, however, must be within Medicare guidelines. These guidelines are quite specific about what will be covered—for example, tube feeding, use of oxygen, medication by injections, dressing changes, decubitis (bedsore) care, and restorative therapy. The maximum coverage or insurance limit under Medicare is one hundred days. Should the patient no longer need these specific services, Medicare coverage can terminate at any time within these hundred days. Therefore, check with the local Medicare office or the facility's social work department to inquire about Medicare or other benefits. Medicare does not pay for skilled nursing services if the patient is admitted directly from home. If a person is discharged from a hospital and is admitted into a skilled nursing facility within fourteen days, Medicare may cover the expenses. Be sure to check with the facility to inquire about eligible coverage.

Once Medicare coverage has been used for the hundred-day maximum period, the patient must make her own payments unless she qualifies for Medicaid or private insurance will cover costs. Eligibility for Medicaid is determined by the person's income and assets. When admitted to a skilled nursing facility after the doctor's recommendation and certification, approval through the Medicaid program is needed before financial assistance can be received. All states except Arizona have Medicaid. (In California, it is called Medi-Cal.) Medicaid is administered through your state's department of social services or public welfare.

Intermediate Care

The next level of care is intermediate care, which tends to those who need restorative and maintenance services due to a chronic illness or disability but do not require care in a skilled nursing facility. Such persons need help with the activities of daily living—grooming, bathing, dressing, eating, using the toilet, and walking. The recommendation and certification of a physician, as with the skilled nursing facility, is also necessary for admission. Payment for this level of care is through private funds or Medicaid. Private insurance companies do not, at this time, cover intermediate care.

Care Homes

The care home is generally for those who are able to walk independently (or with a device such as a walker or cane) and are continent—in other words, in control of their bladder and bowel functions. They may need supervision or assistance with bathing, dressing, and eating, with monitoring of medication or going to the doctor, and with social activities. Such persons are generally in good health or at least their chronic illnesses are stable.

Unless the older adult can make her own payments, financial assistance is given by the Supplemental Security Income (SSI) program of the Social Security Administration. The amount of help depends on the level of care as well as the supervision required by the individual.

Care homes may vary in size from small facilities to institutions caring for a hundred people or more. They are licensed by state government agencies.

Boarding Homes

The boarding home is for those who can handle their daily living requirements independently but need a place to live and assistance with meals. Payments are through the resident's own resources and/or through the Supplemental Security Income program. Boarding homes are licensed in most states, and different payment levels are determined by a state agency. Some states combine care and boarding homes in one category. Check with your state department of health.

Two additional points should be emphasized regarding the different levels of institutional care for older adults. First, your relative's needs may change. An elder may need skilled nursing care immediately following hospitalization, for example, but may be transferred to a lower care level such as intermediate care or a care home as she improves. If, on the other hand, the health of a person residing in a care home deteriorates, she may have to be cared for in an intermediate care or skilled nursing facility. The second point is that there are few care facilities in the United States that offer all the different levels of care within one facility. Therefore, as needs change, transfers to different facilities may become necessary. Such movement can be difficult for the patient as well as the family.

When Is Institutional Care Needed?

Many older persons need special care because of chronic disabling conditions. They may be unable to dress, bathe, or eat by themselves. They may be seriously confused and disoriented. Their dependency on others to manage their daily lives may grow to a point where institutionalization needs to be considered—for instance, when family members are faced with a relative who requires more nursing care than they are able to provide. In that circumstance, the community resources that have been used may now be inadequate and the caregiver may be feeling exhausted.

Families that must decide whether or not to admit a frail or disabled relative into a nursing home never find it an easy decision. If you are considering nursing home placement, you may be experiencing a variety of feelings: guilt, inadequacy, anxiety, fear, frustration. Clearly you want to be sure your elder family member receives the appropriate care. How do you make this decision? First, it helps to be honest. After all, there are limits to your ability to make your older relative "the way she was." Ask yourself the following questions: Do you want to keep your family member at home with you? Are you able to provide the care that she really needs? Are you financially able to stay at home with her or pay for someone else who can? What about your relative? Is she happy in your home? And what of your own family? These are difficult questions, but they must be answered.

Share your concerns with someone—a clergyman, social worker, or friend. Try not to feel guilty about your feelings. There comes a time when round-the-clock care may no longer be expected of you in the child/parent relationship. Discuss your concerns with your doctor or your parent's primary physician or other professional. If you decide to keep your family member at home, the physician may be able to recommend a home health agency or other social service that can lessen the demands on you. Alternatively, your doctor may feel that your parent has reached the point where her needs will be best met in an institutional setting. (Don't forget: There is nothing wrong in getting a second opinion.)

If your parent is confused and you and your family physician agree that institutional care is the best alternative, discuss this prospect with her. If she is alert, by all means include her in the decision. Confusion is no reason to deny her information. Be sure to stress the positive reasons for the move: comfort, professional care, security, companionship, and a concerned staff. Your involvement, your love, and your understanding can assist your parent in accepting the decision.

Choosing a Nursing Home

Dependency, like aging, does not happen overnight unless there has been a traumatic accident. Discussions regarding care outside the home should be held before the actual need arises. Many families find such talk too upsetting and consequently avoid the subject, hoping their parents will never have to be placed in a nursing home. This is a mistake. While the prospect of institutionalization is a sensitive subject, it is possible to bring it up tactfully, caringly, yet realistically. A good opportunity may arise after her recovery from a serious illness. Another opportunity may present itself when a friend or relative needs to make similar arrangements.

Open communication and the participation of everyone involved, including the person about to be placed, become essential. The question of whether or not to admit a parent into an institution often becomes a question of what one generation can expect from the other, owes to the other, and is capable of doing for the other. The prospect of institutional care is a question only you and your family can answer.

When the decision has been made, help is available in most communities. The job before you may seem overwhelming, but there is help. First of all, there are state and local agencies to provide assistance. Many hospitals are equipped with social work departments to help families and patients choose a nursing home when illness prevents them from returning home. If help is not available, here are six steps to follow:

1. Make a list of local facilities.
2. Check out the facilities.
3. Visit the facilities.
4. Prepare a checklist of desirable features.
5. Check the costs.
6. Make your decision.

Now let's look at these steps in some detail.

Making a List

List the local facilities offering the level and types of services you need. You can get such a list from your local and state agency on aging, American Health Care Association affiliates, or the telephone book. Next, review the characteristics of the nursing homes, care homes, and boarding homes in the community. Usually there are various facilities to suit people with differing needs for care: skilled care, intermediate care, care homes, and boarding homes. A physician can also be of help.

Checking Out the Facilities

Check to see if these facilities are licensed and certified. The nursing home you select should be licensed—that is, it must meet basic state requirements regarding staff, programs, sanitation, and the physical environment. A certain number of nursing homes are also certified, which is to say they meet federal standards for participation in the Medicare and Medicaid programs.

To determine whether or not a nursing home complies with federal and state regulations, members of a state department of health or other comparable body conduct unannounced inspections each year to evaluate the facility and consult with staff on ways of improving the care. During these surveys the nursing home is evaluated on numerous basic requirements including fire safety, nursing care plans, and patients' rights.

The regulation of care and boarding homes is slightly different than that of nursing homes. Since there are no federal standards for them, each state is responsible for its care homes. Most states do set specific requirements for these facilities and inspect them annually. Before placing a relative in a care or boarding home, examine its license. All care and boarding homes should have certificates from the department of health or another licensing agency. Some, however, hold only a general excise tax license. Since such a license is only for tax purposes and is held by all private businesses, the home may not be in compliance with state regulations for care and boarding homes. Friends and neighbors may also have firsthand knowledge of the facility from personal experience of having placed a relative. Ask them for their opinion of the facility.

Visiting the Facilities

After preparing the list, the next step is to visit the facilities—an important step that is often omitted. Frequently a facility is chosen because it is known; and, likewise, homes are rejected because people did not know about them. Staff members of the facilities generally are willing to meet with prospective patients and their families. Should they be reluctant to do so, you may wish to seek another facility.

Those looking for a facility should talk with the administrator or director of nursing and other staff. Try to assess the temperament of the staff and how they enjoy their work. Is employee morale good? High morale often reflects high-quality care.

Check recent survey reports from the licensing agency in your state. Skilled nursing facilities, intermediate care facilities, and care homes and boarding homes are surveyed by a state regulatory agency at least once a year and cited if certain conditions are not considered safe. Those cited must correct the deficiencies. Copies of the surveys are available from the administrator. If you are hesitant to check with the administrator, consult your state department of health for a copy. (For facilities certified by Medicare, certain state Social Security offices can furnish a copy.)

When visiting a skilled nursing facility or intermediate care facility, bear in mind that many nursing homes look like hospitals or institutions. They are not private homes. Since the people residing in them need medical care, nursing homes must be equipped and staffed to provide it. Visitors may see patients with nose tubes for feeding purposes or patients bound to their wheelchairs because of confusion. Unpleasant smells and sounds are also disheartening. These are often part of nursing home life, however, and it is rare to find a place which does not present such scenes.

Preparing a Checklist

You might want to devise a checklist of all the services, furnishings, and programs which should be in a nursing home. In fact, the licensing agencies have already done so. Therefore, instead of checking the mattresses and the hot water, evaluate each facility in light of the needs of the person who will be moving in. If it's your mother who needs nursing home placement and she likes certain foods, look at the menus and witness a serving of lunch or dinner. You can also find out whether your mother can have her own food preferences. If, on the other hand, your mother likes all kinds of foods (or, by chance, does not like most dishes no matter how they are prepared), you should focus on other concerns. If she likes to spend time visiting with other women, has special craft interests, or enjoys religious services, you should inquire with the staff about such opportunities or programs. In fact, ask the staff to describe a typical day. Even better, ask another visiting family member to describe a typical day. For those who wish to follow a checklist for choosing a nursing home, the U.S. Department of Health and Human Services has published one in the pamphlet called "How to Select a Nursing Home."[2] Your local hospital association may also have a checklist.

Regardless of how thoroughly you may try to select an appropriate place of residence, it's hard to anticipate every feature related to a comfortable daily existence. In addition to the criteria noted above, try to determine whether or not you or your relative will feel comfortable with the staff. If there are any distressing occurrences observed during the initial visit, review them with the administrator. Remember, though, that the nursing home is a social situation. Use tact and discretion in making your comments. You should also evaluate whether or not the staff seems helpful and reassuring.

Do not, however, make the mistake of anticipating opposition from the nursing home staff. You'll probably be pleasantly surprised. But do be prepared to express your relative's needs (and your own) clearly and to give careful thought to your requests. Many family members are hesitant to bring up concerns, fearful that they will look like troublemakers. Simply stay calm and voice your concerns precisely. You are asking for help. Most people do respond to a request for assistance when it's clearly voiced in a calm, caring manner. If your meeting goes badly, you'll need to consider your alternatives.

Checking the Costs

The monthly cost of nursing home care should cover room, board, housekeeping services, general nursing care, dietitian services, and personal care. Extra costs such as physician services, pharmaceutical services, physical therapy, and diagnostic tests may be incurred, however, along with beautician and dry cleaning services. Before you admit your family member, make sure you fully understand the daily rates, the cost of items not included, and your relative's eligibility for Medicare or Medicaid.

Making the Decision

While many staff take their responsibilities quite seriously, some do not. Choosing a nursing home means choosing additional family members for yourself and your relative. You want to choose a family that will encourage your relative to participate in important decisions and share happy occasions. Making this choice cannot always be based on objective criteria such as how many towels or blankets are allowed each patient. It may be just as helpful to rely on general impressions after meeting the staff and observing their interactions with patients.

In selecting a care home or boarding home, the same considerations apply as in the selection of a nursing home. Care homes, like boarding homes, are usually family operations, and there may be even greater intimacy between the patients and the staff. Again, be sure to select a facility suited to the older person's *needs*. Visit the facility, preferably with your relative, and meet with the care home operator. The visit can be evaluated in a manner similar to nursing homes. You should request information on a typical day and judge how comfortable you and your relative feel about the care home operator personally as well as professionally.

You will be fortunate if you do have an opportunity to select a nursing, care, or boarding home. Often there is no opportunity for selection at all. If there is a shortage of beds at a certain level of care, you may have to accept whatever facility has the first available bed. Moreover, there may be only one or two places able to handle your relative's specific medical and behavioral problems. This does not mean, however, that there is nothing you can do to ensure that your relative receives the best possible care.

What About "Bad" Nursing Homes?

Over the last twenty years, there have been published reports, news accounts, and congressional investigations concerning the deplorable conditions in our nation's nursing homes. Descriptions have appeared in the news media of residents being deprived of all their money, of patients being beaten or left tied in chairs for entire days, of facilities which are unsafe and unsanitary, and of abusive or negligent staff. One way to observe the facility being considered is to visit and check for yourself.

Bear in mind that facilities are not good or bad forever. The care provided can improve or decline. Relatives do influence what happens inside these health care facilities. Nursing, care, and boarding homes are not separate from the community; they are supported financially and socially by community people.

Institutions, more than smaller, family-operated care and boarding homes, are often described as being "outside the community" as if they were isolated in remote places. This, however, is not an accurate picture. Care providers are a necessary part of the community because of their special ability to look after the ill and disabled.

If after having selected a facility you find the place unsuitable either to yourself or to your relative, there are several steps you can take. First, you can move your relative out. If this drastic step seems premature, discuss your concerns with the staff to learn whether changes can be made or there are reasonable explanations for the conditions. It may not be possible for a facility to modify all its practices to suit individual preferences, but the staff should be able to indicate why specific policies are followed. Again, be clear about your concerns and stay calm when expressing them.

Or you can contact the state licensing agency and complain about the facility. Complaints can also be lodged with the ombudsman program at your state's office on aging. The ombudsman/advocate is an independent and politically neutral examiner who investigates complaints made by (or on behalf of) patients and residents against long-term-care facilities and the agencies which regulate them. All information is treated as confidential. If a complaint is verified, the facility is requested to make corrections or provide an explanation within a reasonable period of time. While the purpose of the ombudsman/advocate is to examine complaints, the goals are also to provide an effective means to ensure that the patient or resident is given a sense of participation and self-determination. The ultimate goal is to improve the quality of care.

How Can Nursing Homes Be Improved?

Despite popular wishes to have as many older persons as possible live outside of institutions in private homes, there are people whose medical, psychological and social needs cannot readily be met in the family home. Nursing homes and other care facilities fill a specific need. When not abused by community people as dumping grounds for unwanted people in ill health, they provide an essential function in a community's social and medical life.

How can facilities be made into places that people *want* to visit and, if necessary, live? The best way is for the public to become involved in the daily activities of these facilities. Almost all large places need volunteers. Although you may not be able to volunteer any time except to visit a relative or friend residing in a nursing home, this in itself is helpful to the patient as well as the staff. The staff can see that someone else cares about the patient and, moreover, that someone else will appreciate the staff's work or point out their carelessness. Visitors can also help employees and operators of facilities view patients as members of the community with strengths as well as disabilities.

Many long-term facilities have family/patient/resident councils which meet regularly with staff to discuss mutual concerns, plan programs and activities, and share information. Some facilities publish newsletters to introduce new staff, explain the services of the different departments in the facility, and pass on chatty information about the patients or residents and their activities.

There are support groups in the community—such as the Alzheimer's Disease and Related Disorders Association and Alcoholics Anonymous—which provide information and support to families whose members have such problems. They may be helpful in advocating changes in the nursing home. Look in the newspapers for notices of meetings or inquire at your local information and referral agency.

Sometimes visits can be uncomfortable occasions for family or friends who do not know how to spend time with someone who is ill or confused. Consult with the staff to learn ways of improving your visits. (Specific techniques which might be useful in visiting relatives are described in the next chapter.) It should be stressed that if the facility is to offer high-quality care for a relative or friend, then we must become involved by visiting and discussing our concerns with the staff. Nursing, care, and boarding homes are as good, or as bad, as we choose to make them.

Notes

The author wishes to thank Dr. Patricia Snyder of the Hawaii State Department of Health for her assistance.

1. "A Senior Citizen's Lament," *The Congregational Home's Residential News,* Brookfield, Wisconsin, December 1980.

2. *How to Select a Nursing Home,* HCFA–30043 (Washington, D.C.; Health Care Financing Administration, December 1980). [For information, send request to the Superintendent of Documents, U.S. Government Printing Office, Washington, D.C., 20402, and specify the name of the publication.]

17

Visiting Your Relative in an Institution

PATRICE MURPHY BAIN
VICTORIA GREENE
BERNADETTE LEDESMA

"I don't know why we bring the grandchildren. Grandmother doesn't seem to remember who they are and she even gets me mixed up with Lois, my older sister," one family member recently commented. Another confided: "I don't like to come too often. He has to understand he has to stay here and that this place is now his home." Another family voiced their frustrations this way: "Dad is so senile! He talks about the past over and over again. Sometimes I find him talking to our mother who has been dead seven years." Still another, a woman of forty-two, talked slowly and despondently about her aging mother: "All she does is lie in bed and stare. I don't know what she's thinking about, if she even knows who I am or if I've said the right thing. Frankly, I don't know why I keep visiting!"

These are common reactions we hear from families after a visit with an aging relative in a nursing home. The underlying message seems to be this: We want to visit, but the visits either drive us away or make us feel depressed and guilty. Can anything be done?

Feelings About Institutionalization

Institutionalization holds different meanings for the entire family. Coming to terms with these feelings is often an involved, painful, and difficult process. While the decision to enter a long-term-care facility is often an intense emotional experience for the aged parent, its impact is also felt among family members. The older relative's fear of abandonment is often matched by the family's feelings of guilt, sadness, and helplessness.

Aging, of course, is a natural process. Without the problem of illness, old age can be a time of life as happy and fulfilling as any other. Serious illness is always devastating, though, and the chance of becoming ill increases with age. One must realize, therefore, that the need for long-term care in an institution is usually a result of an individual's physical and emotional disabilities—not a reflection of how much or how little she is loved. In the past, families were criticized for placing their parents in nursing homes. Society judged them as uncaring children who were dumping their parents into institutions. While some people are in fact uncaring, these families are small in number. Studies have proved again and again that families turn to institutional care only after their elder's health has deteriorated to the point where the family can no longer provide the care that is needed. Most families do not abandon their elders. In fact, many continue to go to great lengths to assist their aging parents with shopping, laundering clothes, and other activities even after institutionalization.

There may come a time when a parent's physical and mental health needs are best met in an institution. This decision should be reached only after a careful assessment by the physician, all members of the family, and, most important, the older person. It is no one's fault if an older family member reaches this stage in life and thus there is no place for blame. It is common, however, for feelings of guilt and doubt to persist, and families may find themselves wondering, "Could I have done more?" or "Did I do the right thing?" Such feelings may prevent families from enjoying their visits at an institution. If they are not resolved, visits may become a dreaded event or simply be continuously postponed. Families are not alone with their unhappy feelings. Their older relatives are experiencing feelings of separation and isolation from friends and a past way of life. Understanding an older family member the way she is now and accepting that no one is responsible for her illness can assist the family in improving the quality of visits. Accepting the limitations, disabilities, and behavioral changes as well as one's feelings toward these changes is difficult, but it is the first step toward improved communication. Families tell us that two areas cause them great anxiety with their aging relatives: communication and enjoying visits at a long-term-care facility.

The Art of Communication

Every person holds an estimate of her own worth or worthlessness—her self-esteem or self-concept. For older adults, more than for younger persons, these feelings of worth—or worthlessness—are based on their social interactions.[1] Their interaction with others takes on new importance as the responsibilities of employment and childrearing drop away and their ability to enjoy a hobby or maintain a home weakens. Communication is one way to improve a person's self-esteem.

What is communication and how does the institutional environment affect communication patterns? Communication is a vital process in life allowing for growth, intimacy, and understanding. In its simplest context, it is the exchanging of information.

Many families tell us that communicating with their aging relative in an institution is similar to learning a new culture. There is a new language to be learned—that of medical and health terms—and there are new customs to be followed. A friend of ours visiting his father in a nursing home was surprised recently when he observed his father in a line of wheelchairs waiting to take a bath. "I didn't know that was the way it was done," he told us. Becoming familiar with your parent's treatment plan, medical orders, and house rules will help you to feel more comfortable in the facility. The older family member must also become familiar with this new culture. Sharing this information together will help both of you to understand that adherence to certain rules does not have to mean a total loss of independence.

Family involvement and support continue to be crucial to the older relative's well-being. A major way to show support is to communicate—to talk to the person intimately, warmly, naturally. Admission into an institution often signals the transferring to the nursing home staff of responsibilities for total physical care once held by the family. You probably will no longer be the one to bathe your relative, feed her, or provide the multitude of aids you did prior to institutional care. You do not, however,

relinquish your responsibilities as a caring relative. You must
continue to provide the emotional support and opportunities
for your relative to express feelings and share family events.
You can ensure that her needs are met by informing the staff of
her likes and dislikes and sharing other information that can
alleviate the stress often associated with institutional life.

Why Is Institutional Life Stressful?

Any move to a new place of residence can be stressful. We leave
old friends behind and must learn how to get around in a new
setting. Research has shown that environmental and residential
changes do create stress. It is no wonder, then, that admission
into an institution is stressful. The Ebenezer Center for Aging in
Minneapolis has listed some of the reasons why a person admitted into a long-term-care facility may experience stress and
anxiety.[2]

First, and perhaps foremost, an institution is not a home and
will never be able to duplicate the personal qualities of a home.
While this shortcoming, to a certain extent, is understandable
when you consider the numbers that must be bathed, fed, and
cared for, it is still unpleasant to realize that personal desires
may not be considered. Second, nursing home residents are
usually segregated from younger age groups and from friends
and family members. Third, entering an institution can make
some people feel rejected and can represent a loss of status. For
example, an elderly Japanese man recently admitted into a
long-term-care facility became withdrawn and depressed. After
a great deal of staff discussion, a Japanese aide was able to
decipher the man's state. It seems he was ashamed that his
oldest son was not caring for him at home. In his culture, the
eldest son is responsible for his parent's welfare. By placing his
father in an institution, the son had embarrassed his father
among his peers. When the son's help was enlisted, he was able
to assist his father with his feelings by reassuring him that his
health needs necessitated his residence in the institution.

The fourth reason institutional life is often stressful has to do
with independence. Living in an institution can result in a loss
of independence and control over one's life. It is a real challenge for facilities to provide their residents with opportunities

for growth and independence. Fifth, there is often a loss of former roles after institutionalization—consider, for instance, the community civic leader who no longer feels part of the community he once helped to build. Sixth, choices are often limited and there's often a lack of privacy. And, last, living in a nursing home can symbolize one's approaching death.

Although these characteristics are not necessarily true for all facilities, placement in an institution can present many of these changes for older relatives. Not only is the facility itself stressful, but the family may be undergoing its own stress. The move from home to institution creates a new set of opportunities, responsibilities, and, at times, problems for the older person and family. Rarely is the move to an institution seen as a joyous time for parent and child. Mixed emotions of guilt, anger, frustration, and depression are common reactions to placement—especially in the first few weeks of institutional care. Anger may be directed at staff because of feelings of frustration at the situation. Other families experience a sense of personal failure toward their responsibilities as children as well as friction between brothers and sisters who "should have helped" but didn't. There may be a sense of hopelessness and disorganization, too, culminating in questions of whether or not placement was the right thing to do.

Once the family accepts placement as the most appropriate choice for their elder, however, there is a reorganization of the parent/family relationship. Of course these stages may vary. Some families dwell on one stage longer than the other. Some never do accept the placement, depending upon the past relationship and integrity of the family members. It is important to recognize that these feelings are often the natural result of the stress related to placing a relative in an institution. With understanding and love they can be resolved.

Improving Communication While Visiting

Certain techniques used by staff working with older persons can lead to effective communication. It should be pointed out, however, that not all persons residing in institutions require different communication styles. Rather, these various approaches can be considered guidelines to assist you in becom-

ing more comfortable with the facility and the changing needs
of your elder with the result of more effective communication.

Reality Orientation

The recreation therapist was observed one day as she began her
morning exercise program. "Good morning, Mrs. Swanson,"
she said cheerfully. "My name is Sue, and I'll be leading your
exercise program here at the Harbor Valley Nursing Home. I
hope you'll be able to participate on this very sunny day. It's
nine-thirty and we'll exercise together until ten. How are you
feeling?" (She waits for a response.) This technique, called *reality orientation*, is one method that repeats basic familiar information to the elderly person until she is able to retain it and use
it comfortably. Its goals are to reduce the confusion, disorientation, social withdrawal, and apathy so characteristic of the
institutionalized elderly.[3] It is used to help the older person
keep in touch with reality and the environment and must be
done continuously.

How can you use this technique? When you visit your elder,
use her name and mention the date and where she is. If necessary, state who you are. Review your own activities of the day
and inquire about her day. Repeat these questions every time
you visit. Bring in a calendar for your relative and cross off the
days that have passed. Circle the date of your next visit and
make sure you do visit on that day. Don't bombard your relative
with a dozen questions. This would jar anyone, especially
someone who is already confused. Lawyers know all too well
that asking a barrage of questions one after another can confuse
even a solid witness. Reality orientation is not a test but an aid
to help your elder remember important persons, places, and
events.

Reminiscing

Reminiscing is another approach that can improve communication. Reminiscing allows the person to talk about past events
without being accused of being senile. The listener must help
the older person tie in the past event with the present. Recently
a family member came to see a social worker and was feeling
frustrated and angry. He said that staff were adding to his
mother's confusion by encouraging her to talk about the days

when she was young and a housewife and mother to her family. "She's living in a dream world," the family member complained. The social worker gently disagreed. She was able to explain how a few appropriately worded questions could be used to keep his mother in touch with the present.

The social worker then suggested that he share his memories of childhood with his mother and explain what it's like for him now that he's an adult. In this way, he would help his parent to acknowledge that her middle-aged son has now grown up. The social worker also suggested that he gently remind his mother of the present while concentrating on *her* feelings. For example, the older adult who consistently tells her family she is waiting for her dead husband to visit is really telling them she is lonely and misses him. The family may gently remind her of this fact and then spend more time reminiscing about their father. Now the mother has a way to share her feelings and her grief—something far more important than remembering a correct date or place.

The goal of reminiscing is to recapture feelings that no longer exist or are difficult to express, such as loneliness, fear, or even love and happiness. Reminiscing can be as simple as talking about the past and associating it to the present. Remember: We *all* like to reminisce. Who doesn't like to talk about the "good old days"?

Be a Friend

Another way to improve communication is to treat your parent as a friend. Talk *to* her, not at her; and, even more important, *listen* to her. To promote a conversation, ask questions that cannot be answered with a simple yes or no. When talking to your elder, take into account her limitations, whether it is a vision or hearing impairment or other disability. Surprises often happen when middle-aged children talk to their parents as friends. Families often tell us how interesting their parents are once they talk to them as people.

Common Problems

Sometimes communication problems can persist even with the best intentions. What can you do when your relative begins each visit with the following statements?

- *"You don't visit enough."* You can compare calendars and try the following. "We all have hectic lives, so let's make appointments. If you have bingo on Wednesday and I have to pick up Joey at Little League, what about Friday?" Put an "X" on the date and agree that it is reserved. The important thing is that both of you will know this is your time to be together.
- *"You only visit when you have nothing else to do."* No one likes to feel as this older woman felt. Rather than scheduling your visit *last*, plan in advance for your special time together. It also helps to say no to other demands. A friend of mine put it this way: "One day I realized I was allowing other demands to take precedence over the time with my mother. I gained a great deal more time by saying no to the PTA, to the League of Women Voters, and to being the only chauffeur for our daughter's group of friends." It is hard to say no, especially when certain requests on our time such as running for president of the Lions Club may be flattering. You need to ask yourself, "Is my relationship with my aging relative important? If it is, what decisions can I make, what priorities can I set, to show it?"
- *"Where are the children?"* What do you say when the real answer is: "They hate this place. It scares them. I can't drag them here." The fear of aging and debilitating illness is not only a fear of the young. It crosses all age groups. What can you do about it? Encourage your children to become acquainted with older people who are well so they'll be able to distinguish sick older people from all other elders. Have them bring something to do while you visit so they can become used to the facility. Plan the visit around a theme including your children. What about an old photo album? Encourage empathy and respect. Talk to them about the way your parent was and try to point out that they are still the same person. Remember that your children are watching you. Are they mimicking your own discomfort about aging? Emphasize that "being there" is a gift to their grandparents.

One woman whose son refused to visit the woman's mother broke the ice when she told him: "It's hard for me, too, to come here and see Mom this way. But I love her. She was always here for me when I needed her just as I try to be here for you when you need me. Now I need you to help me with this visit." Without a word, her son accompanied her and became a support to his mother again.

Another difficult situation is the lack of verbal response when visiting. There may be many reasons for this. As an illness strikes, complications may occur in speech and language. Sometimes making the effort to converse is so difficult for the older person that she withdraws into apathy and depression. This may be a way of coping. The person may be severely confused. Families must supply encouragement, understanding, and patience. Continue to talk aloud to older relatives even if you doubt their comprehension. Another approach may be to use the senses to communicate. Touch her blouse and tell her it's pretty. Have her touch yours. Bring in a tasty snack that is sour or tart and make faces together! (Check with the nursing staff for diet approval.) Bring in fresh flowers or body lotion and smell them together. Take her for a walk or wheel her around if she is wheelchair-bound. Enjoy nature together. While you are strolling, point out new sights and sounds. When back in her room, play the radio and find a song you can tap your feet to or beat two sticks together.

Communication approaches take time to master. But with love and respect, patterns of relating can be improved to the benefit of visitor and patient alike. Don't give up! Ask staff members for suggestions and assistance. Talking about your difficulties may help you to cope with them.

The Value of Visits

The need to be placed in an institution is a result of a person's physical and mental disabilities and the lack of community and support services available in the home. The potential problems surrounding residence in an institution can be compounded when the person feels separated from family and past ways of life. You can prevent isolation by visiting older adults in care facilities. According to Betty McMeekin of North Texas State University for Studies in Aging, family and friend visits to older family members improve the resident's health and spirit more than any other treatment approach. The resident's interest in appearance and in the future can be stimulated. Moreover, feelings of isolation and separation from the world beyond the nursing home can be reduced, and, as a result, self-concept can be improved.[4] Other gerontologists (those who study the process of aging) note that maintenance of a long-term intimate relationship is closely associated with positive mental health in nursing homes.[5] Even when the institution has opportunities for socializing among its residents, a visit from family or friends can still be of great benefit to a resident's self-esteem and happiness.

Why, then, do some families find visiting their elderly relative in a nursing home so frustrating and difficult? There are three major reasons: a lack of understanding of aging, a failure to understand the limitations and disabilities associated with the aging process, and unplanned visits which can lead to boredom.

Lack of Understanding

The first problem experienced by families is the lack of true understanding or empathy toward their aging relative. Unless we are old, it is difficult to imagine what being old is really like. It helps for all involved to understand *why* the person has been placed in a facility. An understanding of the aging process and of diseases and disabilities is helpful in becoming more sympathetic toward your aging relative. Ask yourself: How would I feel if I couldn't raid the refrigerator at night any more; if I couldn't walk anymore; or if I had no privacy? Learn all you can about aging as a natural process as well as the specific diseases of your elder. This knowledge will help you to adjust to the new problems and, in turn, help your relative adapt to the changes in her body and living situation.

Limitations and Disabilities

A second consideration in preventing frustration during visits is an understanding of the capabilities and limitations of the institutionalized person (as well as the limitations of the visitors). Everyone, including families, has limits. Once these are accepted, it is possible to work out a compromise concerning visits. Not everyone is comfortable with individual visits, for example. Accept this without guilt. Many institutions organize group activities that are as enjoyable to the resident and visitor as private visits.

It is possible to improve the quality of care that a parent receives in several simple ways. Most care facilities, for example, develop individualized patient care plans that are discussed at resident care meetings. At these meetings, the older person's progress and goals are talked over. These meetings provide an excellent opportunity for families to get acquainted with staff. You will learn your parent's capabilities and progress in physical, occupational, and recreational therapies. The professional participants at these meetings find the family's comments very helpful in planning goals for the patient; therefore, attendance at the meeting is an asset to both family and staff. This translates into more effective care.

Besides attending the resident care meetings, you may be able to attend your relative's individual or group therapy sessions. Her therapist will let you know when visiting is permissible. Not only may family attendance motivate your relative, but it may also be possible for you to go through the specific activities with your parent, within or outside the regular therapy session, if allowed by the therapist and approved by the physician.

Unplanned Visits

Apart from empathy and accepting limitations, a positive attitude toward visiting can be promoted by *planning* the time spent together. Just as other social functions are planned—lunch with friends, a dinner invitation, a movie date—so should your visits with your parents be planned beforehand. Feelings of frustration and wondering "what else will we talk about?" can be reduced if visits are planned ahead of time. The objectives to be accomplished during the visit should be suited to your relative's condition. Certain activities should be approved in advance by the nursing staff if they are particularly vigorous. A favorite activity for many older adults is an outing—but the visitor must be aware of the institution's policies. A Sunday drive, a trip to the hairdresser, or just a wheelchair stroll can provide a welcome change of pace and scenery. The popularity of outings among older adults in institutions is reflected in the overwhelming demand for this kind of activity at local facilities—chances for going on an outing must be rotated among the residents to allow everyone the opportunity.

Suggestions

Here are some general suggestions that may help you make your visits meaningful and fun for both you and your relative:

- Include her in family gossip and decision-making, even though she is physically separated from your home and other family members. Read letters from other family members. Bring in photo albums.
- Bring in fresh flowers and help to arrange them. Encourage your relative to decide where to place the flowers—in her room, a chapel, dining room, or community room.
- Work on a craft project together. If you can't think of an idea, ask the recreation therapist for suggestions. What about a family tree?
- Sing songs. Bring in a tape recorder with her favorite songs. A friend's mother can barely talk after a stroke but it is amazing how she can sing to the Frank Sinatra albums her daughter supplies.
- Play a game of cards, dominoes, table games, jigsaw puzzles. Bring in a newspaper.
- Plan visits at mealtime and eat together.
- Make plans for your next visit.
- On special occasions, check to see if parties are allowed in the facility. Plan with the administrator, the activity director, or nurses. Invite family and friends to meet at the nursing home.

Be prepared to take the lead in initiating activities or finding topics for discussion. At the end of the visit, give your parent something to look forward to by making plans for the next visit.

Not everyone is comfortable in a private visit, but there are other kinds of visits in most facilities. Many families do not realize that visits need not be confined to a resident's room. Changing the setting can be helpful. There are certain to be other areas available for visiting such as a television room, solarium, activity room, dining room, courtyard, or library.

Federal regulations require nursing homes to have a recreational therapy or activity program available to all patients, and with these activities come opportunities for visits in a group setting. Good recreation programs offer a variety of activities suited to a wide range of individual capabilities and interests. Some examples of group-oriented activities are movies, bingo games, church services, monthly birthday parties, and other special events. Some facilities offer classes for older adults in cooking, woodworking, dance, ceramics, health care, painting, and playing musical instruments. Moreover, there may be discussion or storytelling groups and various craft activities that you can attend with your parent.

One idea that has proved successful is the Family Social held at night or on weekends to encourage family visitations—a "Picnic in the Park," "Bingo Night," or a potluck dinner complete with entertainment. These popular events have stimulated family involvement in facility life, and this involvement has been of immeasurable benefit to staff and patients alike. Activities such as these can be suggested to the activity director or social worker at facilities that do not provide them. Staff are almost always open to suggestions from the family.

Understanding Special Needs

More than half the elderly persons in this country have at least one chronic condition such as high blood pressure, arthritis, diabetes, heart disease, or a mental disorder. A chronic illness is, by definition, one that is sustained over a long period of time and for which there is no cure. For these very reasons, chronic ailments can be depressing to the person who suffers from them. More than half of those with a chronic ailment also have some limitations on their activities. Activities, then, must be adjusted to meet the needs and the rights of the elderly. Recently we observed a family visiting their mother whose hands were contracted and deformed because of arthritis. Since they did not want to deny her the pleasure of opening her gift, they wrapped the package loosely, giving their mother the opportunity for self-expression and achievement.

It is painful to watch a parent's capabilities decline as limitations become more constricting on activities. The most important way a family member can demonstrate understanding for the elderly person's new situation is by planning visits that will neither underestimate her capabilities nor exceed her limitations. Often, after participation in various therapy programs, the capabilities of the older adult may have increased beyond her children's expectations. This progress can be another benefit of attending the therapy session.

Older adults who have certain illnesses and disabilities

require special understanding and skills from their families and others around them. Many people continue to enjoy their lives even with chronic ailments. But adaptations must be made. Comprehending how a chronic illness can affect your parent's emotional and physical health will help you to enjoy your visits and support your relative.

Here are some activities you can participate in when visiting a family member with chronic health problems:

- Listen to your relative when you are visiting. She may need to express fear, anger, and other inner feelings.
- Encourage your relative to make her own decisions.
- Encourage your relative to become involved in her own hygiene. For neglect of a paralyzed side, have her rub lotion or powder on the paralyzed side to encourage body awareness.
- If your relative has speech and language problems, bring a large pad or blackboard for writing. If she can't write, use pictures of common items to which she can refer: pillow, magazine, bedpan, floor, and directions such as up and down and right and left.
- Keep your relative as active as possible to build up or maintain endurance. If she's able to walk without support, encourage her to take short walks with you during your visits.
- Provide her with games (checkers, cards, puzzles, and the like), simple crafts (painting, drawing, tile work, and so on), or handwork (crocheting, knitting, and so forth) so that she may keep herself motivated and active. You may have to use adapted materials (such as paintbrushes with built-up handles for a weak or partial grip) so she can continue to enjoy her interests.
- Take photos of your relative and fellow patients, and share the pictures at your next visit.
- Play a radio softly or use a dim light at night to reduce restlessness, confusion, or irritability by providing sensory input.
- Talk to other visiting family members and observe them. Perhaps you can learn some of the methods they use in visiting *their* aging relative.

In summary, then, the aging process, while similar for all of us, is also unique for every individual. Many problems and conditions attributed to aging are actually due to specific diseases. We are not sick because we are old but because of certain disease processes. Society is also discovering the diversity of the older adults' problems and is attempting to find ways to make this period of life one of dignity. For older persons in nursing homes, high-quality care is greatly increased with the involvement of the family and their willingness to understand and accept their parent's disabilities. Involving the institutionalized elder in all aspects of family and community life can make visits to an institution more meaningful and more enjoyable. Remember the following points when you are visiting your relative in an institution:

- Families need not relinquish their responsibilities as caring relatives.
- Family visits are vital to your relative's health and spirit.
- Visits should be planned ahead of time for optimum pleasure and benefit.
- Visits should encourage the creativity and freedom that leisure can allow.
- The capabilities and the limitations of both resident and visitor must be understood.

Families are as much a part of institutional life as the staff and are vital in the support, survival, and livelihood of their relative. The family's participation and welfare should therefore be considered an essential part of the care plan in the institution.

Notes

1. R. MacNeil and M. Teague, "Social Psychological Aspects of Growing Old in America: A Research Review," *Perspectives on Leisure and Aging in a Changing Society* (Columbia: University of Missouri–Columbia, 1982).

2. Kathy Carrol, *The Nursing Home Environment* (Minneapolis: Ebenezer Center for Aging and Human Development, 1978).

3. J. Barnes, "Effects of Reality Orientation Classroom on Memory Loss, Confusion and Disorientation in Geriatric Patients," *Gerontologist* 14 (1974): 138–142.

4. Betty McMeekin, "Family Involvement in the Nursing Home Experience," *North Texas State University Center for Studies in Aging,* no. 5, p. 17.

5. MacNeil and Teague, ibid.

18

Grief and Bereavement

MEMREY CASEY

No one escapes death. No one escapes bereavement. No one escapes grief. And yet these three topics—death, bereavement, and grief—are still considered taboo by many people. People go to great lengths to deny and distort the reality of death for many reasons. For one, we are all powerless to prevent it. Many others have a fear of the unknown and unexpected. Death brings with it a state of loss and deprivation felt by those left behind which we term bereavement. Bereavement then gives way to grief, the interaction of a number of emotions sweeping over and threatening to engulf the person. Grief can consume all of one's time and energy. For the person experiencing grief, the emotions affect the mind, the body, and the spirit. These emotions should not be ignored or dismissed, however, for they need attention. Grieving, like dying, is normal. Grief seeks to give meaning to anguish. It is a means of healing us rather than wounding us further. While grief is a universal emotion, it is experienced by everyone in their own way.

How old will you be when you die? What would you like people to remember about you after you've gone? What do you think others will remember about you? These are questions that cross the minds of the young and healthy only once in a while or maybe never. But these questions come to the minds of the sick and the elderly quite often. Most of us occupy the world of the well, however, so it is hard to understand what the world of the sick and dying is like. The following observation confided by a 49-year-old dying woman may help you to understand her world:

Nothing has changed with my family. . . . They are acknowledging my dying, but it's so casual to them. . . . Death is so casual. . . . I am confined, useless, dependent on others for every need. . . . Overnight I find I can't do simple things. . . . Your whole life changes. . . . I don't want to do *anything*. . . . I think I do exist and yet I feel I do not exist. . . . This whole thing is unreal to me. . . . Physically I don't feel like I'm dying and yet I'm told I'm dying . . . weird. I can't believe life will end so strangely. I don't expect life to end so casual . . . like an animal, not a person. . . . I have mixed feelings about visitors—they're not in my shoes, so how do they know what I feel? No other person feels what I feel—not even my family. I go through this alone . . . they can't feel what I feel. . . . What I *can* do, like reading the papers and watching television, doesn't matter. . . . I love my family. They love me, and yet I'm detaching. . . . I am preoccupied with body functions. . . . I am frustrated. . . . I wonder if my mind is going to go. . . . I am two separate people—my mind can do *but* my body can't.

Living in the world of the sick can thus elicit many feelings: frustration, helplessness, inadequacy, dependency, fear of pain, fear of the loss of mental and physical capacities, sorrow over the loss of life's enjoyments including loved ones, and loss of one's future and dreams for the future.

Five Stages of Dying

Along with these feelings, the sick and dying person experiences several emotions. These emotions are best described by Elizabeth Kubler-Ross in her book *Death and Dying*.[1] A person does not necessarily go through these stages consecutively, however. People can skip stages or be in several stages at once. These stages and their corresponding emotions are also experienced by the family of the sick or dying person. They may help you understand how others feel when a loved one is dying.

The first stage of grief is *shock and denial*. During this time, the person simply cannot hear the diagnosis. Whether the ill person expresses it or not, she is saying, "No, not me!" The reality of the illness is too difficult to bear. At this point, a person may ask for the opinion of another doctor or for new laboratory tests, thinking that perhaps they were mixed up with someone else's. To understand shock and denial, try to remember something serious you have faced in your own life—a divorce, perhaps a serious loss, or an illness. How did you handle it? What do we all do when something tragic happens? We tell ourselves "I don't want to think about that right now." We put it off all day and then go to bed. We wake up the next morning and, while only half awake, we think we must have had a bad dream. Then we shake ourselves and find that we *are* awake and realize that it really did happen. At that point, we take it a step further. We decide whether we can deal with the situation now or must deal with it later.

The same thing happens to a person who is diagnosed with a serious illness. She will deal with it when she is ready. The important thing here is for others not to push; instead, simply be there—open and willing to listen when the time comes. (Be aware, however, that the time may *never* come.)

The next stage that the ill person experiences is *anger:* "Why me?" Wrapped up in this anger are feelings of guilt: "There must have been something I did or did not do in my life to deserve this." There may also be fear of the unknown: "What is going to happen to me?" Her anger may be directed at all members of the family because well family members represent all that the ill person is losing—energy, good health, and a future. There may be anger at God; anger at get-well cards when getting well is impossible; anger at flowers for making a room look like a funeral parlor. The person may become nasty and critical and say hurtful things that are not really meant; or maybe she won't talk at all. It is natural to feel anger when one is seriously ill. Sometimes it seems these feelings are directed at the ones loved most, the person's family. But this anger can be beneficial. She is not necessarily angry at any one person or thing. Rather, she is angry at what is happening to her. The daughter of a dying man confided:

> I think back and feel that maybe I was overreacting to certain situations regarding my dad's doctors, treatment, and chemotherapy, but that's just how I felt at that moment and I couldn't help it. I'm not angry any more with the doctors. . . . I think I was more angry with the cancer—at what it was doing to my dad— and with myself for feeling so mixed up about everything. I was just striking out at others who happened to be there, regardless of whether I agreed or disagreed with them.

Is there ever an answer to the question "Why me?" When someone who is dying asks this question, the best answer is an honest one. You simply say you do not know why. Tell her that it happens to people of every age and every culture. And even if there were an answer, it probably would not make it any better.

Another stage of grief is *bargaining*—when the person says "Yes, me, *but* . . ." Anything may be promised in exchange for a longer life. A man asks only that he may continue to live until June to see his only son graduate from college, and so he is kept alive until June. It doesn't necessarily mean that he will die after the son's graduation, however. After all, if he can be kept alive until June, why not then until December to enjoy Christmas? Most of us would probably do the same as this man. Most of us want to enjoy as many Junes and Decembers as we can.

Another stage of grief is *depression*—when the person admits, "Yes, this is really happening to me." There are two types of depression: reactive and silent (preparatory grief). In reactive depression, the person mourns all the losses she experienced in her lifetime. An elderly woman mourns the sheepdog she had to leave on the mainland when her family moved to Hawaii when she was a child. The memory is still with her. An 83-year-old man mourns the death of his grandson who died at the age of thirty-nine. In silent depression, or preparatory grief, future losses too are mourned. Death will cause one to miss many anticipated events. A 66-year-old woman mourns not being able to grow old with her husband, for instance. Another woman, still in her forties, mourns not being able to watch her children grow up. What can be done during this stage? A person who is depressed may not wish to talk a great deal. Touching, holding hands, or sitting in silence may be more important than words. Don't worry if you do not know exactly what to do or what to say. There is no perfect thing to do or say. Simply be yourself. And do not be frightened by the process.

The final stage of grief is *acceptance*—when the person is done talking. This is a time of victory and peace. Usually, the person wants the company of one or two close friends or family members who can simply be with her. This is a new level of experience. She now knows something about living and life that we, the well, do not.

Accompanying all these stages of grief is that of hope—hope that maybe the ill person will somehow live on, hope that the treatment will work or a cure will be found in time. Even though people accept death, few truly look forward to it.

How to Help

We turn now to ways in which you can help someone close to you who is dying. These suggestions have been offered by those in the dying process:

- Remember that people are alive until the moment they die.
- There is no best age to die.
- People do share feelings. It is a myth that they do not. Be aware of the person's feelings about dying and talk to your physician or other professional about them.
- You don't need answers to everything—the ill person knows there aren't answers to everything.
- Don't abandon the person. Her greatest fear may not be dying but dying alone.
- Don't say "I know how you feel." You don't. You can try to understand, but you don't know the feelings the person is experiencing.
- Find out where the person would prefer to die. Talk to your physician about this.
- Encourage her to seek counsel from competent advisors to get her affairs in order and make a will.
- Hospice programs can offer special support to the dying person and her family. Offered in the home or hospital, hospice care seeks to assuage the physical, emotional, spiritual, and social pain of dying.
- You can be the humor in her life. People want to smile even when they are dying.
- Listen and try to hear. But be comfortable in silence, as well. It is all right to have tears in your eyes. Learn how to touch.
- Talk to people in comas.
- If the person is in an institution and her roommate dies, talk to her about it. She will want to know what happened.
- Come to terms with your own death. Know your own feelings about death. These feelings are usually in flux and depend on where you are in your life.

Grieving does not stop after the person has died. The difference now is that the grieving is carried on by the survivor rather than the dying person. When death occurs, it is up to the survivor to deal with the feelings.

Transition

The following passage from *A Grief Observed* by C. S. Lewis may help you to understand the world of the survivor:

No one ever told me that grief felt so like fear. I am not afraid, but the sensation is like being afraid. The same fluttering in the stomach, the same restlessness, the yawning. I keep on swallowing.

At times it feels like being mildly drunk. There is a sort of invisible blanket between the world and me. I find it hard to take in what anyone says. Or perhaps, hard to want to take it in. It is so uninteresting. Yet I want the others to be about me. I dread the moments when the house is empty.

And no one ever told me about the laziness of grief. Except at my job—where the machine seems to run on as usual—I loathe the slightest effort. Not only writing, but even reading a letter is too much.

At first I was very afraid of going places where we had been happy—our favorite restaurant, our favorite woods. But I decided to do it at once—like sending a pilot up again, as soon as possible after he's had a crash. Unexpectedly, it made no difference. Her absence is no more emphatic in those places than anywhere else.

I have no photograph of her that's any good. I cannot see her face distinctly in my imagination. Yet the odd face of some stranger seen in a crowd this morning may come before me in vivid perfection the moment I close my eyes tonight. No doubt, the explanation is simple enough. We have seen the faces of those we know best so variously, from so many angles, in so many lights, with so many expressions—waking, sleeping, laughing, crying, eating, talking, thinking—that all the impressions crowd into our memory together and *cancel* out into a mere blur. But her voice is still vivid. The remembered voice—that can turn me at any moment to a whimpering child.

I went to tidy up her grave yesterday. Can I honestly say that I believe she now is anything? The vast majority of the people I meet would certainly think she is not. Though naturally they wouldn't press the point on me. Not just now anyway. What do I really think? I have always been able to pray for the other dead, and I still do, with some confidence. But when I try to pray for her, I halt. Bewilderment and amazement come over me. I have a ghastly sense of unreality, of speaking into a vacuum about a non-entity.

The reason for the difference is only too plain. You never know how much you really believe anything until its truth or falsehood becomes a matter of life and death to you.[2]

We see, then, that the world of the survivor can elicit many physical and emotional signs. Here are some of the more common ones:

- Feeling tired or exhausted
- Respiratory distress, sighing
- Digestive symptoms, change in appetite
- Troubled sleep
- Loss of sex drive
- Sense of unreality
- Persistent vision of the deceased
- Disorientation
- Loss of warmth in relationships

Grieving

In learning to leave an old life behind and finding a way to a new life, the survivor has to pass through a personal grieving process. This process entails four stages: shock and denial; intense grief; depression; and readjustment to new relationships and a new environment. Since grieving is personal, the time and intensity of these stages vary from person to person. Nor are the stages entirely separated chronologically; in other words, they are not necessarily followed in this order.

In the first stage, *shock and denial*, the person is on automatic pilot. Anxiety has not yet been activated. This is a time of disbelief and confusion. Many people describe it as a time of numbness when little is actually remembered of what has happened. Not only can the person not feel, but the person does not wish to feel. Since the mind is not ready to handle the reality of the situation, defense mechanisms come into play. Many times, in the stage of shock and denial, the person is sure that the whole thing is a mistake or a bad dream. Surely this cannot be happening!

The person then enters the second stage, *intense grief*, where there is open expression of a number of painful emotions. The grief brings with it intense emotions of anger, hostility, crying, despair, protest, guilt, resentment, fear, and panic. The expression of these emotions usually alarms others around the survivor. For the most part, however, there is no need for alarm. These are extremely sad but entirely natural reactions toward feelings of loss and pain. There may be anger toward people the survivor thinks may have contributed to the present situation. This anger may be directed at doctors and nurses for their handling of medical treatment, or it may be anger directed at the disease itself. It may also be expressed as anger toward the deceased for leaving the person alone to cope with all of this. Those left behind often feel hostile at the world and what life has done to them. There is a need to strike out at someone or something.

The guilt experienced during intense grief may come from feelings of "I should have done more, or I should have got her to a doctor sooner." Guilt can also develop when the survivor thinks about the relationship with the deceased. Every relationship has its frustrations, disagreements, and irritations. The survivor relives these troubled moments and feels guilty about them. "Why didn't I kiss him goodbye before he left the house?" one woman cries. Over and over she punishes herself by reliving this memory of an argument she had with her late husband. He died in an automobile accident and she never saw him alive again. Many people criticize themselves unrealistically and feel they should have been more even-tempered, more loving, more forgiving. The resentment that comes at this time may be directed at the couple across the street who still have each other or toward a teenage daughter who has a boyfriend.

Feelings of panic are often evident during this time. Survivors may convince themselves that something is wrong with them mentally, and perhaps physically. They begin to feel that because they concentrate on nothing except their loss, they must be losing their minds: What am I going to do now? Can I handle all of this? Will I make it?

During intense grief, the reality of the situation and the sense of loss are there, but at the same time the survivor wants to hold onto some fantasy. And so the survivor expects the phone to ring with a call from her partner or waits for the front door to open and to see her partner standing there. Many survivors report seeing the person who has died, hearing a voice, or sensing a presence in the room. Try not to dispute this. One day, you may want to share a similar experience with those around you. Try to concentrate on what the person is feeling as opposed to what she says she is seeing or feeling. One woman kept telling her daughters that her husband, who had recently passed away, would speak to her at night. Her daughters, wisely, encouraged her to share her grief with them, and eventually her visions went away.

When the person is stretched to the breaking point and feels as if she can't take anymore, a third stage sets in: *depression*. This is a time of apathy, disorganization, and loneliness. Often the survivor does not want to leave the house or apartment. Everything becomes an effort. The person appears to have no initiative. The meaning has drained out of much that was previously important. A man ceases to look forward to retirement. Without his wife, what is there to look forward to? Even with family and friends around him, he feels alone.

Do not push the person who is in this stage of grieving. Be available for the survivor, but let the person have time—time to figure out where she's been, where she's at, and where she's going.

The last stage of grief is *readjustment* to new relationships and a new environment. This is when the survivor lets go of old patterns and learns new ones. Freed at last from her bond with the deceased, the person lets go of old attachments and forms new relationships. The survivor's clarity in thinking returns. She also reestablishes a position in the world and begins to develop self-assurance and self-reliance.

During this period the person sees life more clearly than ever before. Those who are close to the survivor are valued with a greater intensity. Energies are now redirected to new things.

This completion of the grief stage does not mean that the person has forgotten the person who has died. One never forgets.

The memories will always be there. Everyone we have ever truly known lives vibrantly inside us. Grief simply means that no one can change what has happened and the survivor accepts this. But meaning can be given to those no longer with us. They have left a gift of themselves, and grieving helps us to find that gift.

There are certain signs of grief, though, where extra precaution is warranted. Suicidal thoughts or actions, postponement of grief, prolonged grief, or personality distortion in grieving are causes for concern by the family. Consult a physician, and possibly a therapist.

Easing the Pain

There are several ways we can support those who are experiencing bereavement and grief:

- Remember that the first year after someone's death is especially difficult. During that time, every holiday, anniversary, and birthday can bring sadness and renewed grieving.
- Give support to both sexes. Men go through the same feelings as women. Although they may not show as much outward emotion, the feelings are still there.
- The grief brought on by a sudden death may be more intense and last longer than that following a long-drawn-out illness. With sudden death, there is no time for preparatory grief. Survivors may therefore need family and friends to stay with them longer for support. The stress may be greater physically as well as emotionally.
- Give specific offerings of help to the survivor. Prepare a meal, take a child to school, clean the house. Close family members can help with the acknowledgment of gifts and letters of condolence.
- Don't be afraid to call the deceased by his or her name. For some reason, the deceased often becomes "him" or "her" to avoid pain (or so some think).
- Check back with the survivor a few weeks after the funeral. Most support has usually disappeared by then, but the need for continued support, attention, and love is crucial.
- Be a friend and a listener. Feelings and stories need to be told

and then told again. Somehow, in sharing stories about the person who has died, people can begin to make sense of what has happened and to relive the uniqueness of the person who has left their presence but remains in the heart.

- Encourage the survivor's strengths in handling life's events. Let her know she is sane and capable of making decisions.
- If you don't know what to tell her, say "I don't know what to say."
- Encourage the survivor to keep a written record of all transactions, because her mind is overloaded and may not initially be clear.
- Don't say "I know how you feel," because you don't. You may wish to understand but you never really know how someone else is feeling.
- It is all right (and may even be helpful) for the survivor either to write or talk to the deceased person. Telling the deceased things that should have been said can be therapeutic and relieve guilt.
- Don't be afraid to talk about the deceased to the survivor. Recalling a funny incident that happened with the deceased will remind the survivor that her loved one is being remembered.

The journey through these stages of grief during the dying process and the survivor's passage through the stages of grief and bereavement are normal and to be expected. These stages enable the dying person to say farewell and allow the survivor to bid goodbye to what has passed and to say hello to new beginnings.

Notes

1. Elizabeth Kubler-Ross, *Death and Dying* (New York: Macmillan, 1969).
2. C. S. Lewis, *A Grief Observed* (New York: Seabury Press, 1961).

19

Reflections of
Three Generations

COLETTE BROWNE
ROBERTA ONZUKA-ANDERSON

While many families do become the mainstay of support for their aging parents, the decision to provide care remains a personal one. The many concerns of old age—loneliness, physical and mental difficulties, financial worries—can result in your family member requiring your help. It is not unusual for middle-aged children to feel stressed as they attempt to fulfill the responsibilities of their various roles in life—that of husband or wife, parent, worker, friend, and now caregiver. Nor is it unusual for aging parents to feel they are burdening their children with their increasing needs.

Individualism is constantly espoused in American society, and dependence is seen as a negative trait in adults. And yet interdependence is more often a characteristic of caring families than dependence. We can learn much from families that are taking the opportunity of caring for an aging relative as a time for growth and togetherness.

We must stress, however, that the decision to care for a frail aging relative is a decision involving your entire family—your elder, your spouse, your children, and other siblings. It must be a family decision because it will affect everyone. Self-evaluation is necessary prior to making your decision. You need to ask yourself honestly: Am I dependable? Patient? Do I enjoy Mama? Do we get along? Am I a good listener? Will I get satisfaction from helping her? Do I want to learn new skills? Can I control my frustrations? Do I have the time? Will my family support me? And be involved? Do I have good health? Only you can answer these questions. You don't need to be a saint to provide home care, but you do need to be aware of your strengths and shortcomings so you can arrange for any additional help you need.

This chapter describes how one three-generation family is adapting to their new interdependence. The daughter's, mother's, and grandchildren's comments are presented so that their feelings and experiences may be shared with others. Helping a loved one who is lonely and in need, along with mutual exchange, is their story. We trust it will lend support to others contemplating such a decision.

The Daughter Speaks . . .

When I was growing up in a small town with a rural atmosphere, my only thought was to become independent and move to the exciting Big City. I never thought that I would one day be back at my parents' home, raising my children in the same environment I was raised in. The return home was a circuitous route; it was a seriously contemplated and deliberately planned move that took into consideration many feelings and events. I married at nineteen and shortly after my marriage moved to another state with my husband. Letters from my mother sounded as if she and my father were having the time of their lives doing all the things they could never do when my sisters and I were young. My husband, in the military for his career, and I spent many nomadic years in different parts of the country. Living away from family and the constant moving were not without problems; but I found the life enjoyable, interesting, and above all independent. Then suddenly my father passed away leaving my mother alone in the large family house.

For five years after his death she managed by herself, making constant adjustments. My sister, Jan, and I both lived out of state and yet we managed to make regular visits and help in whatever way we could. My other sister, Sharon, lived in a neighboring town and was readily accessible to her. But, on the whole, my mother learned to survive on her own. When my two sons were one and four, my husband was transferred to Korea for a one-year unaccompanied tour. My sons and I returned to our family home to live with my mother during this period. It was fun to be back home and to have the kids renew their bonds with their grandmother. I thought everything was fine since she seemed happy and content with what appeared to be a problem-free life. Now, when I look back, I realize there were many hints that life was not so perfect for her. But I was so busy with the children that some of the obvious things I should have noticed slipped right past me.

One day my mother told me quietly that she was thinking of selling the house. It was too large for her. It needed to be painted, the roof leaked, and even cleaning it was difficult. Her arthritis was also worsening and she was developing back problems. The physical and financial burdens of maintaining the house seemed overwhelming to her. To say the least, I was surprised!

My husband was intending to retire from the military in another year and a half, and it was time for us to make a decision on where to live and what to do. A new alternative suddenly hit me. What if *we* bought the family home from Mom? After discussing it with my husband, we offered to buy the house from her. In the many discussions that followed, we decided we would all live together in the house. We would assume all financial responsibilities for maintenance, and we made plans to construct a separate living area for her. Financially, it was ideal for us as Mother certainly sold it to us for a very good price. But it was also good for my mother as she could now remain in the home where she had spent most of her life. My husband still had one remaining military assignment to fill before retirement. My mother agreed to hold down the fort while we moved once again, this time to California. In retrospect, the solution sounds simple, but simple it wasn't! It involved a lot of hard thinking.

When I first broached the idea to my husband, he was totally in favor of it. I was the one who was somewhat reluctant. He was self-assured and wholly convinced that the arrangement would work out without major problems. I thought he was oversimplifying the situation. Although it was a very lucrative financial deal for us, I realized that once we moved back we could never move out without hard feelings. It was a permanent decision. The rewards were many but so would be the repercussions.

I gave the decision more serious thought than I did the decision to get married and have children. There are no romantic thoughts about returning home to live with one's parent—no bells ringing, no birds singing, just a lot of hard thinking. Although my mother was still physically independent, I wondered if I could handle the day when she required more care. I had been independent for many years and had established a good relationship with my husband and children. Could I return home and accept the role of daughter once again? How would three generations live under one roof? Would the children adjust? My husband can be quite stubborn. Could he and my mother live together? Would I end up being an interpreter for the two of them relaying messages between them because neither would give in? With retirement from the military, my husband would be faced with finding a new career. After being a housewife for so many years, I would also be returning to the job market. There seemed to be so many social and financial adjustments to consider. Once the decision was made, however, the three of us worked toward paving the way for the final move back.

I have to emphasize that all three of us made the decisions— my husband, my mother, and I openly discussed everything, and decisions were mutually agreeable to everyone. At times they weren't unanimous but through openly expressing our feelings and thoughts we recognized and appreciated the compromises that each other made.

And how did this work out? There is a happy ending to this tale. We have lived together for many years without any major problems. We all help each other out and work toward living as *one* family—not "my" family plus grandma. It was very important to my mother to be part of the family effort. When I returned to work, for example, she insisted on watching the children before and after school. I didn't want to burden her with two active boys and felt they should go to a sitter. But she insisted on sharing the responsibilities. Wherever she can lend a helping hand, she does so graciously and willingly. And we appreciate it.

Every family encounters crises and we're no different. But I find that it's not the big problems that are dangerous—it's the little ones. Somehow it's those little problems that can grow into big crises without your realizing it. Whatever problems we encounter, we make an effort to clear the air immediately and find a solution. My mother has a lot of friends and they love to chat on the phone. So, rather than inconveniencing each other, we installed a second private line—one listed under her name and one listed under ours. A private entrance was built for her living area so her friends come come to visit freely without feeling they were an imposition. When my mother's arthritis worsened and she began dropping dishes, we simply switched to the cheaper unbreakable type. In this way it doesn't matter if she drops any. There are no recriminations or criticisms. All of us, no matter how young or old, need reassurance and a vote of confidence. And I feel that if you can't say anything positive, don't say it. I still remember the day when my mother dropped one of my favorite crystal pieces while trying to clean. She was horrified and I was terribly disappointed—the piece was irreplaceable. After a few seconds of stunned silence, my son said, "It's okay—at least you didn't hurt yourself. You're more important!" From the mouths of babes. . . .

A common complaint among my friends living in similar situations with their parents is that Grandma or Grandpa always interferes when they discipline their children. We solved that problem by discussing it among the three of us and also with the children. While our values were fairly alike, we differed in our ways and methods. My husband and I tended to be stricter than Grandma. She was more protective and less inclined to let the boys go off on their own and be independent. We decided that when my mother was at home with the boys she was the sole authority and disciplinarian. When my husband and I returned from work, the disciplining problem was ours. For the children it was less confusing and discouraged them from pitting one against the other. They have learned to accept the differences and to adjust accordingly. One reason this arrangement has worked so well is that we support each other's decisions. I know there are times my mother feels I'm too hard on the boys, but she never butts in or contradicts me. If the boys look to her for sympathy, she simply says, "I'm sorry but your parents are right." It takes a special kind of person to say that.

In living together there are a lot of pressures and sacrifices. I find that I not only have the responsibilities of being a wife and mother but also those of being a daughter. Sometimes there just aren't enough hours in the day to satisfy everyone, but we all give and take and compromise. You can also lose a little of your privacy. There's nothing like having a heated conversation with your husband while your mother is looking on!

There are obvious benefits to living with your mother. People will always immediately comment, "You have a built-in babysitter!" She in turn receives comments like these from her friends: "Your daughter can take you everywhere! Your son-in-law sure keeps up with the house and yard!" Yes, there are lots of benefits. And we are careful not to take them for granted. It's a lot better to ask, "Mom, we'd like to go out this Saturday. Will you watch the boys for us?" than to say "We're going out—you can watch the boys."

The boys have grown up with my mother and have come to look at her not just as "Grandma" but also as a second mother. One of the many things I appreciate about my mother is her honesty and willingness to be open and forthright. Living with young children, who are curious and ruthlessly honest, takes a lot of patience and a certain thick-skinned approach. I winced the first time my son asked her, "Grandma, why is your skin all wrinkled?" or "Why are your fingers all crooked?" or even "When are you going to die?" She has answered them candidly and without hesitation.

I realize that as the years continue to pass, our relationship with each other will change. I can see some changes already from when we first moved in with my mother. My mother's arthritis is steadily worsening and as her physical independence is being curtailed, she finds it more and more difficult to be optimistic about each passing year. We make it a point to spend more time with her during the "down days" and do the special things that make her smile. The boys, who were very dependent on her when we first returned, are growing more independent. There are times when they don't want Mom, Dad, and Grandma to meddle in their affairs. I don't tell my mother she shouldn't let her feelings get hurt over it. After all, my husband and I get our feelings hurt, too. We try to adjust constantly— and I fully realize that with each year the boys will be more independent and my mother will become more dependent.

I feel we've been very fortunate with a supportive family. My sisters and their husbands and their children are very helpful. I do not hesitate in calling my sister and telling her that Mom is kind of down today and asking "Why don't you give her a call?" The entire family have reassured us that taking care of

Mom is not solely my husband's and my responsibility. They are there to help in whatever way they can.

What has really helped is our family's sense of humor. We try not to take everything too seriously. We have also been fortunate to have the time to plan, discuss, and make arrangements prior to a real crisis. From the time we decided to move back to the time we actually returned, we had time to build her living quarters, talk to the boys, and mentally prepare for a different type of family. Just as it took a lot of adjustment when we first began living together, we find that we need to keep adjusting. I hope we'll continue to adapt with the years.

The Grandmother Speaks . . .

After years of a busy life, my children were finally grown and married with families of their own. My husband and I were able to live, for the first time, without the financial worries of supporting and educating them. We were at that stage in our lives when retirement was close at hand and we were dreaming about indulging ourselves with a few luxuries. Then, one day, it all ended. My husband died unexpectedly and I thought it was the end of the world. Suddenly I was alone, the house was empty, and my life had turned completely upside down. I didn't know what to do. Well-meaning friends were full of advice: "You shouldn't live alone . . . it's dangerous. . . . You should move to your daughter's home and sell your house. . . . Don't sell your house . . . have your daughter move in with you. . . . Live alone and remain independent." I just didn't know what to do.

Of my three daughters, two were living out of state and my oldest daughter, Sharon, was living in a neighboring town. She and my son-in-law graciously invited me to move in with their family. But they expressed no desire to move into my home, even though it would have been a big help to them financially. They had just bought their home and, like so many other young couples, were saddled with a high mortgage. But it was their home and just as they were reluctant to move, I was reluctant also. I knew that I wanted to remain in my familiar neighborhood. I had so many friends there. So I decided to try it on my own. After a while, it got easier to live by myself and not to be afraid. As the pieces fell together, I began to enjoy my independence but the frustrations of maintaining the house never got easier.

As the years passed I came to realize several things. First of all, I knew I could not comfortably continue to maintain the house by myself and yet I still didn't want to leave my home and neighbors. Having one of my daughters move back home would be the ideal solution. But I also knew I would never *ask* them to come. I didn't want it to be an obligation on their part. The offer would have to come from them on their own. If the offer never came, then I would have no choice but to sell the house and move to an apartment.

Just at the time these frustrations were starting to really worry me, my youngest daughter returned to live with me while her military husband was in Korea for a year. She had two sons, eleven months old and four years old, and my quiet house suddenly was filled with noise and activity. Toward the end of that year she stayed with me, I talked to her about the possibility of selling the house. And then she and my son-in-law countered with what I wanted hear—they offered to buy the house and return to Hawaii when he retired from the military. It was during our conversations that we decided they would come back to live and I would remain in the house with them.

Initially I felt very relieved and happy that the problem was solved. But then I realized that everything in life wasn't that simple. Yes, the financial and physical responsibilities would be lifted, but I realized that I had come to love my quiet life and independence. I was filled with fear and doubts. I wanted the security of having someone there—to take care of the house, to figure out why the electricity suddenly went out, to take care of the painting and the trees in the yard. But I also knew that I didn't want to sacrifice my privacy. I had gotten used to eating when I wanted to eat, sleeping when I wanted to sleep, and doing things at my own pace. I wondered if I could live as part of the active young family. I just didn't know.

During the time after the decision was made but before my daughter and her family actually returned home, I gave it a lot of thought. First of all, I made it a point to talk to my other two daughters individually to tell them of the decision and arrangement. I wanted to make sure that neither of them would misunderstand or resent the change. I didn't want them to feel that their sister was "taking advantage" or "reaping all the benefits" by getting the house and property. Then I honestly discussed with my daughter and son-in-law my fears of losing my privacy. Although I was willing to give up the house, I still wanted to do certain things my way. My daughter also told me of her feelings—my son-in-law, too. As a result we all understood who was going to be doing what and we all reached agreeable solutions to our questions. For example, it was decided that my daughter's family would move into the house and they would build living accommodations for me attached to the original house. They left the planning and design of the addition up to me. It would have a bathroom, living room, and bedroom and also a separate sewing room since my hobby was sewing. The new living area included a separate outside entrance so my friends could come to visit without having to interrupt my daughter's family. Due to the zoning regulations, we could not put in a second kitchen—but that was fine with us since we had decided to cook and eat together. I agreed that my daughter would be in charge of the kitchen. She could change it around and set it up as she wished. My son-in-law staked his claim to the basement where he set up a workshop for his woodworking hobby. We all had our areas laid out.

We discussed everything—starting from the basic living arrangement to the actual division of chores. We didn't assume that everyone else knew what we wanted—everything was clearly stated to avoid misunderstanding. I agreed to keep up with my flowers while my son-in-law and daughter agreed to do the heavy yardwork such as the mowing and tree trimming. My daughter agreed to take care of the housecleaning. And on and on the list went. It may sound strange to some people, but I have to say that working everything out in this way helped us all to adjust to living together. There were still some rough spots but we worked them out right away. Everyone exercised a spirit of patience and understanding.

If I had to put down in words why I think this arrangement worked, I would have to say it was because we defined everything clearly. We decided who was going to pay for what—my daughter agreed to pay for all the groceries, all the house maintenance costs, and the property taxes. I would pay for my own telephone bills and so forth. It left no doubt about everyone's responsibilities and no one felt taken advantage of. Also, it was important to me to help, even though in a small way, with some of the finances.

Living together has had a lot of benefits. I can depend on them to be there and to help. I no longer have to worry about the house and the rising costs of maintenance—and the end result is that I can enjoy my life without financial worries. But there are drawbacks, too. The peaceful home is gone. The boys are typical boys and at times the noise is deafening. I've agreed to help my daughter with the boys while she and her husband are back at work, and I find that I'm not as young as I thought I was. Being with two energetic youngsters can make your blood pressure go up on certain days. But the benefits far outweigh the shortcomings. The love I share with my grandsons is priceless. I grew up with immigrant parents and never knew or even saw my grandparents, so I feel fortunate to share this relationship with my family. It's fun to help raise the boys as a grandparent—I remember when I was raising my children there never seemed to be enough hours in the day to work and keep up with the household chores. And there never was the luxury of being relaxed when it came to money matters. But with my grandkids, I can spoil them a little and do so many of those special things that they love.

I think it's interesting to see people's reactions when they learn I live with my daughter and her family. They're curious to see how it has worked out. And the questions follow, although subtle in nature, for they're still curious about how we manage. I think some of them are actually disappointed to learn that we live together comfortably. I think sometimes they want to hear it's a disaster because they perhaps feel misunderstood and unloved by their own children. But it *has* worked out well. One of my rules is even though there are disagreements and problems, they are to be discussed with the family *first* and worked out. After all, if they are not brought up, no one will know it's a problem and then a solution won't be found. In living together, what one person does affects the other and we've all learned to roll with the punches, laugh together, and even cry together. I feel fortunate to have such a good family. All my daughters are understanding and supportive. My grandchildren are loving. I am indeed lucky to be able to live confidently knowing that I can love them and they love me.

The Grandchildren Speak . . .

When we moved back to live with Grandma, my parents explained to us that things were going to be different. Until then we had just come back for vacations and then we would always go back to our own home. But this time it sure was different. We had a new home, new friends, new school, and things changed a lot. The house was big—and the yard was big—we could play football and baseball without any problems. And, for the first time, we got to really play with our cousins.

Life with Grandma has its ups and downs. When Mom asked us to write what it's like, we couldn't think of what to say. After all, life with Grandma is *life!*

Grandma is a neat person. She smiles a lot and she does a lot of special things for us. She always knows how to make special snacks that Mom can never copy. She sews our scout patches on our uniforms—if Mom had to do it, we'd be waiting forever. With Mom working, she doesn't seem to have enough time to get everything done. But Grandma is always there to help. Grandma knows how to make those yucky days turn into something special.

Grandma also has neat friends who seem to love little kids like us. There's one lady who makes super chocolate chip cookies for us. Grandma tells us we should always take the time to talk to "old people"—a lot of them don't get to see young kids as much as they want to.

But sometimes Grandma is not so neat. She seems to pester us a lot. She's always telling us to clean our rooms, empty the trash cans, comb our hair. And she has eagle eyes that can see and hear everything. Mom and Dad are always at work, so she's the one who knows exactly what we're doing. She always thinks we're younger than we are. Whenever we go anywhere she always reminds us to behave, to be careful, and she asks us a thousand and one questions. She thinks we're still little boys even though we are twelve and nine now. I guess it's hard for her to realize that we're growing up. Maybe that's because she's all grown up and she doesn't have to grow anymore—and once you stop growing you think others stop, too.

Sometimes we think she's nicer to our cousins than she is to us. She never seems to scold them or tell them what to do.

When we asked my mom why, she said that even though we're all her grandchildren, *we're* special because we live with her and see her every day. Our cousins are more like guests. There are times we wouldn't mind being like guests either. But then our cousins will tell us how lucky we are to live with Grandma —and they're right.

Grandma seems to be tired a lot lately. When we first moved back she used to go out a lot and visit her friends. Now she seems to stay at home more and more. We'd hate the idea of getting old and not being able to do all the things we want to. We know there are days when Grandma wishes she could run around like before. Mom and Dad tell us we should help her as much as we can. But that's a funny situation. She doesn't mind help in opening jars and carrying things—but sometimes she doesn't want help. I know if someone offered to do my chores for me, I sure wouldn't argue with them. I guess sometimes it's important to Grandma to know she can still do it.

Several years ago, the cub scout pack I belonged to visited a convalescent home during Christmas to take cookies and sing carols. My mother talked to me before I went and explained what I would see—people in wheelchairs, people who couldn't talk, and people who smelled of urine. It didn't hit me until I got there. Listening to words and actually seeing something are two different things. A lot of people there just wanted to touch us and hug us. When I returned, Mom asked us how we would feel if Grandma became sick and couldn't walk or go to the bathroom. We thought she was crazy—that would never happen to *our* Grandma. But now we can see that maybe it might happen—and, yes, we would help. But I hope it never happens. We love her.

Glossary

Active motion: Movement performed consciously by a person

Activity theory: Theory maintaining that satisfaction in old age is achieved by retaining middle-age activity levels; opposite of the disengagement theory

Acute: State of illness or disability that comes on suddenly and may be of short duration

Ageism: Prejudice or discrimination of one age group against another solely on the basis of age, usually directed against older people

Aging: General term used for various biological, psychological, and social processes and changes whereby a person acquires the socially defined characteristics of old age (see also *senescence*)

Aging population: General term applied to persons approaching retirement, usually persons over the age of sixty-five

Alzheimer's disease: Brain disease in which cell loss is prominent—the most common cause of organic mental impairment in the elderly

Ambulatory: Able to walk

Antibiotic: Drug that prevents disease-causing microorganisms from multiplying in the body

Aphasia: Loss of speech or language abilities due to brain damage that may be either permanent or temporary

Arteriosclerosis: Hardening of the arteries due to thickening of the blood vessel walls

Artery: Blood vessel that carries blood away from the heart

Arthritis: Term used to describe more than one hundred diseases; characterized by inflammation and destruction of the joints

Assessment: Gathering data in order to develop a plan of care

Atherosclerosis: Increased formation of fatty deposits and fibrous plaques that reduce the diameter of the blood vessel

Atrophy: Decrease in size of a normally developed organ or tissue, usually from disuse

Bedpan: Container into which a person defecates or urinates while in bed and unable to go to the bathroom

Bereavement: Stage of life that survivors experience after someone close to them has died; characterized by certain physical symptoms (shortness of breath, headaches, inability to sleep), psychological distress and depression, and changes in social role

Biological aging: Changes in body processes that occur with advancing age; changes may vary from person to person

Bladder (urinary): Membranous sac that serves as a container within the body for holding urine

Body alignment: Proper arrangement of the body in a straight line; placing of body parts in correct anatomical position

Body language: Body gestures that function as a form of communication

Body mechanics: Correct use of the body to do work while avoiding injury and strain

Cancer: A disease characterized by uncontrolled growth of abnormal cells

Cane: A device that can be used for weight bearing or balance to assist when walking

Cardiac arrest: Absence of heart motion

Cartilage: Tough connective tissue that holds bones together

Case management services: A function provided by specially trained social workers and nurses to assist frail older adults identify and obtain the services they need to remain at home

Cataracts: Clouding of the eye lens that can interfere with vision in one or both eyes

Catheter: Tube inserted in a body cavity, usually to withdraw fluid such as urine

Central nervous system: Part of the nervous system; made up of the brain, nerves, and spinal cord

Cerebrovascular accident (CVA): Blockage of a blood vessel within the brain leading to death of brain tissue; a stroke

Chronic: State of disease that lasts a long time and has no known cure

Chronological aging: Use of a birthdate in defining a person's age and appropriate role and function in society

Circulation: Continuous movement of blood through the heart and blood vessels to all parts of the body

Coma: State of deep unconsciousness caused by disease, injury, or drugs

Commode: Portable toilet with a pan or pail into which a person can urinate or defecate

Communicable: Spread from one person to another

Constipated: Unable to move bowels without difficulty

Contagious: Readily transmitted by contact

Continuity theory: Theory which states that the degree of the older person's involvement with society is constantly adapted to meet the changes of age

Custodial care: Institutional care providing for basic physical and emotional needs

Daily living skills: Tasks done each day to meet a person's basic needs such as bathing, eating, and grooming

Day care: A day program of recreational and social activities for older adults in need of supervision

Decubitis ulcer: Open wound which occurs from lack of blood supply to an area usually located on a bony part of the body; a bedsore

Dehydration: Condition in which the body is suffering from a lack of fluid

Dementia: Confusion and memory loss

Dependency: Social state in which a person must rely on others for well-being and safety

Depression: Extreme sadness and despair; a common psychiatric problem among the elderly

Diabetes: Condition that develops when the body cannot change sugar into energy because of deficient insulin

Diagnosis: Physician's identification of a disease producing a specific condition

Diarrhea: Abnormally frequent discharge of liquid fecal matter

Disability: Loss of the use of a part or parts of the body; may be permanent or temporary, partial or complete

Disengagement theory: Theory which states that older people disengage, or withdraw from society in response to a decrease in capacities

Diuretic: Drug or substance that increases the flow of urine

Edema: Abnormal swelling of a part of the body caused by fluid collection in the area; usually occurs in the legs

Empty nest: Period in life, usually middle age, when the children leave home

Escort services: Services that accompany and assist older adults to reach necessary services and/or places

Extension: Straightening of an arm or leg

Extremities: Medical term for the arms, legs, hands, and feet

Fahrenheit: System for measuring temperature. In the Fahrenheit system, the temperature of the body is 98.6°F

Feces: Fecal matter; bowel movement

Filial responsibility: Willing support or care given by children to their aging parents

Friendly visiting: In-home visits to isolated older adults to provide opportunities for social contact

Functional: Capable of being used

Geriatrics: Pertaining to medical treatment of diseases characteristic of the aged

Gerontology: Science and study of aging, including biological, psychological, and sociological processes

Gerontophobia: Fear of aging or older people

Glaucoma: Condition in the eyes causing damage to the optic nerve and resulting in loss of vision

Health maintenance: Programs which enable frail, disabled older adults to maintain healthy functioning

Hearing aid: Mechanical device used to help a person hear and perceive sounds

Heart attack: Everyday term referring to damage to the heart

Hemiplegic: One who is paralyzed on one side of the body

Home care: Personal care given in a home setting; can include many of the services of skilled professionals that are provided in nursing homes and hospitals as well as essential housekeeping tasks

Hospice: Facility that specializes in caring for the terminally ill; can also refer to a philosophy which recognizes the role of the family and the need for pain-controlling drugs in working with the terminally ill

Hypertension: High blood pressure

Incontinence: Inability to control bowel or bladder functions

Institution: Housing facility organized primarily to perform personal care, housekeeping, mental health care, and medical care to those who reside there

Intergenerational: Occurring between generations or persons of different age groups

Intermediate care facility (ICF): Nursing home that provides supervised care on a 24-hour basis but is not as intense as found in a skilled nursing facility (SNF); services are mainly restorative, supportive, and preventive

Joint: Part of the body where two bones come together and there is movement

Level of ability: Amount of activity a person is capable of doing

Life cycle education: Education dealing with all the major processes and milestones of life

Lifelong learning: Education throughout life as opposed to education for only the young

Long-term care: Care rendered to people on a sustained basis and offered in a variety of settings with the goal of promoting maximum functional capacity

Medicaid: Federal/state program that provides reasonably complete medical care to the needy regardless of age; financial need must be demonstrated; available in all states but Arizona

Medicare: National health insurance program for older Americans, the blind and disabled, in two parts (Part A and Part B), and administered by the Social Security Administration. Most persons sixty-five and over are eligible for hospital coverage (Part A) without payment; medical coverage (Part B) requires payment of a monthly premium by the older person. Neither Part A nor Part B covers all the costs of health care

Muscle: Tissue composed of fibers with the ability to elongate and shorten causing joints and bones to move

Myocardial infarction (MI): Death of a part of the heart due to blockage in a blood vessel; commonly called heart attack

Nervous system: Group of organs that control and stimulate the activities of the body and the functioning of the other body systems

Nursing home: Intermediate care facility or skilled nursing facility

Occupational therapist: Trained health professional who assists people in their daily living tasks and increasing their upper extremity strength

Organic disorder: Disorder that has a biological or physical basis

Organic mental disorder: Disorder (such as Alzheimer's disease or multi-infarct dementia) caused by physical disease or injury and with symptoms of confusion, loss of memory, incoherent speech, and poor orientation and judgment

Oriented: Aware of one's position in relation to time, place, and other people

Osteoporosis: Reduction in both mass and density of bones; common among older women and associated with a lack of calcium in the body

Pacemaker: Modern electrical device used to stimulate the heart

Paralysis: Loss of ability to move part or all of the body

Paraplegic: One who is paralyzed in half of the body, usually the lower half (the legs)

Physical therapist: Health professional trained to assist people with activities related to motion and movement

Postmortem: After death

Prognosis: Expectation from physician's diagnosis and judgment

Psychological aging: Changes and degrees of change in sensory functions and in perceptions, learning, intelligence, and feelings as well as personality that occur with age

Psychotropic medication: Drugs that affect the mind's state such as tranquilizers and antidepressants

Quadriplegia: Paralysis of both upper and lower parts of the body

Range of motion: Exercises which take a body through the entire repertoire of its movements

Reality orientation: Therapeutic technique that helps people maintain their present abilities and contact with reality

Recreation therapist: Skilled professional trained to work with those who require assistance in learning and relearning leisure activities that have specific goals for increased functioning

Rehabilitation: Process by which people who have been disabled by injury or disease are assisted in recovering their original abilities and in living positively with the remaining disabilities

Reminiscence: Form of therapeutic intervention whereby the older person is encouraged to discuss the past, giving the present meaning

Residential care home: Room, board, and supervised care provided in boarding or care homes

Respiratory system: Group of body organs that provide for the function of breathing; the system brings oxygen into the body and eliminates carbon dioxide

Retirement community: Age-segregated community that is composed almost entirely of retired people

Senescence: Biological aging whereby a person becomes more vulnerable; manifests itself in increased probability of disease, injury, and death

Senility: Term generally used to describe mental problems (incorrectly thought to be the result of aging); senility is not a definitive diagnosis (see also *organic mental disorder*)

Senior center: Nonresidential organization for older people that offers a range of services such as recreation, nutrition, education, transportation, and referral services, usually in a specific facility

Senior citizen: Generally anyone over the age of sixty-five, an age established by Medicare and Social Security for eligibility of benefits

Sensory loss: Reduction in amount or strength of nerve impulses from the sense organs to the nerve centers

Skilled nursing facility (SNF): Long-term-care facility for an individual who requires extensive professional nursing services twenty-four hours a day but is not in need of acute care in a hospital; support services, such as physical and occupational therapy, are also provided

Social Security: Colloquial term referring to the general public retirement pension administered by the federal government; technically, Social Security also provides a number of other benefits to survivors and disabled persons and administers Medicare

Social worker: Trained professional, usually with a master's degree, who has skills in counseling, assessment, and community resources

Sociocultural aging: Changing roles, functions, and status with aging as defined by various social institutions including the family, church, government, and business

Sprain: To twist a ligament or muscle without dislocating the bones

Stroke: See *cerebrovascular accident (CVA)*

Supplemental Security Income (SSI): National income maintenance program for older Americans that guarantees a minimum income to those with insufficient resources; replaced the state/federal Aid for the Aged welfare program

Support system: Arrangement that gives aid and comfort to a person; usually refers to the family

Therapeutic: Service that helps in the treatment of disease or discomfort

Varicose veins: Abnormal swelling of veins, usually in the legs

Vein: Any blood vessel carrying blood to the heart

Vital signs: Temperature, pulse, respiration, and blood pressure

Walker: Device used for security and balance while walking

Common Abbreviations

ADL	activities of daily living	MD	medical doctor
A.M.	morning	O₂	Oxygen
bid	twice a day	OT	occupational therapy or oral temperature
BM	bowel movement, feces, stool		
		oz.	ounce
BR	bedrest	P.M.	afternoon
C°	centigrade or Celsius degree	prn	whenever necessary; when required
CVA	cerebrovascular accident or stroke	PT	physical therapy
		qd	every day
d/c	discontinue	qid	four times a day
Dr.	doctor	qod	every other day
DX	diagnosis	RN	registered nurse
F°	Fahrenheit degree	rom	range of motion
H₂O	water	℞	prescription or treatment ordered by a physician
hr	hour		
HS	bedtime or hour of sleep	stat	at once, immediately
ht	height	tid	three times a day
in.	inch	w/c	wheelchair
lb	pound	wt	weight
LPN	licensed practical nurse		

A Guide to
Long-Term Care Services

Long-term care can be defined as a complex of services intended to support one's abilities to function as independently as possible. Long-term care services can be provided at home, in the community, or in an institution. The following list of services and brief descriptions of what they offer has been adapted from *Long Term Care for the Elderly,* a 1981 report prepared by the State of Hawaii Long-Term Care Planning Group.

Institutional Setting

Acute Care: Acute care provides medical, diagnostic, therapeutic, and related services to injured, disabled, and sick patients at a round-the-clock nursing/medical facility, after which patients are returned home or go to other facilities.

Skilled Nursing Facility (SNF): The SNF provides inpatient nursing services to chronically ill or disabled patients in need of frequent and emergency professional services or treatment. The facility provides round-the-clock nursing care under supervision of a physician as well as physical and/or occupational therapy, recreational activities, and social services.

Intermediate Care Facility (ICF): The ICF provides inpatient health-related care and services to physically or mentally disabled persons who require periodic nursing care. A nurse is on duty during the daytime hours seven days a week. ICF services are intended for persons whose medical condition is stabilized and who do not require round-the-clock nursing service. Recreational activities and social services are also provided.

Institutional/Community Setting

Hospice: This is a special program for the care of the dying. It is not limited by age. Many are terminal cancer patients. The care setting may be freestanding, part of a hospital's regular inpatient program, or part of a home health care program. Characteristics common to most hospice programs are: (1) the goal is to improve the quality rather than quantity of life for the dying patient; (2) the care emphasis is upon reducing and controlling pain, continuity of care, and maintenance of patient's normal life-style for as long as possible; and (3) family members and the dying individual are considered collectively as the patient with care extending through the mourning period.

Community Setting

Adult Day Care Center: The adult day care center is a place maintained and operated by an individual, organization, or agency for the purpose of providing supportive and protective care to a disabled or aged person during the day. Lunch, social and recreational activities, and other nonmedical services are provided. Adult day care programs enable some persons to reside at home and to maintain their social ties in the community. They also encourage families to care for elderly dependents by providing relief from the burden of constant care.

Adult Family Boarding Home: This facility may be any family home providing, for a fee, living accommodations and minimal assistance with activities of daily living.

Care Home: A care home is an institution, place, or building in which accommodation is maintained, furnished, or offered for round-the-clock care to persons in need of personal services, supervision, or assistance essential for sustaining the activities of daily living. The care home category includes family care homes and residential care homes.

Congregate Housing (Elderly Housing): There is no single definition of elderly congregate housing. At a minimum, it is age-segregated housing built for the elderly that may provide an on-site meal program, minimal surveillance, and shelter. Most residents are functionally and emotionally independent but benefit from assistance with meal preparation and social interaction with other residents.

Congregate Dining: One hot meal a day, usually lunch, is served in a congregate setting.

Day Hospital and Day Health Care: These are special programs which provide daytime physical therapy and restorative services, medical monitoring, and social services. Day hospital is provided in a medical setting. Day health care may be provided in a nonmedical setting. In both programs the patient returns home at night.

Food Stamps: This program offers counseling and assistance for senior citizens eligible for subsidized food purchases.

Information and Referral Service: The I and R Service provides information and refers persons seeking help to appropriate agencies.

Legal Services for Elderly: These are legal services focusing on problems affecting the elderly. They offer assistance to help elderly with legal problems.

Senior Employment: Senior employment offers job counseling and placement for senior citizens.

Social Programs: These are regular, but not necessarily daily, social and recreational activities conducted for the elderly at senior centers, community centers, or congregate meal sites.

Transportation and Escort Services: Transport and/or escort services are provided to physically, mentally, and/or socially handicapped adults who are unable to use public transportation, or when public transportation is not available.

Home Setting

Chore Services: These are services performed in the home of an elderly or physically disabled person by a person who is not a trained, professional homemaker. The services need to be supplemented with essential housekeeping and related activities in cases of illness, disability, absence of spouse, or some other crisis in the home.

Companion Services: Persons may be assigned to isolated or potentially isolated adults primarily to serve as a companion and assist with limited chores. Usually companion programs are sponsored by church and civic groups with volunteers serving as companions to visit and spend some time with isolated homebound adults.

Foster Home (FH): A foster home is usually a private home owned and occupied by an individual or family who offers a place of residence, meals, housekeeping services, and personal care. Coordination of medical services is provided by the placement agency.

Home Health Care: Home health care consists of medically oriented services rendered in the person's home. It includes, but is not limited to, skilled nursing, physical therapy, occupational therapy, speech therapy, home health aide assistance, medical social services and medical supplies and appliances provided in the home.

Homemaker Services: Homemaker services are those performed in the home of an elderly or physically disabled person by a trained, professional homemaker. Services include essential housekeeping, personal care, training for in-home management, and skilled observation to help persons maintain their own home or to help a family remain intact during periods of crisis.

Meals on Wheels: Through this program hot meals are delivered to people who cannot adequately prepare their own meals at home.

Monitoring Services: Although some aged or disabled persons need extensive in-home services, others need only minimal monitoring, such as friendly visiting, daily telephone calls, or periodic inquiries. More passive monitoring networks also exist in the form of apartment-building supervisors and emergency alarm systems. Most monitoring programs are initiated by volunteer community groups.

Personal Care Services: Services to assist with personal hygiene, dressing, feeding, and household tasks essential to a person's health are personal care services. This category of long-term care may also include some other supportive services such as assistance in routine household chores. Providers may be self-employed or employed by a certified home health agency, nursing placement service, private social service agencies, and governmental agencies.

Respite Care: This program provides temporary care to frail or impaired persons by someone other than the regular caretaker in order to offer relief to the caretaker from daily care responsibility.

State Governmental
Agencies on Aging

Alabama

Commission on Aging
740 Madison Avenue
Montgomery, Alabama 36130
(205) 832-6640

Alaska

Office on Aging
Department of Health and
   Social Services
Pouch "H"
Juneau, Alaska 99811
(907) 586-6153

Arizona

Aging and
   Adult Administration
1400 W. Washington
Box 6123
Phoenix, Arizona 85007
(602) 255-4446

Arkansas

Office on Aging and
   Adult Services
Department of Social and
   Rehabilitation Services
Donaghey Building, #1031S
Little Rock, Arkansas 77201
(501) 371-2441

California

Department of Aging
918 J Street
Sacramento, California 95814
(916) 322-3887

Colorado

Division of Services for the Aging
Department of Social Services
1575 Sherman Street
Denver, Colorado 80203
(303) 839-2586

Connecticut

Department on Aging
80 Washington Street #312
Hartford, Connecticut
(203) 566-7725

Delaware

Division of Aging
Department of Health and
   Social Services
New Castle, Delaware 19720
(302) 421-6791

District of Columbia

Office on Aging
Office of the Mayor
1012 14th Street, N.W. #1106
Washington, D.C. 20005
(202) 724-5622

Florida

Program Office of Aging and
  Adult Services
Department of Health and
  Rehabilitation Services
1323 Winewood Boulevard
Tallahassee, Florida 32301
(904) 488-2650

Georgia

Department of Human Resources
618 Ponce de Leon Avenue, N.E.
Atlanta, Georgia 30308
(404) 894-5333

Guam

Office of Aging
Social Service
Department of Public Health
Government of Guam
P.O. Box 2816
Agana, Guam 96910
749-9901 x423

Hawaii

Executive Office on Aging
Office of the Governor
State of Hawaii
1149 Bethel Street #307
Honolulu, Hawaii 96813
(808) 548-2593

Idaho

Idaho Office on Aging
Statehouse, Room 114
Boise, Idaho 83720
(208) 334-3833

Illinois

Department on Aging
421 East Capital Avenue
Springfield, Illinois 62706
(217) 785-3356

Indiana

Commission on the
  Aging and Aged
Graphic Arts Building #201
215 North Senate Avenue
Indianapolis, Indiana 46202
(317) 633-5948

Iowa

Commission on Aging
415 West Tenth Street
Jewett Building
Des Moines, Iowa 50319
(515) 281-5187

Kansas

Department of Aging
610 West 10th
Topeka, Kansas 66612
(913) 296-4986

Kentucky

Center for Aging Services
Bureau of Social Services
Human Service Building,
  6th Floor
275 East Main Street
Frankfort, Kentucky 40601
(502) 564-6930

Louisiana

Office of Elderly Affairs
P.O. Box 44282
Capitol Station
Baton Rouge, Louisiana 70804
(504) 342-2747

Maine

Bureau of Maine's Elderly
Community Services Unit
Department of Human Services
State House
Augusta, Maine 04333
(207) 289-2561

Mariana Islands

Office of Aging
Community Development
   Division
Government of the
   Trust Territory
   of the Pacific Islands
Saipan, Naruaba Uskabds 96950
Overseas Operator: 2143

Maryland

Office on Aging
State Office Building
301 West Preston Street
Baltimore, Maryland 21201
(301) 383-5064

Massachusetts

Department of Elder Affairs
38 Chauncy Street
Boston, Massachusetts 02111
(617) 727-7751

Michigan

Office of Services to the Aging
300 E. Michigan Avenue
P.O. Box 30026
Lansing, Michigan 48913
(517) 373-8230

Minnesota

Minnesota Board on Aging
Metro Square Building #204
Seventh & Robert Streets
St. Paul, Minnesota 55101
(612) 296-2544

Mississippi

Council on Aging
P.O. Box 5136
Fondren Station
510 George Street
Jackson, Mississippi 39216
(601) 354-6590

Missouri

Division on Aging
Department of Social Services
Broadway State Office Building
P.O. Box 570
Jefferson City, Missouri 65101
(314) 751-3082

Montana

Aging Services Bureau
Department of Social and
   Rehabilitation Services
P.O. Box 4210
Helena, Montana 59601
(406) 449-3124

Nebraska

Commission on Aging
State House Station 94784
300 South 17th Street
Lincoln, Nebraska 68509
(402) 471-2307

Nevada

Division of Aging
Department of Human Resources
505 East King Street
Kinkead Building, Room #101
Carson City, Nevada 88710
(702) 885-4210

New Hampshire

Council on Aging
14 Depot Street
Concord, New Hampshire 03301
(603) 271-2751

New Jersey

Division on Aging
Department of
    Community Affairs
P.O. Box 2768
363 West State Street
Trenton, New Jersey 08625
(609) 292-4833

New Mexico

State Agency on Aging
440 St. Michael's Drive
Chamisa Hills Building
Santa Fe, New Mexico 87503
(505) 827-2802

New York

Office for the Aging
New York State Executive
    Department
Empire State Plaza
Agency Building #2
Albany, New York 12223
(518) 474-5731

North Carolina

North Carolina Department of
    Human Resources
Division of Aging—Suite #200
708 Hillsborough Street
Raleigh, North Carolina 27603
(919) 733-3983

North Dakota

Aging Services
Social Services Board
    of North Dakota
State Capitol Building
Bismarck, North Dakota 58505
(701) 224-2577

Northern Mariana Islands

Office of Aging
Department of Community and
    Cultural Affairs
Commonwealth of
    Northern Mariana Islands
Civic Center, Susupe
Saipan, Northern Mariana Islands
    96950

Ohio

Commission on Aging
50 West Broad Street, 9th Floor
Columbus, Ohio 43215
(614) 466-5500

Oklahoma

Special Unit on Aging
Department of Institutions
Social & Rehabilitative Services
P.O. Box 25353
Oklahoma City, Oklahoma 73125
(405) 521-2281

Oregon

Office of Elderly Affairs
Human Resources Department
772 Commercial Street, S.E.
Salem, Oregon 97310
(503) 378-4728

Pennsylvania

Department of Aging
Room #307, Finance Building
Harrisburg, Pennsylvania 17120
(717) 783-1550

Puerto Rico

Gericulture Commission
Department of Social Services
P.O. Box 11368
Santurce, Puerto Rico 00908
(809) 722-2429

Rhode Island

Department of Elderly Affairs
150 Washington Street
Providence, Rhode Island 02903
(401) 277-2858

American Samoa

Territorial Aging Program
Government of American Samoa
Office of the Governor
Pago Pago, American Samoa
  96799
Samoa 3-1254 or 3-4116

South Carolina

Commission on Aging
915 Main Street
Columbia, South Carolina 29201
(803) 758-2576

South Dakota

Office on Aging
Adult Services
S.D. Department
  of Social Services
State Office Building
Illinois Street
Pierre, South Dakota 57501
(605) 773-3656

Tennessee

Commission on Aging
535 Church Street
Nashville, Tennessee 37219
(615) 741-2056

Texas

Governor's Committee on Aging
8th Floor, Southwest Tower
211 East Seventh Street
P.O. Box 12786, Capitol Station
Austin, Texas 78711
(512) 475-2717

Utah

Division on Aging
Department of Social Services
150 West North Temple
Box #2500
Salt Lake City, Utah 84102
(801) 533-6422

Vermont

Office on Aging
Agency of Human Services
State Office Building
Montpelier, Vermont 05602
(802) 241-2400

Virginia

Office on Aging
830 East Main Street
Suite #950
Richmond, Virginia 23219
(804) 786-7894

Virgin Islands

Commission on Aging
P.O. Box 539
Charlotte Amalie
St. Thomas, Virgin Islands 00801
(809) 774-5884

Washington

Office of Aging
Department of Social and Health
    Services
OB-43G
Olympia, Washington 98504
(206) 753-2502

West Virginia

Commission on Aging
State Capitol
Charleston, West Virginia 25305
(304) 348-3317

Wisconsin

Bureau on Aging
Division of Community Services
One West Wilson Street
Room #685
Madison, Wisconsin 53702
(608) 266-2536

Wyoming

Wyoming State Office on Aging
720 West 18th Street
Cheyenne, Wyoming 82002

Further Readings

The books listed below, while not an exhaustive bibliography, will provide you with a good introduction to aging and eldercare.

American Foundation for the Blind. *Facts About Aging and Blindness.* New York: American Foundation for the Blind.

Bumagin, Victoria E., and Kathy F. Hirn. *Aging Is a Family Affair.* New York. Thomas Crowell, 1979.

Burger, Sarah Green, and Martha D'Erasmo. *Living in a Nursing Home.* New York: Ballantine Books, 1976.

Butler, R. N. *Why Survive? Being Old in America.* New York: Harper and Row, 1975.

Butler, R. N., and M. I. Lewis. *Sex After Sixty.* New York: Harper and Row, 1976.

Butler, R. N., and M. I. Lewis. *Aging and Mental Health.* St. Louis: C. V. Mosby Co., 1977.

Carey, J. R. *How to Create Interiors for the Disabled.* New York: Pantheon Books, 1978.

Curtin, Sharon. *Nobody Ever Died of Old Age.* Boston: Little, Brown and Co., 1972.

Dept. of Health and Human Services, Public Health Service, National Institute on Aging. *Age Page.* Washington, D.C.: Government Printing Office. Ask for free sheets on aging information.

Kubler-Ross, E. *On Death and Dying.* New York: Macmillan, 1970.

Mace, Nancy, and Peter Rabins. *The 36-Hour Day.* Baltimore: Johns Hopkins University Press, 1981.

Otten, J., and F. Shelly. *When Your Parents Grow Old.* New York: Thomas Crowell, 1976.

Sayre, Joan M. *Handbook for the Hearing Impaired Older Adult—An Individual Program.* Danville: Interstate, 1980.

Schwartz, Arthur N. *Survival Handbook for Children of Aging Parents.* Chicago: Follett Publishing Co., 1977.

Silverstone, Barbara, and Helen Kendall Myman. *You and Your Aging Parents.* New York: Pantheon Books, 1976.

Thornton, Susan M., and Virginia Fraser. *Understanding "Senility"— A Layperson's Guide.* Denver: Loretto Heights College, 1978.

Troccio, Julie. *Home Care for the Elderly.* Boston: CBI Publishing Co., 1981.

Contributors

Patrice Murphy Bain, B.A., recreational therapist, Nashville, Tennessee

Hazel Beh, M.S.W., Ph.D., social worker, Honolulu, Hawaii

Mary Breneman, R.P.T., chief physical therapist, Kuakini Medical Center, Honolulu, Hawaii

Colette Browne, M.P.H., M.S.W., director, Elderservice Associates, Honolulu, Hawaii

Memrey Casey, M.S.W., chief social worker, Kuakini Medical Center, Honolulu, Hawaii

Cathy Collado, O.T.R., occupational therapist, Kuakini Medical Center, Honolulu, Hawaii

Billie DeMello, R.P.T., physical therapist, Rehabilitation Center of the Pacific, Honolulu, Hawaii

Elaine Fiber, M.S.W., social worker, former director of Social Work Services, Convalescent Center of Honolulu, Hawaii

Carole Fujishige, R.N., Children's Pediatric Arthritis Center of Honolulu, Hawaii

Linda Gerson, O.T.R., occupational therapist, private practice, Honolulu, Hawaii

Victoria Greene, certified occupational therapy assistant, Kuakini Medical Center, Honolulu, Hawaii

Grace Ihara, M.S., C.C.C., speech pathology consultant, Honolulu, Hawaii

Beverly Klopf, M.S.W., social worker, Kuakini Medical Center, Honolulu, Hawaii

Bernadette Ledesma, M.P.H., director, Adult Day Care/Adult Day Health, Kuakini Medical Center, Honolulu, Hawaii

Diane Murayama, M.P.H., Hawaii Housing Authority, Honolulu, Hawaii

Otto Neurath, M.D., physician, former clinical faculty, John Burns School of Medicine, University of Hawaii, Honolulu, Hawaii

Roberta Onzuka-Anderson, A.C.S.W., social worker, Veterans Administration, Honolulu, Hawaii

Mildred Ramsey, M.P.H., R.P.T., director, Honolulu Gerontology Program, Honolulu, Hawaii

Jane Rogers, O.T.R., chief occupational therapist, Kuakini Medical Center, Honolulu, Hawaii

Aileen Sakado, M.S., R.N., inservice coordinator, Kuakini Medical Center, Honolulu, Hawaii

Alice Talbott, R.N., patient education coordinator, Kuakini Medical Center, Honolulu, Hawaii

Rita Vandivort, M.S.W., assistant director, Social Work Department, Queens Medical Center, Honolulu, Hawaii

Herbert Yee, R.P.T., physical therapist, Physicians Physical Therapy Service, Honolulu, Hawaii

Index

HAWAI Production Notes

This book was designed by Roger Eggers.
Composition and paging were done on the
Quadex Composing System and typesetting
on the Compugraphic 8400 by the design
and production staff of University of Hawaii
Press.

The text typeface is ITC Garamond Book
and the display typeface is ITC Garamond
Bold.

Offset presswork and binding were done by
Vail-Ballou Press, Inc. Text paper is Writers
RR Offset, basis 50.